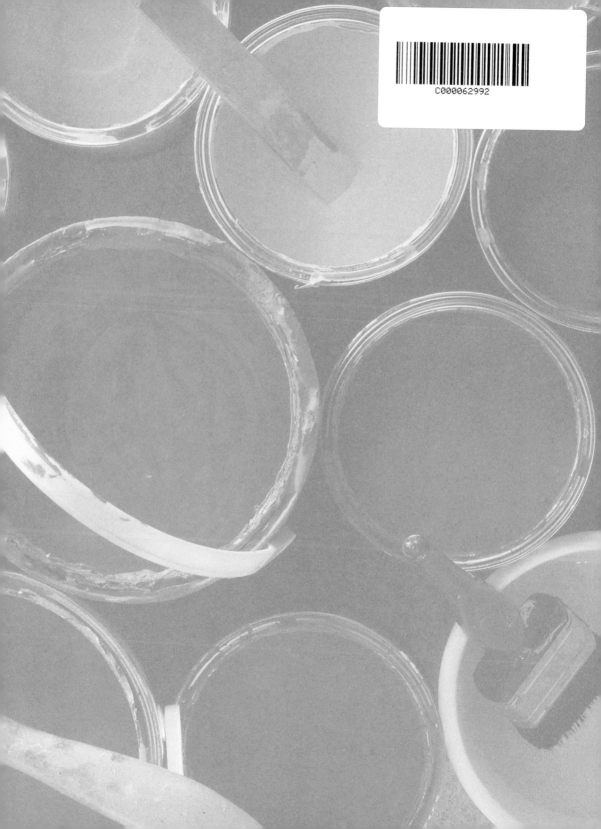

THE COMPLETE ILLUSTRATED
ENCYCLOPEDIA OF

PAINT EFFECTS

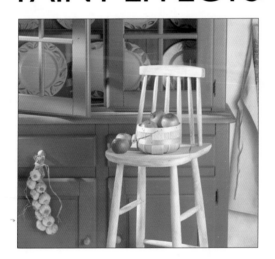

THE COMPLETE ILLUSTRATED
ENCYCLOPEDIA OF
PAINT EFFECTS

Over 150 fabulous projects and 1700 photographs – the complete practical guide and ideas book for decorating your home with special finishes, including step-by-step instructions for guaranteed results

SACHA COHEN AND MAGGIE PHILO

LORENZ BOOKS

This edition is published by Lorenz Books

Lorenz Books is an imprint of
Anness Publishing Ltd, Hermes House
88–89 Blackfriars Road, London SE1 8HA
tel. 020 7401 2077; fax 020 7633 9499
www.lorenzbooks.com; info@anness.com

© Anness Publishing Ltd 2006

UK agent: The Manning Partnership Ltd,
tel. 01225 478444; fax 01225 478440;
sales@manning-partnership.co.uk
UK distributor: Grantham Book Services Ltd,
tel. 01476 541080; fax 01476 541061;
orders@gbs.tbs-ltd.co.uk
North American agent/distributor:
National Book Network, tel. 301 459 3366;
fax 301 429 5746; www.nbnbooks.com
Australian agent/distributor: Pan Macmillan
Australia, tel. 1300 135 113; fax 1300 135 103;
customer.service@macmillan.com.au
New Zealand agent/distributor:
David Bateman Ltd, tel. (09) 415 7664;
fax (09) 415 8892

A CIP catalogue record for this book
is available from the British Library.

Publisher: Joanna Lorenz
Editorial Director: Judith Simons
Project Editor: Felicity Forster
Photographers: Paul Bricknell, Rodney Forte,
    John Freeman, Tim Imrie, Lizzie Orme,
    Debbie Patterson, Graham Rae, Lucinda
    Symons, Steve Tanner and Adrian Taylor
Stylists: Diana Civil, Katie Gibbs, Andrea
    Spencer, Fanny Ward, Tamsin Weston and
    Judy Williams
Additional text: Petra Boase, Lucinda
    Ganderton, Elaine Green, Emma Hardy,
    Alison Jenkins, Cheryl Owen, Sandra
    Partington, Judy Smith, Liz Wagstaff,
    Stewart and Sally Walton
Copy Editor: Judy Cox
Designers: Bill Mason and Ian Sandom
Production Controller: Lee Sargent

Previously published as two separate volumes,
Paint Effects Projects and *The Practical Encyclopedia
of Paint Recipes, Paint Effects and Special Finishes*

10 9 8 7 6 5 4 3 2 1

CONTENTS

INTRODUCTION

Recent years have seen a surge in interest in decorative paint effects. Perhaps as technology plays an increasing role in our lives we are eager to counteract its seeming impersonality by creating our own style and expressing our individuality more clearly in our homes.

This book aims to help you explore a wide variety of techniques for making a decorative impact on your own interior. There are inspirational effects, from simple colour treatments for the walls to fantasy decoration for furniture and accessories. All are described in easy-to-follow steps and there are project ideas for themes to follow or adapt as you wish.

ABOVE: *An ordinary box is transformed with a dark wood effect. The black fern effect is painted freehand.*

OPPOSITE: **This Roman fresco of the 1st century AD from the House of Livia, Rome, features a dark green wall painted with garlands of flowers.**

THE DECORATIVE USE OF PAINTING

People have used paint to decorate the walls of their homes since the time of the Stone Age cave dwellers. These early hunters used simple earth pigments to adorn their caves with huge scenes of wild animals.

By the time of the early civilizations wall decoration was becoming more sophisticated and reflected the great advances that mankind had made. The ancient Egyptians painted the walls of their temples and tombs with scenes of everyday life, and decorated furniture and architectural detail. They used a range of pigments that included a wondrous, brilliant blue made by crushing the mineral stone lapis lazuli.

In the Minoan Palace of Knossos on the Mediterranean island of Crete, amazing frescoes have been found that date from around 1600 BC. These are startling in their apparent modernity. Many of them feature the plant and marine life that is found in and around the island, yet they are painted in such a stylized fashion that they seem almost like abstract shapes. Mycenaean pottery that dates from about the same time also displays stylized naturalistic forms with banding and stripes.

A thousand years later on mainland Greece the great temple of the Parthenon was decorated with a profusion of bright colour, which seems strange to us today when we view the white marble of the building sparkling in the sun on top of the Acropolis in Athens. Greek pottery featured painted and engraved decoration, with geometric borders that are still regularly used. Designs such as the Greek key pattern immediately convey a classic look to any item or area they decorate.

It was the Romans who invented what we now know as mural painting. With the frontiers of their empire ever widening they were able to obtain many new pigments and increase the colour range of their paints.

BELOW: This cave painting of bison from Altamira in Spain dates from Palaeolithic times.

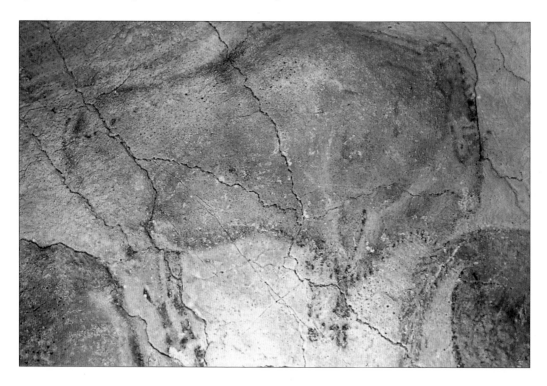

ABOVE: The Throne Room of the Minoan Palace of Knossos, Crete, dates from the 16th century BC. The decoration here shows a fresco of a griffin and plants. It is painted with red earth pigments and a double white stripe borders the room.

The city of Pompeii lay covered and protected under the volcanic ash of Mount Vesuvius for hundreds of years, yet many of the colours are still as bright as when they were first painted. These houses of the 1st century AD are painted with frescoes that depict full-scale modelled lifelike figures and a wide variety of activities and subject matter from mythology to eating and drinking. The decorations were used to display the social status and wealth of their owners and the Romans enhanced their villas with clever creativity. They became masters of faux effects, extending and manipulating space in interiors by painting realistic architectural detail with marbling and graining and painted entire *trompe-l'oeil* settings.

The tradition of fresco painting came to the fore some hundreds of years later in the religious painting of the Renaissance when artists revived the classical rules and attitudes of the ancient Greeks and Romans. In terms of the decoration of interiors, supreme art and craft came together in the work of Leonardo da Vinci and Michelangelo. Leonardo's *Last Supper* in the convent of Sta Maria delle Grazie in Milan is a monumental wall painting within a false room that stretches back into the landscape, while Michelangelo's frescoes on the ceiling of the Sistine Chapel in Rome are among the greatest works of Western art.

At about this time the nature of paints also began to develop, and oil-based binders led to new possibilities for artists and craftsmen. Oil-based paints took longer to dry and gave the opportunity for further experimentation. Artists used oil paints to create free-standing paintings, and the art of fresco wall painting was abandoned. In the meantime technical ability developed and it became essential for artists to be able to imitate surfaces and fabric textures accurately in paint and to render perspective correctly. The trade routes to the East were a source of new colours and pigments.

Trompe-l'oeil ceiling decoration continued right through the 18th century, and with the revival of neoclassicism in architecture new paint effects were used for walls. Proportions became important and rooms were divided by panels and ornamental details. Travel became easier and more popular in Europe and colours and ideas were gathered and exchanged. Faux effects were used for marbling columns and for decorating furniture and small items with expensive woods and tortoiseshell in an effort to display the appearance of wealth. Layers of thinned paint were used on top of each other as glazes to achieve depth of colour.

Aniline dyes were invented in the 19th century. This meant that new, vibrant pigments that were not as costly as natural earth resources could be used. The art of paint effects became within everyday financial reach, though they were still executed by specialist craftsmen. Public buildings such as public houses and theatres were decorated in a grand style that we associate with the Victorians, with wood graining, marble effects, ornamented patterning and gilding.

By the 1930s and the arrival of the Art Deco style, paint effects had become simpler. Combed and textured techniques were more prominent and a limited, though specific, colour palette was used. In the following decades paint effects were used only by specialist craftsmen as wallpaper and, later, flat surfaces became the fashion. Matt, soft sheen and gloss paints meant that light could be played with in a simple way in keeping with the modern feel for space.

Meanwhile, parallel with the efforts of the well-to-do to appear even more grand by copying rich and expensive materials, country people were using their own paints in effects and designs that were individual to their own cultures. This simple and easy-to-live-with look has much character and appeal to today's technological age. The use of natural paints and their soft colours allows the creation of a comfortable home rather than one that is painted to reflect status.

In Eastern Europe and Scandinavia bright colours were used, probably as a foil against the cold, white winters, with simple painted patterns that became traditional and were passed down through the generations. In the United States the pioneering spirit of the early settlers led to the development of freehand designs that were influenced by the many countries from which they had originated, producing a style of their own. They used milk paints in muted colours to decorate walls and furniture and simple storage items, such as wooden boxes, were painted in flowing naturalistic designs both for protection and decoration.

OPPOSITE: This 16th-century fresco from the Villa Barbaro in Maser, Italy shows a trompe-l'oeil *garden scene.*

ABOVE: *The technique of pargeting was popular in houses in the countryside of France. Here, dark brown thinned paint outlines a design incised with a stick on a cream-coloured wall.*

BELOW: *This bathroom, cleverly tiled in diamonds rather than squares, is decorated with a stamped French fleur-de-lis motif.*

Texture, too, was an intrinsic part of decoration for many country people. In France, for example, the craft of pargeting was used. This is a method of decoration in which a design is incised into wet plaster. Many effects can be produced in this way, from all-over geometric designs to randomly placed motifs.

The current interest in traditional folk decoration runs hand in hand with a respect for natural materials. Thus wood graining, marbling and other special effects such as gilding have been revived for new and exciting uses. As we try to recapture our past, effects such as distressing and ageing, and the look of antique materials such as bronze and copper with verdigris, have become fashionable.

Many new paints are available to today's decorators. No longer do we need to rely on local resources. The invention of synthetic paints means that we can choose to paint with any colour we desire. We also have a massive choice of finishes for different effects and numerous paints for various surfaces. There are special quick-drying formula paints that allow us to achieve a new decoration for a room in a matter of hours. Painting equipment, too, has improved, with softer paintbrushes and new solvents that make cleaning up easy. There are specialist brushes for specific techniques and to help you reach into any niche or corner.

Paint is now one of the easiest ways to transform your home, allowing you complete freedom in choosing any style you wish with a multitude of colours and textures. You can choose to recreate a historic period from the past or let your imagination create a futuristic setting quite unlike anything anyone has yet seen. Ranges of traditional paints are being revived from every era and location so you can decorate authentically if desired. Manufacturers produce a constant stream of new paints, such as interference paints, metallic finishes and pearlescent effects.

Many people now enjoy refurbishing junk furniture into new items through simple paint techniques. This is an inexpensive way to add even more style to your home. Car boot and garage sales, junk shops and flea markets are an amazing source of items that have been thrown away as useless. In most cases it is easy to make a few easy repairs and paint the piece to give it new life at a fraction of the cost of a new item. Even plastic items such as bowls and containers can be painted to look as if they are made from expensive metals.

The use of natural colours and finishes is popular. If you cannot afford wood panelling or new floorboards it is easy to paint them, with the added advantage that you can always repaint them at some time if you decide on another scheme.

Foreign travel has had a great influence on lifestyles and decoration. The clean, bright colours found in the Mediterranean and the rich reds and browns of Africa can be adapted to create an unusual or exotic setting in which you can instantly relax. Remember, however, that you might need to lighten the tones for a climate that does not receive such fierce sunlight. As well as using the colours and patterns from exotic places, bring in the textures. Try to match colours to materials. For instance, purples and dark brown wood effects go well together and create a luxurious look.

The world of decorating has no limits. With paint effects you can create whatever look you want. So enjoy the planning and preparations in anticipation of a great result.

BELOW: A tiled look painted in natural earth colours of grey-blue and terracotta. The diamond shapes incorporate a combed effect.

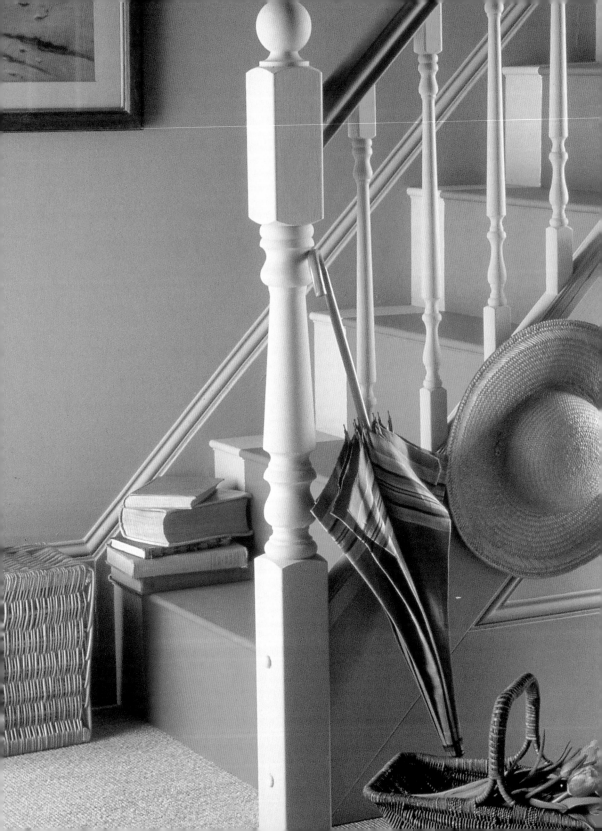

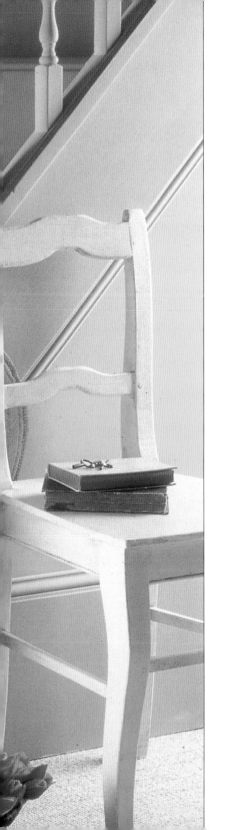

USING COLOUR

Colour can have tremendous impact in our homes. The colours we choose for our surroundings reflect our personalities, lifestyles, travels and interests. They set the scene for an atmosphere of relaxation or stimulation, for quiet contemplation or family get-togethers and parties.

We live in a world that contains millions of natural colours. Today, using synthetic dyes and stainers, we can match almost any colour found in nature in the form of paint, fabrics and other materials. An understanding of the visual effects that these different colours can produce will help you plan creative and successful decorating schemes.

ABOVE: For special effects watercolour, acrylic and special stencil paints are invaluable. The colour palette is more restricted than with household paints, but you can have great fun mixing your own shades.

OPPOSITE: The coolness or vibrancy of a colour has a major effect on the appearance of a room. Here, pale blue walls are prevented from looking cold by being teamed with warm yellow and orange colours.

COLOUR TERMINOLOGY

Knowing some of the generally accepted theories of how colour works will enable you to use colours to their best advantage and for particular purposes. Artists, designers and decorators use precise terms to describe colours and the differences between them.

Red, yellow and blue are known as primary colours. These are colours that cannot be produced from a combination of other pigments. Mixing two primary colours produces the secondary colours: red and yellow results in orange, yellow and blue in green, and blue and red in violet.

Placing primary and secondary colours in a circle in their appropriate positions forms a colour wheel. Tertiary colours can then be produced by mixing a primary colour with a secondary colour that is next to it. For instance, red mixed with violet gives red-violet. Experiment by making your own colour wheel, mixing adjacent colours for an infinite variety.

ABOVE: *Colours that are immediately opposite each other on the colour wheel are termed complementary. For example, violet is complementary to yellow, and green to red. These opposites enhance each other and make each appear more intense. Here green is painted next to a tint of its complementary red (pink). The colours really seem to glow against each other.*

BELOW: *Tints are made by adding white to a colour, and shades by adding black. These pastel stripes show tints of colours. They are all also similar in tone - they have the same amount of light or dark.*

ABOVE: Colours that are near each other on the colour wheel are called harmonious. Having elements in common, they relate and work well together. For instance, the swatches of main colour shown here work well with the dashes of colour painted below them.

BELOW: Contrasting colours can also give a dramatic effect. These are colours that are not related at all, but create impact because they are of the same tone. The main colour swatches shown here are matched in intensity by the dashes of colour painted below them.

DENSITY OF COLOUR

The amount of colour used in a room and where it is placed can create a dramatic or a subtle effect. Use it in large areas to create an overall atmosphere or in selected small areas to emphasize particular features. Clever use of colour can appear to change the proportions of a room, making it appear bigger or smaller than it really is. Remember that your furniture and fabrics are all part of the same scheme. Be careful not to use too many colours or the effect will be unbalanced.

LEFT: *The more intense a colour is, the more we notice it. Adding a gloss finish or glazing surfaces can make them look much brighter. This chair is varnished, making it stand out as well as protecting the distressed paint effect.*

BELOW: *It is generally accepted that colours towards the red end of the spectrum appear to advance. However, an intense red used in a large area can look overpowering. Here, a dramatic effect is produced by using areas of different reds, allowing the eye to move constantly forwards and backwards.*

ABOVE: Towards the other end of the spectrum from red, blue is a colour that seems to recede. It is therefore useful to use in decorating schemes where you want to increase the feeling of space. Here intense blue and yellow accessories balance each other visually on the sill, but the pale blue shutters beyond lead the eye out of the window, making the room seem bigger.

COLOUR AND LIGHT

When you are choosing paints or coloured materials for your home make sure that you look at the colours in natural daylight at different times of the day. A colour in a room facing the sun varies from morning to night, while a colour in a room that does not receive much, if any, direct sunlight remains largely consistent. Colours can look quite different in artificial light too.

Seasons and geographical location also have an influence on our impressions of colour. A bright colour that you see on vacation under a glaring Caribbean sun may not work as well in your own living room, but you may be able to modify it. You can also tone colours down by adding a little of the complementary colour.

RIGHT: This Indian-style room is decorated with just two bright primary colours – red and yellow. However, the jewel-like scarlet is balanced by the natural ochre colour so that the effect is rich and warm rather than garish. The sheen finish on the walls reflects the light in the room and the sheer curtain fabric gently diffuses light coming through the window.

COLOUR AND TEXTURE

Textures can emphasize the general effect given by colour. We associate hard, glossy finishes with streamlining and efficiency and so they tend to look cold, especially when used with colours in the blue range. Warm-looking traditional surfaces such as soft, grainy woods and rich, textured fabrics that suggest age and reliability enhance the effect of reds, oranges and browns. General paint effects such as combing and rag rolling can be lightly or heavily textured, so when you are choosing colours think carefully about the overall effect you want to create.

RIGHT: Colour and texture combine here to produce a restful environment, yet one full of visual interest. The walls have been dry-brushed in green and purple – two shades that always work well together – creating an illusion of texture, while the grapevine border was made using a bought stencil.

BELOW: Everything in this room speaks of warmth and comfort. The faux-effect wood panelling sets the scene, and the soft, grained effect is enhanced by the cream walls. Furniture with traditional coverings such as leather and rush are timeless and lend an air of comfort.

NATURAL SHADES

The colours and textures of nature can be brought into home decoration and used over and over again to add a calming note. They are surfaces that are always interesting and diverse, yet complement any environment and style, old or new, classic or modern. The shades you choose may be bright or subtle.

Greens and blues are perennial favourites in home decoration, either used singly in toning shades or together. Browns, soft oranges, buttermilk yellows, beiges and creams are also natural colours that harmonize well in the home; they are often seen in country-style kitchens, reinforcing the sense of warmth and comfort. Neutral colour schemes allow you to use a mixture of textures for visual variety. They can also act as a foil to small areas of bright colours that can be changed from time to time to give a different accent to a room.

RIGHT: These pale greens and blues in a matt (flat) finish suggest the places in which we find escape in the heat of summer, such as cool water or shady areas. The walls are defined by clean white lines of matt skirting (base) board, and the wood-washed floor looks as if it has faded in the sun.

RIGHT: This entire scheme relies on a neutral palette of off-white, accessorized with metal furniture and gold-accented ornaments. The wall motifs were created using a stamp dipped in a mixture of stone white and interior filler (spackle) and add subtle highlights and texture to the wall.

COLOUR GROUPS

You can achieve stunning effects with monochrome schemes using colours of one hue, or black and white, or black and cream, or the many tones of grey that can be mixed from these combinations. Other greys can be mixed by using exact proportions of two complementary colours, so they can be used as a neutralizing effect in conjunction with a bright decorative palette.

Various browns also work well together visually, since they are based on earth pigments and thus have a natural affinity with each other. They are good for rustic looking decorating schemes, since these are the colours that would most commonly have been used in country interiors.

RIGHT: Try seeing how many tones of black, brown and grey you can make by adding water to thin down the pigment. The addition of white or cream gives further ranges of colours. These can be combined in a scheme or used as neutral background or relief with other colours.

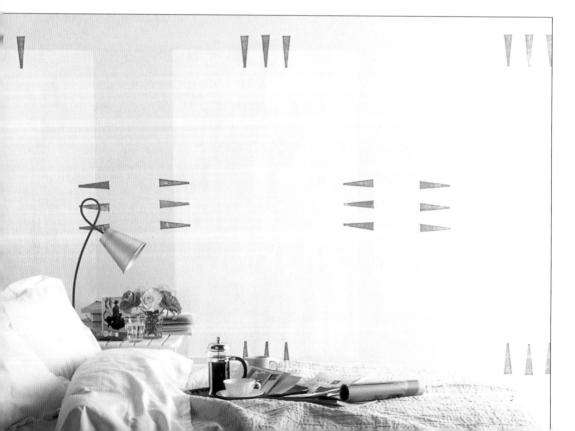

ABOVE: The aged look of this painted brown door makes a backdrop to a palette of warm earth colours in the form of items made from natural materials. These include iron, terracotta, buff clay, hessian, raffia and wood.

OPPOSITE: This is a powerful 'no colour' scheme. It combines strong bands of cream with white painted panels defined by unusual greys. The look is softened by the textures of white cotton sheets and a cream quilted bedspread.

RIGHT: Here, soft greys ranging towards white are used for a restful, but interesting, scheme. The matt painted effects of the wood-washed floor and distressed chair are enhanced by the textures of velvet, sequins, satin ribbons and silk muslin.

YELLOW, ORANGE AND RED

Red is a very versatile colour, able to conjure up many different moods. Used at full strength in its purest form it is dramatic and powerful. Yellow is the colour of sunshine and summer. Its visual warmth is intensified by the addition of red to make glowing oranges that cheer the heart. Use yellow and orange in rooms that receive little natural light to give them an instant lift. You can choose clear pastel tints for a gentle ambience or bright hues to create a bolder effect. The lighter yellows tend to give a fresh look that can appear surprisingly cool, while the redder oranges can look even more dramatic teamed with complementary blues.

LEFT: Mix a variety of yellows to achieve colours that similarly range from clean bright oranges to burnt and brown tones.

RIGHT: Painted in yellow, this kitchen has a sunny feel, slightly cooled by touches of blue, violet and white. The fresh, country-style gingham effect on the wall is quickly achieved by painting two lines at a time from a roller with the middle section cut out.

BELOW: Here a richly worked orange-brown wall links a number of elements in different colours from the same part of the colour wheel – yellow curtains, bright red accessories, tan cushions and a cream sofa.

BELOW: This lovely old folk chest is decorated with freehand traditional flower motifs in red and brown. Warm red is balanced by creamy yellow panels and the colours are enhanced by just a little soft blue from the cooler part of the colour wheel.

PINK, LILAC AND PEACH

Red is a very strong colour in its purest forms. Yet, when diluted to its minimum, or added to white, red gives the softest of pinks for a sophisticated dining room or a new-born's nursery. Add it to blue and relax into a completely new world of lilacs, mauves and violets. Add it to pale yellow and you can enjoy gentle shades of orange from the palest warm beige to a soft terracotta.

RIGHT: These pinks, mauves and oranges are based on red mixed with white. The more intense colours in the range work well with similarly intense colours such as lime green or turquoise.

OPPOSITE: Here different shades of pink have been combined to produce a fresh and modern colour scheme – ice-cream pastel pink on the walls harmonizes with the mauve-blue wash, peach towel and bright fuschia soap.

BELOW: A diluted red used as a pink wood wash gives a rosy tinge to old floorboards. Some of the natural colour of the wood is allowed to show through, adding yellow-orange tints to the effect.

BLUES AND GREENS

Blues and greens are relaxing to look at and to live with. They are familiar to us because they make up so much of our world. The sky displays a vast area of constantly changing blues, as does the sea. Green, of course, is the colour of plant growth, from soft greyish leaves to bright yellow-green buds. Blues and greens in their myriad variants seem to bring a breath of outdoors into the home. Use pale blues and greens for a cool, airy feel or deep, brilliant tones for a more exotic effect.

LEFT: Blue is closely related to green, needing the addition of just a little yellow to produce a colour that displays new characteristics. Although from the cool part of the colour wheel, these colours can appear quite warm if a warm yellow or red is added to blue.

OPPOSITE: A vivid yellow-green combined with brilliant white paintwork brings a fresh feel of spring. Small silver diamond motifs on the wall keep the green from looking too dense.

LEFT: A blue colourwashed shade on the walls is accented with bright blue and orange in a hand-painted tile effect. The whole scheme is simple and fresh.

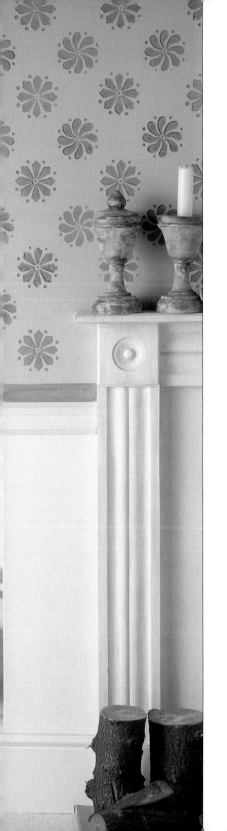

DECORATING SCHEMES

The most exciting part about using paint effects is planning how they will work together. You may want to decorate a room with a particular theme, or combine specific effects with distinctive colours. The following pages suggest all the factors to consider, and give some ideas for decorating schemes based on colour, patterns and styles from around the world. You can follow the steps for the projects exactly or use elements from them, adapting them to your own taste. Most describe a basic treatment for the walls and show some simple finishes for added decoration.

ABOVE: A flag motif stamped on to the wall of this kitchen instantly gives the room a nautical feel.

OPPOSITE: The pattern on the walls perfectly complements the Scandinavian theme of this living room.

CHOOSING A SCHEME

Before dashing straight for the colour cards and paint pots take time to think exactly what you want to achieve when you decorate your home. You need to consider if the scheme you are choosing will succeed in the room you wish to paint.

Take a good look at the room. Take into account the size and how much light it receives. This can make the difference between a room that receives almost no direct sunlight and one that will be sunny and bright for much of the day. If east or west facing it may receive sunlight only in the morning or afternoon. Light can radically change the appearance of colours. The shape of the room can also have some bearing, as light may be angled more strongly in some areas depending on the position of the windows, doors and alcoves. Make sure you see the colours in the actual room at different times of the day.

Look at the colours that are already in the room. There may be much that you cannot change, such as furniture, carpets and curtains, and you will have to plan your colours and effects around these. Figure out your scheme with these fixed items in mind.

Choose colours and effects for the atmosphere that you want to create – warm and cosy or cool and spacious. They can also be used to give the visual impression of changing the shape of a room. Warm colours seem to advance, so use these if you want to make a room look smaller. Cool colours recede and are

OPPOSITE: The light colours used in this scheme give the kitchen a suitably fresh and airy feel.

BELOW: A wall decoration could be influenced by the soft colours, textures and shapes of a collection of ceramics.

BELOW LEFT: A frottage effect above dado height teams perfectly with wallpaper below. The soft green colour is a restful shade to choose for any room, including a narrow hallway.

ABOVE: Trompe d'oeil *china plates painted over antiqued shelves immediately suggest a country home interior.*

BELOW: A hand-painted and stamped frieze adds colour and decoration to a child's room. Here the frieze is just part of the overall design with the green skirting (base) board standing in for grass and the walls decorated with a sky effect.

useful for making a room look bigger. Similarly, dark tones tend to advance and light tones recede, so use shades of colour to visually move space. For instance, if you have a high ceiling that you wish to appear lower, paint the walls in a dark colour to picture rail height, then white above this and over the ceiling to reduce the wall height. You can also emphasize certain elements in the room in this way.

Patterns can be used to change space, too. Large, bold-coloured motifs tend to attract the eye, so use them in areas that you wish to bring forward. Small muted patterns tend to merge into an overall textured effect unless you are close to them. Vertical patterns such as stripes will give the impression of heightening an area, while horizontal ones will widen it. Remember that texture will also have some effect by breaking up the surface and disguising imperfections.

Bear in mind the age of the building you are decorating. Consider whether a particular style or theme is appropriate to the architecture. There may be existing original features that you can plan a theme around. Perhaps you can adapt elements in the design of the furniture or fittings to create a completely original theme. A motif from the design of the curtains, for instance, can be used as a basis for a stencil or stamp pattern. The overall style of the room could be

ABOVE: A stamped rose motif on a neutral background is quick and simple to do. The motif has been used again to decorate a cream-upholstered director's chair to pull the scheme together.

enhanced with faux effects such as verdigris candlesticks, pewter vases or copper plates. Let your imagination run wild.

Flick through magazines and books, find a colour scheme that appeals and see how you can interpret it into your own interior. Try out your ideas on paper – even a rough sketch with the colours and the main elements of the room in place will help you see whether the scheme will work. Use paint samples so that you are accurate in your choice of colour. The more care you take in planning, the more successful the result is likely to be.

The amount of time and money you have available for decorating are important considerations. If you have only limited time, choose an effect that you will be able to complete without leaving the job half done. Practise the paint techniques before starting on a large-scale project for a room. Check that the type of paint you are going to use is suitable for the particular technique you have chosen. Also figure out how much paint and other materials you will need so that the cost for completing the whole scheme falls within your budget.

Another important point to remember is paint safety. Make sure you have all the equipment you need before you start. Take great care when using stepladders. Make sure they are safe before climbing them. Do not lean out in an effort to paint an odd corner, but get down and move the ladder nearer to the place you want to paint. Keep paints and solvents well out of the way of children and animals. Store solvents and thinners tightly capped in their original containers with the relevant labels intact. Put them in a dark, cool area away from heat.

Finally, have fun with your decorating scheme. With careful planning and a bit of practice you will find that not only do you have a new skill, but you can change the interior of your house with the stroke of a brush.

WHERE TO USE SPECIAL EFFECTS

Agate
Use on small objects that would realistically be made from agate.

Ageing/Antiquing
Use to mimic age on painted or bare woodwork.

Animal prints
Each of the zebra, cowhide and giraffe patterns is quite "loud", so use them sparingly, probably with a plain scheme.

Bambooing
Use where bamboo would realistically be used.

Basket weave
Walls are suitable for this effect, which is a controlled version of colourwashing.

Beech
Use where beech would realistically be used.

Bronze
Use on objects that might realistically be made from bronze.

Colourwashing
A basic effect often used for walls. Can also be done on furniture with a different paint mix, using eggshell finish mixed with 50 per cent white spirit (turpentine).

Combing
Can be used on various surfaces. An integral part of woodgraining

Copper
Use on objects that might realistically be made from copper.

Crackle glaze
Furniture is suited to this medium. In most cases it must be used with emulsion (latex) paint, so several coats of varnish are necessary.

Distressing
Use to imitate old painted woodwork, worn and chipped away. Suitable for wood.

Dragging
Traditionally used for woodwork (doors, door and window frames, skirtings (base) boards etc) and furniture as it gives the impression of wood grain.

Dry brushing
Suitable for large walls especially those with various imperfections. Use for an aged paint effect on furniture working in the direction of the wood grain or lengthways.

Faux plaster
Suitable only for a wall finish.

Frottage
Use on any surface with a suitable type of paint.

Granite
Use on surfaces that realistically could be made from this type of stone.

Wrought Iron
Use on surfaces that might realistically be made from iron.

LEFT: Combing is a very versatile effect and looks surprisingly good on floors, especially in bright colours.

Lacquering
Use only on furniture.

Lapis lazuli
Use on small objects that would realistically be made from lapis lazuli.

Leather
Use where leather would realistically be used.

Lining
Use on any surface with the correct type of paint slightly diluted so that it flows easily.

Mahogany
Use where mahogany would realistically be used.

Malachite
Use on small objects that would realistically be made from malachite.

Maple
Use where maple would realistically be used.

Marbling
Use on any surface where marbling would be appropriate, but floating marble must be done on a flat surface.

Oak
Use where oak would realistically be used.

Pewter
Use on objects that might realistically be made from pewter.

Pine
Use where pine would realistically be used.

Ragging
Generally used for walls. Can also be used on furniture with suitable paints.

Roller fidgeting
Use only on walls because of the large flat area needed to achieve the effect. It masks imperfections.

Sky
Ceilings and walls naturally lend themselves to this effect.

Spattering
The easiest way to use this technique is on to a flat surface.

Sponging
Usually used on walls, but can also be effective on furniture.

Steel
Use on surfaces that might realistically be made from steel.

Stippling
Suitable for walls or furniture using water-based or oil-based paint respectively.

Stone blocking
Use on surfaces that realistically could be made from this type of stone.

Tartan (Plaid)
Can be used on any surface as a panel or border of any width or size.

Tortoiseshell
Use on small objects that would realistically be made from tortoiseshell.

Trompe l'oeil panelling
Walls are suitable. Requires

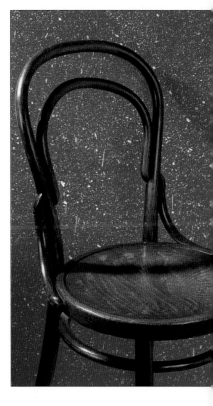

ABOVE: Choose a wide expanse of wall for spattering, as it can get a bit messy!

extensive marking up to make sure all the panels are well proportioned and evenly spaced.

Verdigris
Use on objects that might realistically be made from copper.

Walnut
Use where walnut would realistically be used.

Wood graining
Use where the particular type of wood would realistically be used.

Woodwashing (wood staining)
Use only on bare wood.

GETTING STARTED

The most important requirement for successful results in paint effects is the proper use of the correct materials and tools. With many of the techniques you can achieve stunning decoration with ordinary household paintbrushes, rollers, sponges and artist's brushes, but specialist equipment is needed for some effects. These items are available in decorators' suppliers and craft shops, where you can also ask for advice on their use.

Choose good quality materials. Make sure that you have the right type of paint suitable for the specific technique you are planning. Read carefully through the steps to check that you have everything you need before you start.

ABOVE: A selection of pigments and stains that can be stirred into water-based paint mediums to create unique colours and textures.

OPPOSITE: You can get a different brush for just about every effect, but special brushes are not always necessary for the different techniques.

PAINTING MATERIALS

Acrylic or emulsion (latex) paint and acrylic scumble glaze are the main painting materials that you will need to put a wide variety of paint techniques into practice.

Acrylic primer is a quick-drying water-based primer. It is used to prime new wood.

Acrylic scumble is a slow-drying, water-based medium with a milky, gel-like appearance, which dries clear. It adds texture and translucency to the paint, and the marks you make with brushes, sponges and other tools are held in the glaze.

Acrylic varnish is available in a satin or matt (flat) finish. It is used to seal paint effects to give a more durable and protective finish to the surface. Acrylic floor varnish is extremely hardwearing and should be used on floors.

Artist's acrylic paint can be found in art and craft shops and comes in a wide range of colours. It gives various paint effects a subtle translucent quality.

Crackle glaze is brushed on to a surface, causing the paint laid over it to crack in random patterns to create an aged appearance.

Emulsion paint is opaque and comes in a choice of matt (flat) or satin finish. Satin finish is best for the base colour and matt for paint effects. Use sample pots of paint if you need only a small amount.

Methylated spirits (methyl alcohol) is a solvent that will dissolve emulsion (latex) paint and can therefore be used to distress paint. It is also used as a solvent, thinner and brush cleaner for shellac.

Pure powder pigment can be used to colour paint and can be mixed with acrylic scumble, clear wax or emulsion (latex) paint. It is also used for vinegar graining.

Shellac is a type of varnish, which is available in clear and brown shades. French polish and button polish are in fact shellac and may be easier to find. Shellac can be used to seal wood, metal leaf and paint.

Wax is available in neutral and in brown. It will seal and colour paint. Neutral wax can be mixed with powder pigment.

RIGHT: 1 powder pigments, 2 emulsion (latex) paints, 3 acrylic primer, 4 artist's acrylic paint, 5 acrylic scumble, 6 crackle glaze, 7 neutral wax, 8 brown wax, 9 methylated spirits (methyl alcohol), 10 brown shellac, 11 clear shellac.

STENCILLING MATERIALS

A variety of materials can be used for stencilling, from specialist stencilling paints and sticks to acrylics and emulsion (latex). Each has its own properties and will create different effects.

Acrylic stencil paints

These are quick-drying paints, reducing the chance of the paint running and seeping behind the stencil. Acrylic stencil paints are available in a wide range of colours and can be mixed to create more subtle shades.

Acrylic varnish

This is useful for sealing and protecting finished projects.

Emulsion paints

Ordinary household emulsion (latex) can also be used for stencilling. It is best to avoid the cheaper varieties as these contain a lot of water and will seep through the stencil.

Fabric paints

These are used in the same way as acrylic stencil paints, and come in an equally wide range of colours, which can be mixed to create your own shades. Fixed with an iron according to the manufacturer's instructions, they will withstand washing and everyday use. As with ordinary acrylic stencil paints do not overload the brush with colour, as it will seep into the fabric. Always back the fabric you are stencilling with scrap paper or newspaper to prevent the paints from marking the work surface.

Gold leaf and gold size

These can be used to spectacular effect. The actual design is stencilled with gold size. The size is then left to become tacky and the gold leaf rubbed over the design.

Metallic creams

These are available in many different metallic finishes, from gold through to bronze and copper and silver. Metallic creams can be applied as highlights on a painted base, or used for the entire design. They can be applied with cloths or your fingertip.

Oil-based stencil sticks and creams

The sticks can be used in the same way as a wax crayon, while the creams can be applied with a brush, cloth or your fingertip. With any method, there is no danger of overloading the colour, and they won't run. The disadvantage is their long drying time (can be overnight in some cases); also, the colours can become muddy when mixed. Sticks and creams are also available for use on fabrics.

RIGHT: *1 acrylic stencil paints, 2 oil-based cream and metallic creams, 3 fabric paints, 4 oil-based stencil sticks, 5 emulsion (latex) paints, 6 gold leaf, 7 acrylic varnish, 8 gold size.*

STAMPING MATERIALS

Stamps can be constructed from a variety of materials, and a whole range of exciting and stylish effects can be achieved by combining different paints and inks with your chosen stamps.

Dutch metal leaf and gold size
Metal leaf is a cheap, easy-to-use alternative to real gold leaf. Use a sponge stamp to apply gold size in a repeating pattern. When the size is tacky, apply the gold leaf.

Inks
Water-based inks are too runny to use on their own but can be added to wallpaper paste or varnish to make a mixture thick enough to adhere to the stamp. Use them for paper or card (stock), but not for walls. If you are using rubber stamps, inkpads are commercially available in a range of colours.

Interior filler
Add filler, in its dry powdered state, to emulsion (latex) paint to give it body without diluting the colour.

Paint
Water-based paints such as emulsion and artist's acrylics dry quickly to a permanent finish. Use emulsion paint straight from the can or dilute it with wallpaper paste or varnish. For wall treatments, emulsion paint can be thinned with water and sponged or brushed over the wall as a colourwash.

Pre-cut stamps
Rubber stamps are widely available in thousands of designs. Finely detailed motifs are best suited to small-scale projects, while bolder shapes are best for walls and also furniture.

Sponge or foam
Different types of sponge are characterized by their density. High-density sponge is best for detailed shapes and will give a smooth, sharp print. Medium-density sponge or low-density sponge will absorb more paint and give a more textured result.

Varnish
Use water-based acrylic varnish (sold as quick-drying) for stamping projects. It can be mixed with emulsion paint or ink to thicken the texture and create a range of different sheens. The varnish will also protect and preserve the design of your stamp.

Wallpaper paste
This allows you to thin emulsion paint without making it too runny to adhere to the stamp. Mix up the paste with the required amount of water first, then add the emulsion.

RIGHT: 1 Dutch metal leaf and gold size, 2 coloured inks, 3 low-density sponge, 4 pre-cut stamp, 5 high-density sponge, 6 medium-density sponges, 7 interior filler, 8 emulsion (latex) paint, 9 varnish, 10 wallpaper paste.

PAINTING EQUIPMENT

Different paint effects require different tools. Most of the tools illustrated are cheap and they are easily found in do-it-yourself or decorating suppliers.

Abrasives include abrasive paper and wire (steel) wool, which come in many grades. They are used for distressing paint.

Artist's paintbrushes are needed to paint fine detail.

Decorator's paintbrushes are used to apply emulsion (latex) paint, washes and glazes. They come in a wide range of sizes.

Flat varnish brushes can be used for painting and varnishing. They are often the choice of the experts.

Masking tape comes in many types. Easy-mask and low-tack tapes are less likely to pull off paintwork, and flexible tape is good for going around curves. Fine line tape is useful for creating a narrow negative line.

Measuring equipment such as a ruler, spirit level, set square (T square) and plumbline are needed to mark out designs.

Mutton cloth is very absorbent and can be used for paint effects. Cotton cloths are also used for ragging and polishing.

Natural sponges are used for sponging. They are valued for their textural quality. Synthetic sponges can be used for colourwashing.

Paint containers such as paint kettles, trays and pots are used to mix and store paint.

Paint rollers, small and large, are used to provide an even-textured base colour without brushmarks. They are also used to create textured paint effects.

Rubber combs and heart grainers are used to create textured patterns in paint glazes. Heart grainers (rockers) create an effect of the heart grain of wood.

Softening brushes are used for blending colours together.

Stencil brushes are for stippling paint on to smaller surfaces.

Stippling brushes are usually rectangular, and are used to even out the texture of glaze and to avoid brushmarks.

RIGHT: 1 paint containers, 2 spirit level, 3 plumbline, 4 kitchen paper, 5 artist's brushes, 6 decorator's brushes, 7 flat varnish brushes, 8 hog softening brush, 9 stencil brush, 10 paint rollers, 11 gloves, 12 stippling brush, 13 masking tapes, 14 measuring equipment, 15 craft knife and pencil, 16 heart grainer (rocker), 17 combs, 18 natural and synthetic sponges, 19 mutton cloth (stockinet), 20 rag, 21 wire (steel) wool and abrasive paper.

STENCILLING EQUIPMENT

Stencilling does not require a great deal of specialist equipment; many of the items used are commonly found in most households. Some additional items, however, will make the job easier.

Brushes

It is worth investing in a set of good stencil brushes. The ends of the brushes should be flat and the bristles firm, to allow you to control the application of paint. A medium-sized brush (3cm/1½in diameter) is a useful, all-purpose size, but you may want to buy one size smaller and one size larger as well. You will need a selection of household paintbrushes for applying large areas of background colour, and small artist's paintbrushes for adding fine details.

Craft knife

Use for cutting out stencils from card (stock).

Self-healing cutting mat

This provides a firm surface to cut into and will help prevent the craft knife from slipping. Mats come in a range of sizes and are commonly printed with a grid and imperial or metric measures for accurate and quick cutting.

Masking tape

As the stencil may need to be repositioned it is advisable to hold it in place with masking tape, which can be removed fairly easily.

Paint-mixing container

This may be necessary for mixing paints and colourwashes.

Pencils

Keep a selection of both soft and hard pencils to transfer the stencil design on to card (stock). Use an ordinary pencil to mark the positions of the stencils before applying.

Stencil card

The material used to make the stencil is a matter of personal preference. Special stencil card (stock) is available waxed, which means that it will last longer, but ordinary card or heavy paper can also be used. It is worth purchasing a sheet of clear acetate if you wish to keep your stencil design. This means that you will be able to reuse the design for future projects.

Tape measure and straight-edges

Many stencilling projects require accurate positioning. Measuring and planning the design and layout of your stencils before you begin will aid the result.

Tracing paper

Use this to transfer your stencil design on to stencil card (stock).

RIGHT: 1 sraight-edges, 2 tape measure,
3 stencil brushes, 4 household
paintbrush, 5 self-healing cutting mat,
6 stencil card (stock), 7 tracing paper,
8 soft pencil, 9 craft knife, 10 paint-
mixing container, 11 masking tape.

STAMPING EQUIPMENT

Stamping is a very simple craft and does not require a great deal of specialist equipment. Most of the items illustrated here will already be found in an ordinary household.

Craft knife and self-healing cutting mat

A sharp-bladed craft knife is essential for cutting your own stamps out of sponge. Use a self-healing cutting mat to protect your work surface, and always direct the blade away from your fingers.

Linoleum blocks

These are available from art and craft shops and can be cut to make stamps which recreate the look of a wood block. You'll need special linoleum-cutting tools, which are also easily available, to scoop out the areas around the design. Always hold the linoleum with your spare hand behind your cutting hand for safety.

Masking tape

Use for masking off areas of walls and furniture.

Natural sponge

Use for applying colourwashes to walls and other larger surfaces before stamping.

Paintbrushes

A range of decorator's brushes is needed for painting furniture and walls before stamping. Use a broad brush to apply colourwashes to walls. Stiff brushes can be used to stipple paint on to stamps for textured effects, while finer brushes are used to pick out details or to apply paint to the stamp.

Pencils, pens and crayons

Use a soft pencil to trace templates for stamps, and for making easily removable guidelines on walls. Draw motifs freehand using a felt-tipped pen on medium- and low-density sponge. Use a white crayon on black upholstery foam.

Rags

Keep a stock of clean rags and cloths for cleaning stamps and preparing surfaces.

Ruler and tape measure

Use these to plan your design.

Scissors

Use sharp scissors to cut out medium- and low-density sponge shapes and also for cutting out templates.

Sponge rollers

Small paint rollers can be used to load your stamps. You will need several if you are stamping in different colours.

RIGHT: 1 scissors, 2 craft knife, 3 masking tape, 4 paint rollers, 5 ruler, 6 tape measure, 7 pencils, 8 self-healing cutting mat, 9 rag, 10 natural sponge, 11 paintbrushes.

PAINT REMOVAL

Over several years and many applications of paint there can be quite a build-up of layers on a surface. This is not really a problem on walls and ceilings, but on woodwork and metalwork it is a different matter. Attractive mouldings, especially on skirting (base) boards, window frames and architraves, can become clogged and their features indistinct. In addition, moving parts on doors and windows, such as hinges, and the edges of the frames can start to become ill fitting. The answer to this is to strip off the old paint right back to the wood or metal.

Stripping is also the best option if the paintwork looks in poor condition. It may be deeply chipped or have been badly painted, leaving drips and blobs on the surface. In these cases it is unlikely that a new coat of paint will disguise the imperfections on the surface.

You can remove thick layers of old paint with a chemical paint remover in the form of a paste or a liquid stripper that you brush over the paint surface. Wait for the chemicals to react with the paint, then scrape it off with a paint scraper. These chemicals are strong, so read the manufacturer's instructions carefully before applying them and use them properly.

Another way to strip off old paint is to use an electric heat gun. Again, keep safety well in mind and

ABOVE: The chipped paint on this old chair can easily be removed using one of the techniques shown, and then transformed with a new paint effect.

wear safety glasses or goggles to protect your eyes. Too much heat can scorch the wood or crack glass if you are not careful. Put the old scrapings in a metal container as you work and cover surrounding areas such as the floor to protect them.

Using liquid stripper

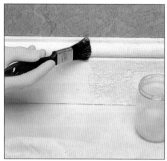

1 Carefully pour some of the stripper into an old glass jar. Then, wearing rubber gloves to protect your hands, brush the stripper on to the painted surface. Leave it until the paint starts to bubble, following the manufacturer's instructions.

2 Scrape off the peeling layers of paint with a paint scraper. Use a shavehook for intricate mouldings.

3 Wash the surface with water or white spirit (turpentine), as recommended by the manufacturer. This will neutralize the chemicals. Then leave to dry.

Using a heat gun

1 Move the heat gun over the surface so that the air stream heats and softens the paint evenly. Scrape off the paint as you work.

2 Be careful not to scorch the wood, especially when working on intricate areas such as mouldings. Use a shavehook to scrape out the paint from these areas.

3 Wearing rubber gloves to protect your hands, rub off any remaining bits of paint with wire (steel) wool soaked in white spirit (turpentine). Work in the direction of the grain of the wood.

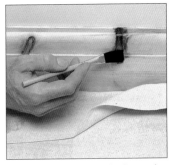

4 Clean any particles of paint out of the crevices in the mouldings with a hand vacuum cleaner.

5 Lightly sand the surface of the wood to smooth it. Wipe any dust away with a clean cloth dampened with a little white spirit (turpentine) or a tack cloth.

6 Finally, seal any knots in the wood so that the resin cannot escape. Do this by brushing on liquid knotting or shellac. Leave to dry.

Using paste remover

1 These strippers dry slowly and are ideal for stripping intricate mouldings. Wear rubber gloves to protect your hands and apply a thick coating of paste remover to the woodwork.

2 Leave the paste to work, following the manufacturer's instructions. Thick layers of paint will need more time. Use a paint scraper to scrape off the paint. Then wash the surface well with water.

SURFACE PREPARATION

Perhaps the most important factor in achieving a successful result in decorating is to make sure that the surfaces are clean and smooth. Careful preparation can seem rather tedious but it is worth the time spent.

Wash walls with a solution of sugar soap, then rinse them well with clean water. Scrape off any pieces of flaking paint and fix any dents and cracks in the plaster with filler (spackle) and a filler knife. When the filler (spackle) has hardened, sand it smooth with fine-grade sandpaper. Similarly, fix any defects in the woodwork. If knots are showing through the existing paintwork, sand them back and apply knotting or shellac. When dry, paint on primer and undercoat to bring the area level with the rest of the surface of the woodwork.

Clean surfaces such as ceramic tiles, china or glass with soapy water and dry them well with a lint-free cloth. You will then need to use specialist paints, as emulsion (latex) and acrylic paints will not adhere well to these smooth surfaces.

Preparing woodwork

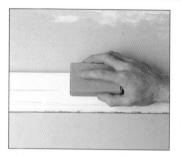

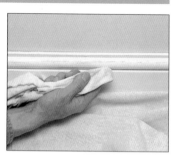

1 Sand down the surface with fine-grade sandpaper over a sanding block. This smoothes the surface of old bits of paint and provides a key to which the new paint can adhere.

2 Wash the paintwork with water and detergent to make sure that it is completely clean of grease and dust. Then rinse it well with clean water so that there is no detergent left to prevent the new paint from adhering.

3 Dampen a clean cloth with white spirit (turpentine) or a tack cloth to remove any dust from intricate mouldings and corners.

Filling defects in woodwork

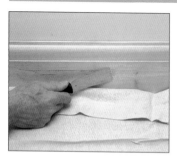

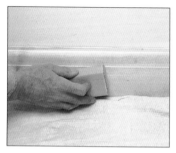

1 With a putty knife, stop any holes, dents or cracks in the wood. Use ordinary filler (spackle) for wood that will be painted, and tinted wood filler for wood that will be varnished.

2 Work the filler into corners with your finger or the corner of a putty knife. Smooth off any excess or edges before the filler dries.

3 When the filler is hard, sand it down so that it is flush with the surface of the wood. The best way to do this is by using fine-grade sandpaper wrapped around a sanding block.

Preparing shiny surfaces

1 Wash shiny surfaces such as tile, china or glass with soapy water. Then rinse them well.

2 Wipe them with a clean cloth dampened with methylated spirits to make sure no grease remains.

Filling cracks in plaster

1 Rake out loose material from the crack with the corner of a putty knife. Undercut the edges of the crack slightly to provide an edge to which the filler (spackle) can grip.

2 Use an old paintbrush to brush out any debris and dust. You could also use the crevice fitment of a vacuum cleaner for this job.

3 Use a water spray to dampen the plaster around the crack so that the filler will not dry too quickly and cause further cracks.

4 Mix up some powdered filler (spackle) on a board, following the manufacturer's instructions. Or use ready-mixed filler if you prefer.

5 Press the filler into the crack with a filling knife. Draw the blade of the knife across the filled crack and then along it. The filler should stand slightly proud of the surrounding surface.

6 When the filler is completely hard sand it smooth so that it is level with the surrounding surface. Do this with a piece of fine-grade sandpaper wrapped around a sanding block.

USING BRUSHES AND ROLLERS

Paint is applied using brushes, rollers or paint pads (pad painters). Brushes are available in a range of widths, so choose one that is suitable for the surface you are painting – for instance, use a narrow brush for the glazing bars of a window. For large areas use a wide brush, or a roller for fast coverage.

If you wish to paint with a previously used brush that has not been kept covered, wash it well first to remove any bits and pieces. Leave it to dry before using it. Check that the ferrule of the brush is securely fixed to the handle and clean off any traces of rust with wire (steel) wool or sandpaper.

Rollers are excellent for large flat areas. Choose a suitable sleeve depending on whether you are painting on smooth plaster or a textured surface. You may also need to use a brush in corners where the roller will not fit. Paint pads (pad painters) cover less quickly than brushes or rollers, but they apply paint more smoothly.

Preparing the paint

1 Wipe the lid of the can first to get rid of any dust. Prise the lid off gently with a wide lever so that you do not damage the lip.

2 Pour some paint into a clean paint kettle (pot) or bucket. You will find a container with a handle easier to work with and replacing the lid on the can will keep the rest of the paint fresher.

3 Use up old paint by first removing any skin from the top, then straining it through a clean piece of cheesecloth (muslin) or an old, fine silk stocking.

Using a brush

1 When using a new brush for the first time remove any stray hairs by working it vigorously across the palm of your hand.

2 Use small or medium brushes by placing your fingers on one side of the ferrule and your thumb on the other. This gives you better control.

3 Hold wide brushes by the handle or your hand will quickly become tired.

Using a roller

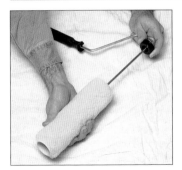

1 Choose a sleeve with a suitable pile and place on the sprung metal cage.

2 Pour the paint into a roller tray until it just overlaps the deeper part.

3 Paint a band in the corners and angles where the roller will not fit.

4 Load the roller by rolling it down the slope of the tray into the paint.

5 Apply the paint by using the roller in overlapping diagonal movements.

6 Blend the sections together by working in parallel to the edges.

Applying the paint

1 Dip only a third of the bristles into the paint. If you put too much paint on the brush you will cause paint to run down the handle or make drips.

2 Tie a piece of wire or string across the top of the paint kettle (pot) or bucket so that you can scrape off excess paint against it.

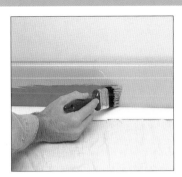

3 Use long sweeping strokes to apply the paint, working in the direction of the grain, until the paint on the brush is used. Then reload with paint and apply it to the next section.

4 Blend the two sections together with short, light strokes. Paint edges and corners by letting the brush run off the edge and repeating the process on the opposite edge.

PAINTING TECHNIQUES

Most of the projects in this chapter are based on a few simple techniques. These can be used on their own, or combined to produce an infinite variety of paint effects. The techniques shown here all use ultramarine blue emulsion (latex) paint. This has been mixed with acrylic scumble glaze and/or water, as appropriate, to achieve the desired effect. Two coats of satin finish white emulsion paint were rollered on as a base. This provides an even-textured, non-absorbent finish, which is ideal to work on as it allows glazes to dry more slowly and evenly than emulsion paint. It also means that if you make any mistakes they are easily wiped off. All these techniques, except the crackle glaze, can be done with artist's acrylic paint mixed with scumble, in which case the effects will look more translucent.

Sponging

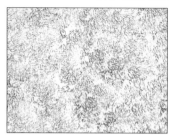

Dilute a little paint with a little water in a paint tray or on a saucer. Dip a damp natural sponge into the paint and wipe off the excess on kitchen paper. Dab the sponge evenly on to the prepared surface in different directions.

Sponging and dispersion

Follow the technique as for sponging, then rinse the sponge in clean water and dab it over the sponged paint before it dries to soften the effect.

Combing

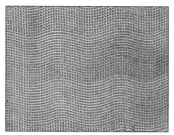

Mix the paint with acrylic scumble and brush on with cross-hatched brushstrokes. Run a metal or rubber graining comb through the wet glaze to make a pattern. This pattern was done with straight vertical strokes followed by wavy horizontal ones.

Colourwashing

Dilute the paint with water and brush on randomly with cross-hatched brushstrokes, using a large decorator's brush. Alternatively, a damp sponge will give a similar effect.

Rubbing in colourwash

Dilute the paint with water and brush on. Use a clean cotton rag to disperse the paint. Alternatively, apply it directly with the rag and rub in.

Frottage

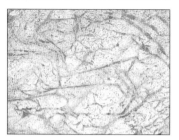

Apply paint with cross-hatched brushstrokes, then press a piece of tissue paper over the wet surface and peel it off. The paint can be diluted with water or scumble.

Dabbing with a mutton cloth

Brush on paint mixed with scumble, using cross-hatched brushstrokes. Dab a mutton cloth (stockinet) over the wet glaze to even out the texture and eliminate the brushstrokes.

Ragging

Mix paint with scumble and brush on, using cross-hatched brushstrokes. Scrunch up a piece of cotton rag and dab this on the wet paint in all directions, twisting your hand for a random look. When the rag becomes too paint-soaked, use a new one.

Rag rolling without brushmarks

Brush on paint mixed with scumble and dab with a mutton cloth (stockinet) to eliminate brushmarks. Scrunch a cotton rag into a sausage shape and roll over the surface, changing direction as you go. Use a new piece of rag when it becomes too wet.

Stippling

Brush on paint mixed with acrylic scumble, using cross-hatched brushstrokes. Pounce a stippling brush over the wet glaze, working from the bottom upwards to eliminate brushmarks and provide an even-textured surface. Keep the brush as dry as possible by regularly wiping the bristles with kitchen paper.

Dragging

Mix paint with scumble glaze and brush on with cross-hatched brushstrokes. Drag a flat decorator's brush through the wet glaze, keeping a steady hand. The soft effect shown here is achieved by going over the wet glaze a second time to break up the vertical lines.

Crackle glaze

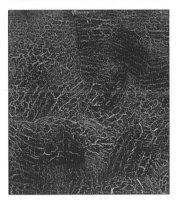

Brush on a coat of water-based crackle glaze and leave to dry according to the manufacturer's instructions. Using a well-laden brush, apply paint carefully on top so that you lay, rather than brush, it over the surface. Work quickly and do not overbrush an area already painted. If you have missed an area, touch it in when the paint has dried. Seal with acrylic varnish.

STENCILLING TECHNIQUES

Stencilling is not difficult to master, but it is worth practising on a small area to get used to handling the stencil brush and to become accustomed to the properties of the various paints you use. The techniques illustrated below show you how to make your own stencils and different ways in which to use them.

TRANSFERRING TEMPLATES

1 To transfer a template on to a piece of stencil card (stock), place a piece of tracing paper over the design, and draw over it with a hard pencil.

2 Turn over the tracing paper, and on the back of the design rub over the lines you have drawn, this time using a soft pencil.

3 Turn the design back to the right side and place on a sheet of stencil card. Draw over the original lines with a hard pencil.

CUTTING STENCILS

1 Place the tracing paper design on to a self-healing cutting mat or piece of thick card (stock) and secure in place with masking tape. Use a craft knife for cutting along the pencil lines.

2 It is safer to move the cutting board towards you and the craft knife when you are working round awkward shapes. Continue to cut out the design, moving the board as necessary.

STENCILLING EFFECTS

Block stencilling in a single solid colour

Use for filling in large areas in a single solid colour. As in all stencilling, remember not to apply the paint too heavily – less is more. Always blot out the paint on to a piece of blotting card (stock) before you begin.

Block stencilling with second colour stippled

When applying two colours, always apply the lighter shade first, then the darker. Do not cover the entire surface with the first colour; leave a gap for the second shade, then blend later. Use a separate, clean brush for each colour.

Block stencilling in two colours

When you apply the first colour, do not fully block out the petals; instead, outline them with the first colour and leave the centres bare. Use the second colour to fill. Take care not to apply the paint too heavily.

Rotating with blocked leaves

Using a very dry brush with a tiny amount of paint, rotate the bristles in a circular motion. This rotating action leaves enough paint on the surface for a lighter, softer look than a block application. Use the same effect in a darker colour on the inside of the petals.

Rotating and soft shading

Using a very dry brush with a tiny amount of paint, place your brush on one side of the stencil and rotate the brush in small circles. Repeat this action, using a slightly darker colour on the edges of the stencil, to create the effect of soft shading.

Rotating and shading in two colours

This is a similar effect to rotating and shading, but is more directional. Using a very dry brush with a tiny amount of paint, place your brush in the centre of the flower and rotate the bristles slightly outwards. Repeat this action, using a slightly darker colour.

Brushing up and down

Using slightly more paint on your brush than you would for rotating, brush up and down only, taking care to keep the lines vertical.

Dry brushing with curve

Using the rotating technique, start at the centre of the design and work outwards in big circles.

Dry brushing and rotating

Apply a tiny amount of paint by rotating the bristles from the centre, and from the outside tips, to give more paint in these areas. Work along the line, using less pressure than on the centre and the tips. This gives a softer effect on the areas in between.

Rotating brush with leaves flicked

Fill in the petals by rotating a very dry brush and a tiny amount of paint. For the flicking effect on the leaves, use slightly more paint on the brush. Working from the centre, flick the paint outwards once or twice. Do not overdo.

Dry brushing, rotating from edge

Using big circular strokes, work from the outside of the whole stencil, moving inwards. This should leave you with more paint on the outside, as there will be less and less paint on your brush as you move inwards.

Brushing up and down from the sides

This is similar to flicking. Using slightly more paint on your brush than you would for rotating, brush up and down, then from side to side. Keep the brushmarks vertical and horizontal to give a lined effect.

Rough stippling

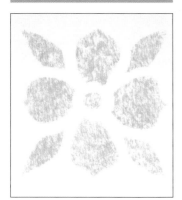

This method uses more paint and less pressure than rotating or flicking. Taking a reasonable amount of paint on the bristles of your brush, simply place it down lightly. This gives a rougher look. Do not go over it too many times as this spoils the effect.

Two-colour stippling

Use less paint than for rough stippling. The second colour is stippled out from the centre, to blend with the first colour.

One-sided stippling

Apply the lighter colour first, up to a point just past the centre. Apply the darker colour, and stipple to the centre. Always start on the outer edge so that you leave more paint on the edges of the stencil design.

Stippling with a dry brush

This is similar to stippling, except that it is essential to dab most of the paint off the bristles before you start. This gives a softer stippling effect.

Gentle stippling from the edges

Using a very dry brush (dab most of the paint off the bristles before you start), stipple from the outside, working inwards. By the time you get to the centre, there should be hardly any paint left on your brush, ensuring a very soft paint effect in this area.

Stippling to shade with two colours

Using a reasonable amount of paint, apply the lighter shade first. Apply the darker shade to one side only of each window. (Here, the second colour is applied to the right-hand side.) A few dabs of the darker colour paint will be quite sufficient.

Flicking upwards with the brush

Using a reasonable amount of paint (not too wet or too dry) on your brush, flick upwards only. This creates a line at the top of the petals and leaves.

Flicking in two directions, up and down

Using a reasonable amount of paint on your brush, flick up and down. Do not use too much paint as it will collect on the edges of the petals and leaves.

Flicking from the outside to the centre

Using a reasonable amount of paint on your brush, flick from the outside edges in to the centre of the design. Flick from the top to the centre, from the bottom to the centre, from the left to the centre, and from the right to the centre.

Flicking from the top to the centre

Using a reasonable amount of paint on your brush, flick from the top edge of the window to the centre of the design, then from the bottom edge of the window to the centre.

Drop shadow, using a block effect

Apply the first colour, which should be the lighter shade, using a block effect. Concentrate on one side of each window (here, the right-hand side). Move the stencil slightly to the left – a few millimetres is sufficient – taking care not to move it up or down. Block again, using a darker colour, to create a drop shadow effect.

TIPS

Check the amount of paint on the stencil brush by practising on a piece of scrap paper. Excess paint can be removed by dabbing the brush on an old saucer or clean cotton cloth.

Clean the stencil brush before using a different colour to keep the colours fresh. It is a good idea to invest in several different-sized brushes.

If you want to use a different colour scheme to that shown in the project, for example to suit your existing decor, see Working with Colour at the beginning of the book for advice and inspiration.

Finally, do not aim for perfectly identical stencilled motifs. Much of the appeal of stencilling lies in its handpainted look and irregularities.

STAMPING TECHNIQUES

Stamping is a quick and effective method of repeating a design on a wide variety of surfaces, using many different mixtures of paints and inks. Ready-made stamps are widely available, usually mounted on wooden blocks, but they are also easy to make yourself using foam or sponge.

MAKING STAMPS

1 Use high-density sponge to create sharply defined and detailed designs. Trace your chosen motif using a soft pencil to give dark, clear lines.

2 Roughly cut around the design, then spray the piece of tracing paper with adhesive to hold it in place on the sponge while you are cutting it out.

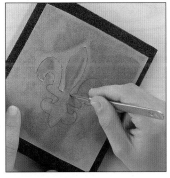

3 Cut along the outline of the motif using a craft knife, then, pinching the background sections, cut them away holding the blade away from your fingers.

4 The surface of low-density sponge is too soft to use tracing paper as a guide for cutting out the stamp. It is easier to draw the design straight on to the sponge using a felt-tipped pen.

5 Sharp scissors can be used to cut out stamps made from low-density sponge and they are especially useful for cutting out the basic shapes of the motif.

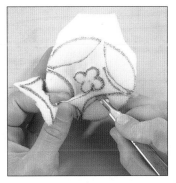

6 As with high-density sponge, the unwanted background areas should be cut away with a craft knife when the outline has been cut, but care is needed as this sponge will tear more easily. Rinse the completed stamp to remove the remains of the felt-tipped pen ink.

PAINT MIXTURES

Wallpaper paste and emulsion paint

Add 50 per cent paste to the emulsion (latex) paint to give a watercolour effect without producing a mixture that is too runny to work with. Apply the mixture using a roller, sponge or paintbrush, or dip the stamp into the paint on a flat plate.

Wallpaper paste and ink

Wallpaper paste thickens the texture of ink, while keeping the rich colour. The effect produced depends on the proportion of ink in the mixture. It will give a more even spread of colour than using emulsion (latex). Apply using a roller or paintbrush.

Varnish and emulsion paint

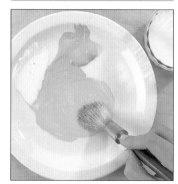

The density of the emulsion (latex) paint is diluted as with wallpaper paste, but this can also be used to create different sheens according to the type of varnish used. Apply with a roller, paintbrush or sponge, or dip the stamp into the paint on a plate.

Varnish and ink

This effect is similar to the wallpaper paste mixture, but creates a smoother mix as both materials are fine in texture. Again, different sheens can be obtained depending on the varnish used. Apply with a roller.

Wallpaper paste and woodstain

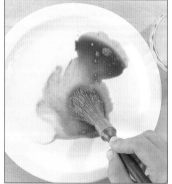

The wallpaper paste dilutes the colour density of the woodstain while thickening the mixture for ease of use. Use quick-drying, water-based woodstains, which are available in a range of colours. Apply with a roller.

Interior filler and emulsion paint

This mixture thickens the paint as opposed to diluting the colour, and is good for creating relief effects. Apply the mixture generously, using a paintbrush, or dip the stamp into the paint on a plate.

HOW TO APPLY PAINT

Using a roller

Pour a little paint on to the side of a flat plate, then, using a small sponge roller, pick up a small amount of paint and roll it out over the rest of the plate until you have an even covering. Roll the paint on to the stamp.

Using a paintbrush

Use a fairly stiff brush and apply the paint with a dabbing or stippling motion. This technique enables more than one colour to be applied and for detail to be picked out. Be careful not to overload the stamp, as this may cause it to slip when stamping.

Dipping into paint on a plate

Brush a thin coat of paint on to a flat plate, then press the stamp into the paint. You may need to do this several times to get an even coating. Initially the stamp will absorb a good amount of paint. Keep brushing more paint on to the plate as you work.

Using a roller and brush

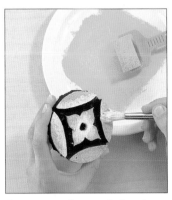

Use a sponge roller to apply the paint evenly over the whole stamp. Use a brush to apply a second colour to act as a highlight or shadow, or to pick out details of the design.

Using a sponge

Spread an even coating of paint on a plate, then use a natural sponge to pick up the paint and dab it on to the stamp. This method allows you to put a light, even covering of paint on to the stamp.

Using an inkpad

Press the stamp lightly on to the inkpad. You may need to do this several times to ensure a good covering. It is difficult to overload the stamp using inkpads. This technique will give a dry look to the stamped motifs.

PREPARING SURFACES

Tiles, china and glass

These are all prepared in the same way, using soapy water to remove dirt and grease, then drying with a lint-free cloth. Appropriate special paints, such as enamel or ceramic paints, must be used as normal emulsion (latex) and acrylic paints will not adhere well and are not sufficiently durable for these surfaces. It is often necessary to strengthen the finished design by applying a coat of varnish.

1 Wash the tile or glass with soapy water and rinse thoroughly. To remove any remaining traces of grease, give the surface a final wipe with a cloth dipped in methylated spirits (methyl alcohol) and leave to dry.

2 When printing on a curved surface, carefully roll the stamp while holding the object securely. Sponge stamps are best suited for this purpose. Rubber stamps are less suitable.

Fabrics

Fabrics must be washed and ironed before stamping to remove any dressing and allow for any shrinkage. Use special fabric paint or ink so that the item can be washed after stamping. Fix the paint to the fabric according to the manufacturer's instructions.

1 Once ironed, lay the fabric on a flat surface and tape down the edges to hold it firmly in position.

2 Place a piece of card (stock) or scrap paper under the area to be stamped to stop any of the paint bleeding through the fabric.

Wood

Wood should be lightly sanded before stamping and varnished afterwards. New wood should be sealed with a coat of shellac to stop resin leaking through the grain. When using woodstains, keep the stamp quite dry to stop the stain bleeding into the grain of the wood.

1 Sand the surface of the wood, then wipe down with a soft cloth to remove any loose dust.

2 Once dry, the stamped design can be rubbed back with abrasive paper to create a distressed effect.

PLANNING A DESIGN

1 With the aid of a spirit level, draw a faint pencil line to use as a guide when stamping.

2 Stamp the motif several times on scrap paper and cut out the prints. Tape them to the wall so that you can judge how your design will look.

3 When using a stamp mounted on a block, you can draw a straight line on the back to help with positioning. Align the block with the pencil guideline on the wall.

4 A piece of card (stock) held between the previous print and the stamp will ensure that there is consistent spacing between the motifs.

5 For a tighter design, butt the stamped motifs together without any spacing.

6 Once the paint is dry, the pencil guideline can be removed using a clean cloth wrung out in soapy water and rubbed along the line.

STAMP EFFECTS

Although basic stamping is a very simple and straightforward technique, you can achieve many different and subtle effects with stamps, depending on the paint mixture you use and the way in which it is applied. The same stamp, cut from high-density sponge, was used to make all the following prints.

Half-shade

Roll the first, paler colour over the stamp, then roll a second, darker shade over one half only, to create a three-dimensional shadowed effect.

Two-tone

Using a paintbrush, load the stamp with the first colour, then apply the second colour to the top and bottom edges only.

Two-tone with dry roller

For an even subtler colour mix, roll the second colour right over the first using a very dry roller.

Contrasting detail

To pick out details of the design in a contrasting colour, apply the first colour with a roller, then use a paintbrush to apply the second contrasting colour in the areas you want.

Partial outline

This shadow effect is produced by stamping the motif in one colour, then partially outlining the print using a paintbrush or felt-tip pen. For a natural shadow effect, place all the shadow on either the right-hand or left-hand side.

Drop shadow

Another, very subtle, effect of shadows and highlights can be produced by stamping the motif in the darker colour first. When this is dry, load the stamp with the paler colour and print over the first image, positioning the stamp slightly to one side.

Stippled

This stippled effect gives the stamped print lots of surface interest. Apply the paint with a stiff paintbrush and a dabbing, stippling motion.

Wallpaper paste

Adding wallpaper paste to emulsion (latex) paint gives the stamped print a translucent, watercolour quality.

Light shadow

Here the paint has been applied with a roller, covering each element of the motif more heavily on one side to create a delicate shadow effect.

Second print

After loading the stamp with paint, print first on a piece of scrap paper. This very delicate image is the second print.

Sponge print

Apply a sponge print in one colour over a rollered colour in another colour for a different effect, as shown here.

Distressed

A single colour of paint applied with a dry roller produces an aged, distressed paint effect.

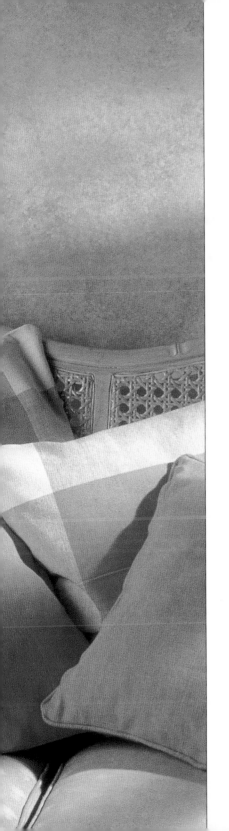

CREATING THE EFFECTS

The following pages show how to create the paint effects that are used later in the projects. They also provide a wealth of further techniques that will inspire you to try out new decorating ideas in your home. All the methods are described in clear steps so that you can produce stunning results with the simplest of instructions. The effects range from basic background techniques, then progress on to planning patterned effects and painting a variety of faux finishes. Read through each one before you start it so that you know what it entails and what you will need in terms of materials and equipment.

ABOVE: Sometimes the simplest effects work best – for a really contemporary feel, combine a beechwood effect on the table with a broad stripe on the wall behind.

OPPOSITE: The soft muted shade on the walls perfectly complements the light wood furniture and the green and burnt-orange cushions.

BASIC FINISHES

The techniques demonstrated in this section are
traditional paint effects, most of which can be used
for all-over impact. They are mainly suitable for
decorating large areas quickly and with ease.
Several, such as distressing, antiquing and
lacquering, are ideal for putting your own personal
stamp on furniture, while others, such as crackle
glaze and gilding, will enable you to transform
small items and home accessories into something
decorative and special.

COLOURWASHING

Colourwashing is usually done with a broad brush using emulsion (latex) paint diluted with water, wallpaper paste and emulsion glaze to make a mixture known as a wash. The effect varies depending on the consistency of the paint mixture and the method of applying the colour. Here, two different tools are used: a large household paintbrush and a synthetic sponge.

COLOURWASHING ONE LAYER

Colourwashing is a quick and flexible effect and is particularly good at disguising small imperfections. Generally, a good guide for mixing is to use 50 per cent emulsion (latex) paint with 50 per cent wallpaper paste. The stronger the paint colour, and the paler the basecoat, the stronger the effect.

ABOVE RIGHT: The broad strokes used in colour washes work well in bathrooms where the humidity can sometimes leave marks on flat, plain walls.

Using a brush

1 Using a paint kettle (pot), mix 50 per cent emulsion (latex) paint with 50 per cent wallpaper paste (premixed to a thin solution). Using at least a 10cm/4in brush (up to 15cm/6in), dip the tip into the mixture and wipe off the excess on the side of the kettle (pot). Add the first dashes on to the wall, well spaced.

You will need

- emulsion (latex) paint
- wallpaper paste
- paint kettle (pot)
- large paintbrush

2 Without adding more paint, brush out these dashes in random directions using broad sweeping strokes.

3 Continue along the wall adding a little more paint as you go and using quite a dry brush to blend the joins (seams).

Using a sponge

1 Mix the paint in a paint kettle (pot) using 50 per cent emulsion (latex) paint and 50 per cent wallpaper paste (premixed to a thin solution). Dip the side of the sponge in to the kettle, scrape off the excess on the side of the kettle and add random dashes on to the wall.

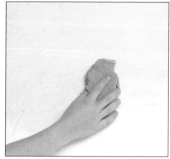

You will need

- emulsion (latex) paint
- wallpaper paste
- paint kettle (pot)
- synthetic sponge

2 Using broad strokes, smear the paint across the wall in varying directions in a large wiping motion.

3 Continue the next section by adding more paint and soften the joins (seams).

COLOURWASHING ONE LAYER

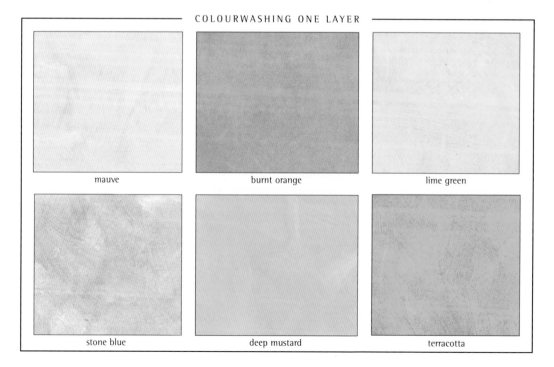

mauve

burnt orange

lime green

stone blue

deep mustard

terracotta

COLOURWASHING TWO LAYERS

This is done in the same way as colourwashing one layer but once the first layer is dry a second colour is applied on top. This layering will soften the overall effect of the brush or sponge marks. Try different colour variations and layering combinations.

You will need

- emulsion (latex) paint in two colours
- wallpaper paste
- paint kettle (pot)
- large paintbrush

Using a brush

1 Mix the paint in a paint kettle (pot) using 50 per cent emulsion (latex) paint and 50 per cent wallpaper paste (premixed to a thin solution). Apply with random strokes to the wall, varying the direction as you go. Continue over the whole surface.

2 When the first layer is completely dry repeat step 1 using a second colour of paint.

3 Add more paint and soften the joins (seams). The overall colourwash effect will be much softer than with using just one colour.

Using a sponge

1 Mix the paint in a paint kettle (pot) using 50 per cent emulsion (latex) paint and 50 per cent wallpaper paste (premixed to a thin solution). Apply with a sponge using random strokes. Continue over the whole surface.

You will need

- emulsion (latex) paint in two colours
- wallpaper paste
- paint kettle (pot)
- synthetic sponge

2 When completely dry apply a second colour with a sponge in the same way as in step 1.

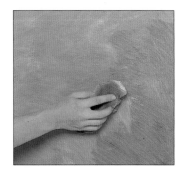

3 Add more paint and soften the joins (seams) as you work.

COLOURWASHING TWO LAYERS

camel under cream

purple under mauve

jade green under pale green

blue under cream

burnt orange under mustard

red under pale yellow

LEFT: Colour-washing is ideal for covering large surfaces quickly and easily. By mixing two shades of blue, one darker than the other, a strong, Mediter-ranean hue can be achieved.

SPONGING

Sponging is a simple technique that is perfect for the beginner because of the ease and speed with which large areas can be covered. It literally consists of dipping a sponge into undiluted paint, scraping off the excess and dabbing on to the wall. Varied effects can be made by using either a synthetic sponge or a natural sponge. A natural sponge will produce smaller, finer marks while heavier marks can be created with a synthetic sponge, such as a car washing sponge, by pinching out small chunks from it. You may find edges and corners are a bit tricky with a larger sponge, so use a smaller piece of sponge for these.

SPONGING ONE LAYER

Much of the effect you achieve with this technique relies on your choice of colour over a base coat. Experiment with colour variations and layering.

You will need

- emulsion (latex) paint
- natural sponge

Using a natural sponge

1 Dip the sponge into the paint and scrape off the excess, ensuring that there are no blobs left on the sponge. Lightly dab on the paint, alternating the angle of application.

2 Add more paint, continuing to work over the surface. Fill in any gaps and make sure the overall pattern is similar.

Using a synthetic sponge

1 Take an ordinary synthetic sponge and pinch chunks out using your forefinger and thumb. Do this especially along the edges so that there is no sharp line left, and also remove pieces from the middle. Dip the sponge in the paint, scrape off the excess and dab on to the wall in alternating angles.

You will need

- emulsion (latex) paint
- synthetic sponge

2 Continue over the surface, making sure the pattern is even and filling in any gaps.

SPONGING

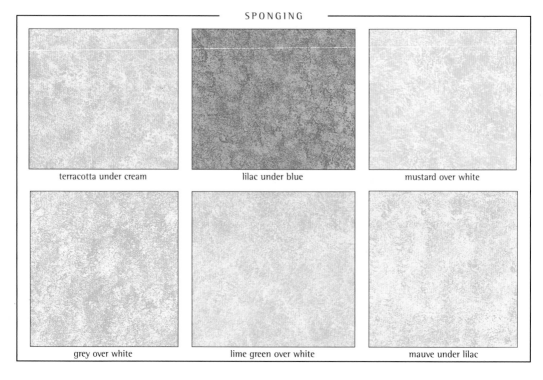

terracotta under cream   lilac under blue   mustard over white

grey over white   lime green over white   mauve under lilac

SPONGING TWO LAYERS

The technique is the same as for sponging one layer, but the overall effect is deepened by the addition of another colour.

You will need

♦ emulsion (latex) paint in two colours
♦ natural sponge

Using a natural sponge

1 Apply a single layer by dipping the sponge into the paint, then scrape off the excess and dab on to the wall for an even pattern. Making the pattern even is not quite so important when applying two colours because the second layer will soften the effect. Allow the surface to dry completely.

2 Wash the sponge out and dry it thoroughly. Dip it into the second colour paint, scraping off the excess as before and dabbing on to the surface. Do not over-apply it, however, as you must make sure the first colour isn't totally covered.

Using a synthetic sponge

1 Pinch out the sponge to remove the harsh edges and large chunks in the middle. Dip into the paint, scrape off the excess and dab on to the wall in varying angles. Allow the surface to dry completely.

2 Wash the sponge out and ensure that it is completely dry before applying the second colour as before by dipping in the paint, scraping off the excess and dabbing on to the wall. Use a lighter movement so that the first colour is not totally covered.

You will need

◆ emulsion (latex) paint in two colours
◆ synthetic sponge

RIGHT: Sponge a plain lamp base to make a bold decorative statement.

SPONGING LAYERS

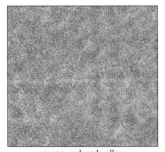

orange, red and yellow

pale green, jade and grey

turquoise and lime green

pale terracotta and yellow

purple and grey

cornflower blue and grey

DRAGGING

A special dragging brush is often used to achieve this effect, but it can also be done with a household paintbrush or even the end of a sponge, though the coarseness of the tool used will determine the finished effect. The actual technique is very simple – the brush is pulled down over wet paint in a clean line to produce a striped effect. These lines must be unbroken, so doing a full-height room may prove extremely difficult. To overcome this a horizontal band can be added, perhaps as a dado (chair) rail, which will break up the height of the room and allow a full reach of the brush within each of the sections.

You will need

- pencil
- ruler
- emulsion (latex) paint
- wallpaper paste
- paint kettle (pot)
- large paintbrush
- dragging brush
- damp cloth

1 Draw a baseline. Mix emulsion (latex) paint with 50 per cent wallpaper paste (premixed to a thin solution) in a paint kettle (pot) and brush on in a lengthways band, slightly overlapping the baseline. Work on one small section at a time, about 15-25cm/6-10in wide.

3 Brush on more paint mixture, joining up with the last one and slightly overlapping.

2 Dampen the dragging brush with the wash before use, as it will initially take off too much paint if used dry. Then take the brush in one hand and flatten the bristles out with your other hand. Pull the brush down in as straight a motion as possible. This will create deep groove lines in the paint mixture.

4 Drag straight over the join (seam) and continue dragging.

5 Once this top section has been done, take a damp cloth and, pulling along the pencil line, remove the excess paint.

6 Drag in a horizontal motion across the bottom of the baseline, creating subtle stripes in a different direction.

RIGHT: To achieve this effect on a simple wooden picture frame, paint a layer of pale orange emulsion (latex) on the frame, masking the corners to create crisp angles. Then paint on a second coat in a deeper shade and drag the brush through this layer before allowing it to dry.

DRAGGING

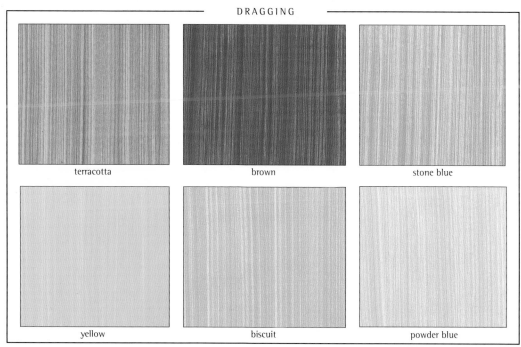

terracotta

brown

stone blue

yellow

biscuit

powder blue

DRY BRUSHING

This is a technique that uses very little paint. The tips of the bristles of the brush are literally dipped into the paint kettle (pot) and as much paint as possible is removed. Then the brush is held almost parallel to the wall and, with little pressure applied, the paint is brushed on in varying directions. The technique is similar to colourwashing but the paint does not totally cover the surface and creates a more textured effect. However, it also emphasizes any dents or imperfections in the surface and you should consider whether this technique is appropriate before application. It suits a rustic setting, perhaps in a kitchen or outdoor room.

DRY BRUSHING WITH ONE COLOUR

As with colourwashing, you can apply just one layer of colour. To enhance the textured look make sure that the base coat remains visible underneath.

RIGHT: Use this technique over bare wood, such as this kitchen stool in white.

You will need
◆ emulsion (latex) paint
◆ wallpaper paste
◆ paint kettle (pot)
◆ large paintbrush

1 Dip the tip of a large household paintbrush into undiluted paint. Scrape off as much as possible and brush on to the wall in varying directions, covering about 2,000 sq cm/2 sq ft.

2 Continue working in the same way, only adding more paint to the brush when there is hardly any paint left at all. But do ensure that the base coat still appears underneath.

3 Add a little more paint to the surface until the whole effect is evened up and slightly softened. The more the surface is brushed over the softer the effect.

DRY BRUSHING WITH TWO COLOURS

Adding a second layer of colour slightly deepens the overall effect. Make sure the amount of paint going on to the wall is actually lighter than the first coat, as the base coat and the first colour still need to be visible.

1 When the first colour is dry add a second colour, working in the same way.

2 Add more paint all over so that the effect is even.

3 Go back over the entire surface filling any gaps or holes that have been created. This is often best achieved by standing as far back as possible and viewing the wall as a whole.

You will need

- emulsion (latex) paint in two colours
- wallpaper paste
- paint kettle (pot)
- large paintbrush

DRY BRUSHING

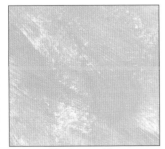

biscuit over white

lime green over white

powder blue over white

cornflower blue under white

deep mauve under pale mauve

red under camel

STIPPLING

Stippling gives a delicate and subtle finish. The technique consists of making fine, pinpoint marks over a wash of emulsion (latex) paint and it creates a soft, mottled effect. However, it can be quite tiring to do as the brush has to be dabbed over the surface many times applying a good amount of even pressure. A two-man team can speed up the process with one person applying the paint and the other stippling the surface.

A specialist (specialty) stippling brush is useful as it provides a large area of compact bristles, but it is not essential. A wallpaper pasting brush or large household paintbrush is suitable and will create a more obvious stippled effect because of the coarseness of the bristles. Whichever large brush you use, you will also need a small household brush (probably about 2.5cm/1in) to achieve the effect in the edges and corners.

You will need

- emulsion (latex) paint
- paint kettle (pot)
- wallpaper paste
- household paintbrush

Using a household paintbrush

1 Mix up a wash of 50 per cent emulsion (latex) paint and 50 per cent wallpaper paste (premixed to a thin solution) in a paint kettle (pot). Brush on a thin, even coat of the mixture over an area of about 2,000 sq cm/2 sq ft.

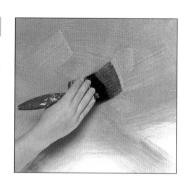

2 Take the brush and dab over the surface with the tips of the bristles until the effect is even all over.

3 Continue stippling over the surface until there are no obvious joins (seams) and the whole effect looks soft and even.

LEFT: Dark green acrylic is stippled over light green on this picture frame.

Using a stippling brush

1 Mix 50 per cent emulsion (latex) paint
with 50 per cent wallpaper paste
(premixed to a thin solution). Brush a
thin, even coat of the mixture over an
area of about 2,000 sq cm/2 sq ft.

You will need

- emulsion (latex) paint
- paint kettle
- wallpaper paste
- stippling brush

2 Dab over the surface with a
stippling brush. Continue dabbing
over the area with the stippling brush
until the entire effect is even and
pleasing to you.

3 Repeat the process until the whole
area is finished.

STIPPLING

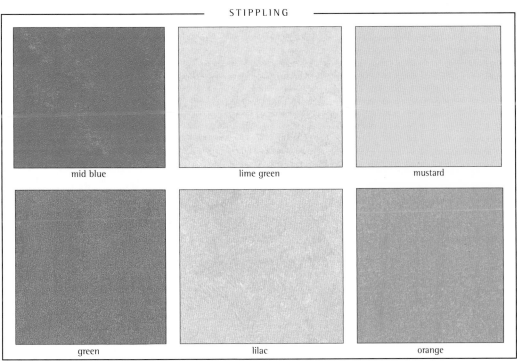

mid blue   lime green   mustard

green   lilac   orange

ROLLER FIDGETING

This is a quick and simple technique and consists of pouring two undiluted emulsion (latex) paint colours into a roller tray, one at each side. You will find that the two paints will sit quite happily together and do not instantly mix. Then, a long pile masonry roller is skimmed over the surface of these colours until a good thick coat is applied. This is rollered on to the wall at varying angles. Little pressure is needed as the texture of the roller and the two colours will do most of the work.

The more the paint is rollered on, the more the colours will blend together, giving an overall dramatic effect. The impact of the effect will depend on the strength of the colours that are used and how many times the wet paint is rollered over. For the edges and corners use a 2.5cm/1in brush and stipple the surface so that it blends in to the rest of the effect. This technique covers a large area in a short time and is simple enough for even the most novice of decorators.

Interesting colour combinations to use are red and camel, powder blue and cream, yellow and cream, pale and dark mauve, mid (medium) blue and mid (medium) green, purple and shocking pink, terracotta and pale terracotta, and sage green and mint.

1 Pour two colours into each side of the pool of the roller tray. Apply a thick coat from here onto the roller so that it will look like a two-tone effect. Apply the roller to the wall at varying angles using short strokes.

2 Continue to work without applying any more paint to the roller until the colours are slightly softened together. The roller can be turned round so that you do not end up with a slightly striped effect on the wall. Keep the angles as random as possible.

3 Go over the whole effect with the roller to soften it. Add more paint when starting another area. Stand back every so often just to make sure there is no heavy concentration of one colour in any particular area.

You will need

- paint tray
- emulsion (latex) paint in two colours
- long pile masonry roller
- 2.5cm/1in household paintbrush

OPPOSITE: Using a mixture of muted colours on your roller looks good in a living room and helps to creates a calm place in which to relax and entertain.

ROLLER FIDGETING

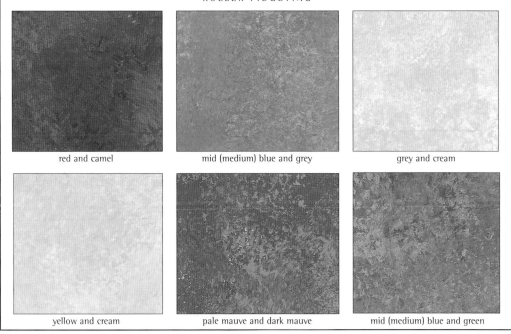

red and camel

mid (medium) blue and grey

grey and cream

yellow and cream

pale mauve and dark mauve

mid (medium) blue and green

RAGGING

Ragging can be done in two ways – ragging on and ragging off – and both techniques are as simple as they sound. With ragging on you dab the rag into the paint then dab on to the surface . With ragging off you brush paint on to the surface and then use a rag to remove some of the paint, leaving a ragged print.

The recommended "rag" to use is a chamois, as it creates a definite print, though you can use most types of cloths for a particular effect. When using either of the techniques, the chamois leather should be periodically squeezed out, as too much paint will result in blobs and drips on the wall.

RAGGING ON

This technique is as simple as sponging, but leaves a sharper effect. Again, the choice of colour you rag on over a base coat will dictate the impact of the finished effect. Make sure that the ragging is evenly applied.

You will need

- emulsion (latex) paint
- wallpaper paste
- paint kettle (pot)
- roller tray
- chamois

1 Mix 50 per cent emulsion (latex) paint with 50 per cent wallpaper paste in a paint kettle (pot). Pour into a roller tray. Scrunch up a chamois, dip it into the paint and dab off the excess, then dab the "rag" on to the wall.

2 Continue rescrunching the chamois and dipping it into the paint as before, then dabbing it on to the wall until the wall is covered evenly.

LEFT: Ragging can also be used to create a patterned effect, as on this colourful harlequin screen.

RAGGING OFF

Ragging off produces a stronger effect, like crumpled fabric.

1 Mix 50 per cent emulsion (latex) with 50 per cent wallpaper paste (premixed to a thin solution) in a paint kettle (pot). Brush the wash on over a large area.

2 Take a chamois, scrunch it up into a ball and dab on to the wall to gently remove small areas of paint. Vary the angles with each dab. Wring out the chamois and scrunch it up again at any time when it is a bit too heavy with paint or the ragging marks are looking a little too repetitive.

3 Continue working over the surface until the entire effect is even. If you find you are taking off too much paint, apply more immediately with a brush and then dab the chamois over the surface again as before.

You will need

- emulsion (latex) paint
- wallpaper paste
- paint kettle (pot)
- chamois

RAGGING

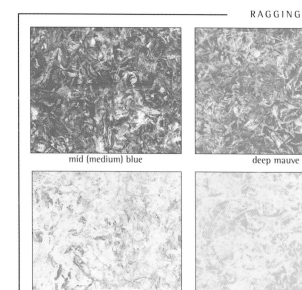

| mid (medium) blue | deep mauve | biscuit |

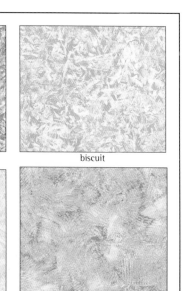

| grey | pale mauve | terracotta |

COMBING

Combing is an easy technique that also enables you to use your own imagination to create a variety of patterns. The basic method involves pulling a comb through paint that is still wet, in order to give a lined effect. A specialist (specialty) rubber combing tool is a recommended purchase, as it is sturdy as well as being flexible and washable, but you could make your own comb if necessary using stiff cardboard with teeth cut out of it. The number of patterns that can be produced is almost endless but you should practise each effect beforehand to test the ability to reproduce it over and over again. Make sure that the surface you are working on is totally smooth or the comb will jump and miss sections and the overall effect will look messy.

BASIC COMBING

Basic combing involves pulling the comb down in a straight line. When straight combing you must also remember that the comb needs to be pulled down in a clean sweep. You may find it difficult to comb an entire wall by pulling the comb all the way from the top to the bottom in one stroke. A straight combing effect is more suitable for a small area.

1 Mix 75 per cent emulsion (latex) with 25 per cent wallpaper paste (premixed to a thin solution) in a paint kettle (pot) and brush on in a vertical direction.

2 Hold the comb at a 90-degree angle to the wall and pull down in a straight line. If the comb wobbles or you make a mistake, just brush more paint over it immediately and rework the combing in the same way as before.

LEFT: A chequerboard floor is given the extra effect of a combed texture.

MAKING PATTERNS

Practise continuous patterns and broken patterns where you lift the comb from the surface at regular intervals. There are endless variations you can try, and they work particularly well if you combine them with contrasting colours. Always allow the base coat to dry before applying the top coat and comb the pattern immediately, while the paint is still easy to manipulate.

Vertical and horizontal stripes.

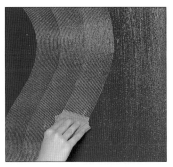

Long wave using parallel strokes.

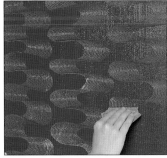

Scrolls using elongated "S" shapes.

Chequerboard made by crossing vertical and horizontal lines at regular intervals.

COMBING

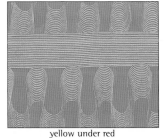

yellow under red

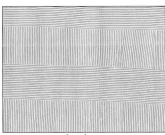

camel under cream

grey under green

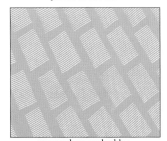

grey under powder blue

cream under yellow

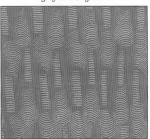

white under deep mauve

FROTTAGE

Frottage consists of brushing a wash on to the wall or surface and then taking either a piece of paper or plastic, placing it over the top while the paint is still wet, scrunching it slightly and then lifting it away. Once removed, the paper or plastic leaves quite an obvious folded-fabric effect. The amount of diluted paint mixture is integral to the success of this technique. Too much will result in the paint dripping with only some patches picking up the effect, while too little will not show any print at all. A good even coat should be applied – practice will help you gauge the amount – and the surface can be brushed over with paint mixture again if the first attempt is not as successful as you would like.

USING PAPER

As the newspaper is absorbent, it will remove more of the paint than if you use plastic. Replace the paper with a clean piece as often as is necessary.

You will need
⟡ emulsion (latex) paint
⟡ wallpaper paste
⟡ paint kettle (pot)
⟡ household paintbrush
⟡ newspaper

1 Mix 50 per cent emulsion (latex) paint with 50 per cent wallpaper paste (premixed to a thin solution) in a paint kettle (pot) and brush on the mixture in a large area of about 3,000 sq cm/3 sq ft.

2 Slightly scrunch the paper and lay it flat on to the wall, scrunch it again slightly while it is on the surface and then lift it away cleanly.

3 Finally, scrunch the paper into a ball and dab to remove any large blobs and even up the surface pattern.

LEFT: *The subtle decorative effect of frottage helps to freshen up a plain expanse of wall in a hallway.*

USING PLASTIC

Using plastic for frottage gives a slightly different effect from paper. Instead of removing much of the paint, it will just make a print within it on the surface.

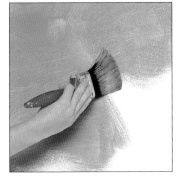

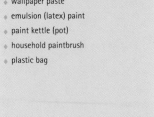

- wallpaper paste
- emulsion (latex) paint
- paint kettle (pot)
- household paintbrush
- plastic bag

1 Mix 50 per cent wallpaper paste with 50 per cent emulsion (latex) in a paint kettle (pot). Brush on to the wall in a large area of about 3,000 sq cm/3 sq ft.

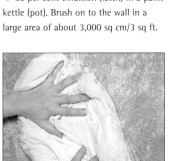

2 Take the plastic bag and scrunch it slightly before applying it to the surface. Once you have placed it against the surface, scrunch it again slightly and then lift it away cleanly.

3 Scrunch the plastic into a ball to remove any excess blobs and soften the overall effect.

FROTTAGE

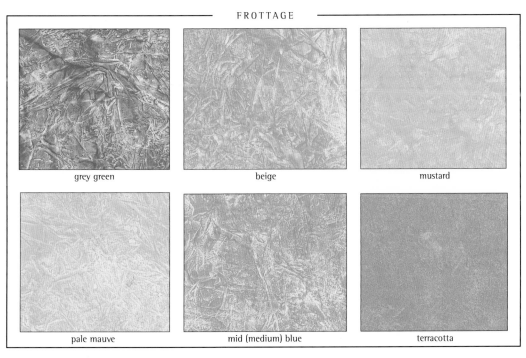

| grey green | beige | mustard |
| pale mauve | mid (medium) blue | terracotta |

SPATTERING

Spattering is produced by layering small dots of different coloured paint. It is an incredibly simple technique when applied to a flat surface, as the consistency of the paint mixture is not crucial to the final effect. If you are spattering an upright surface, however, consistency is a key element because if the paint is too thin it will simply drip down. Test the paint mixture beforehand to prevent any mistakes, which are almost impossible to correct and may result in having to start again. The basic technique of spattering is to load a paintbrush with paint and then knock this against another to launch small dots and spatters of paint onto the surface, moving the position constantly to control the distribution.

The colour of the base coat is important as this will probably remain the overall dominant colour since the spattering itself is a purely decorative rather than a covering effect. You can use a number of different colours to spatter, but simple colour combinations to try are sage over jade green, navy over lilac, mustard over terracotta, cream over camel, mauve over purple and lime green over turquoise.

You will need

- emulsion (latex) paint in at least three colours
- paint kettle (pot)
- household paintbrush
- medium artist's brush

1 Apply the first coat of base coat of emulsion (latex) paint.

2 Once this is dry, add a second coat of the base coat for a solid finish.

3 Mix the second colour with about 25 per cent water in a paint kettle (pot) until it is thin and creamy. Take an artist's brush and dip it into the mixture. Scrape off excess paint on to the side of the container and flick the bristles to create large dots.

4 Once the second colour is dry, take a third colour and mix with 25 per cent water in a paint kettle (pot) until it has a creamy consistency. Again, take the artist's brush, dip it into the paint, and scrape the excess on to the side of the kettle (pot). Create dots on the surface by tapping one brush on to the other.

5 Make finer dots with the third colour by flicking the bristles with your index finger.

RIGHT: This wall is spattered with a mixture of slightly diluted white and yellow emulsion paint over a navy blue base coat.

SPATTERING

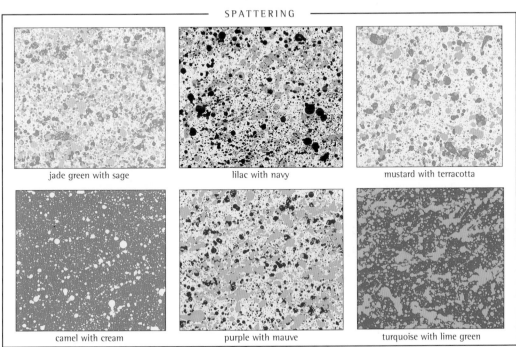

jade green with sage

lilac with navy

mustard with terracotta

camel with cream

purple with mauve

turquoise with lime green

DISTRESSING

Distressing is a way of ageing paint to create chips and scratches that would occur naturally on a painted piece of furniture over a matter of time. The two mediums used here are wax and petroleum jelly. These both create a barrier between the surface and the paint, so once the paint is dry it can be lifted away in certain areas where the medium has been applied. Therefore the careful placing of either wax or petroleum jelly is the key to the success of this technique. Concentrate on areas that would receive more wear and tear, such as edges and corners and around handles; this way the effect will look more natural. Using this technique through layers of different colours creates a more intense distressed effect. Water-based paints must be used, but you will need to varnish the surface for durability.

USING WAX

The easiest way to apply wax to distress a piece of furniture is to use a candle, as you can manipulate it across the edges and into corners. If you are applying two or more layers of paint you will need to wax and rub after each one. Once you have mastered the technique, however, it is a very inexpensive way to age new looking furniture.

Distressing one layer using wax

1 Rub with a candle over the surface in the direction of the grain. Even if the surface is not wooden, rub in a lengthways direction over a suitable coloured base coat. Concentrate on the edges where more wear would occur naturally.

You will need
◆ candle
◆ emulsion (latex) paint
◆ household paintbrush
◆ paint scraper
◆ fine-grade sandpaper
◆ varnish

2 Paint over the whole surface with a thin layer of emulsion (latex) paint and leave it to dry thoroughly.

3 Use a paint scraper to remove the paint. The paint will be removed very easily in the areas where the wax was applied as it acts as a barrier and stops the paint adhering to the surface beneath. If there is any residual wax left, remove it using fine-grade sandpaper before varnishing.

Distressing two layers using wax

1 If you wish to paint on another layer of colour, first rub over the surface again with a candle in the same direction as in the previous technique. Again concentrate on the edges. Apply the wax quite heavily, as you will need to remove more paint from the second layer to expose areas of both the first coat of paint and the original base coat or wood.

2 Paint over the whole surface with emulsion (latex) paint in a contrasting colour and then leave to dry thoroughly.

3 Again, use a paint scraper to remove the wax and reveal both the first coat and the base coat. Use sandpaper to remove any remaining wax. Varnish to protect the surface.

DISTRESSING WITH WAX

cornflower blue over wood

mauve over wood

terracotta over wood

purple over green over wood

pale yellow over burnt orange over wood

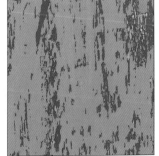

orange over blue over wood

USING PETROLEUM JELLY

Distressing with petroleum jelly produces a far more dramatic effect than using wax. The blobs of petroleum jelly used to create a barrier are bulkier and create tears in the paint that look far less scratchy than with wax. This is a good technique to use for the first layer of distressing, followed by a wax layer on top.

You will need

- petroleum jelly
- small paintbrush
- emulsion (latex) paint
- household paintbrush
- paint scraper
- soapy water
- varnish

1 Using a small brush, load it with petroleum jelly and apply blobs in an elongated motion in the direction of the grain of wood over a suitably coloured base coat. Even if the surface is not wooden, rub in a lengthways direction. You can apply quite a lot of petroleum jelly but try and keep it in long blobs.

2 Carefully paint over this, ensuring that the petroleum jelly is not dragged too much as it will move under the paintbrush.

3 Once thoroughly dry, use a paint scraper to remove the blobs as these acted as a barrier between the top coat and the base coat.

4 Wash down with soapy water, as the paint that is sitting on top of the petroleum jelly will not actually dry and you will not be able to totally remove the petroleum jelly surface using the scraper.

5 Once dry, rub over with a wax candle and then paint as before. (You could use another layer of petroleum jelly, following the same procedure as for the first layer, but the finished effect would not look as subtle.)

6 When the paint is dry remove with a paint scraper. Wipe down to remove all the flakes and then varnish to protect the surface.

RIGHT: Give an old junk table a lift by applying a light blue distressed paint effect to the wood.

DISTRESSING WITH PETROLEUM JELLY

blue over yellow over wood

mauve over blue over wood

green over blue over wood

orange over yellow over wood

purple over red over wood

blue over burnt orange over wood

AGEING AND ANTIQUING

These two techniques are basically a way of eliminating the too perfect and too new look from a newly made piece of furniture. Some of the effects are more dramatic than others, some are more suitable for painted surfaces and others for wood, and sometimes the use of two effects together can achieve a successful finish. Practise on an area that is not normally visible before starting the whole piece.

Generally, ageing adds a distressed appearance to the surface while antiquing is a more delicate and refined approach, which is perhaps better suited to small decorative accessories, such as picture frames.

AGEING

These three effects are all suitable for a painted surface. You can combine them to give a more authentic aged look to a new piece of painted furniture, but be careful not to overdo the effect.

You will need

- burnt umber artists' oil colour paint
- white spirit (turpentine)
- paint kettle (pot)
- fine artist's brush
- household paintbrush

Applying age spots

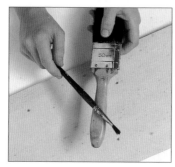 

1 Mix burnt umber artists' oil colour paint with white spirit (turpentine) into a thin wash in a paint kettle (pot). Spatter lightly on the surface of the area with a brush, slightly dotting the surface.

2 While the spattered dots are wet, take a dry brush and brush in one direction. This technique will add random-shaped age spots to the surface.

For a heavy aged look

You will need

- heat gun stripper
- knife
- wire (steel) wool

1 Remove random strips of paint from the surface of the piece of furniture with a heat gun stripper and a knife.

2 When you have finished stripping off the slivers of paint, smooth off with wire (steel) wool to slightly age the remaining paintwork.

For a lighter chipped look

You will need

- paint scraper
- fine-grade sandpaper
- varnish

1 Run a paint scraper across the newly painted surface. This will remove small chunks of paintwork.

2 Soften the effect with fine-grade sandpaper, giving more attention to the edges. Then wipe down with a damp cloth and, when dry, varnish to protect the surface.

RIGHT: You can give a very plain looking mirror an attractive rustic look by applying a heavy aged surface to it. By removing slivers of paint from the top layer of paint, the appearance of the frame is instantly transformed.

ANTIQUING

Here are three different effects that give an older look without making the surface appear too distressed. They can be done on newly painted surfaces for a subtle finish.

You will need

- tinted varnish
- household paintbrush

Applying tinted varnish

1 Apply a tinted varnish over the painted surface. These are available in various ranges of tinted colours. If you are applying the varnish to unpainted wood choose one that will complement it. For instance, use antique pine for a newly made piece of pine furniture.

2 While wet, wipe away the excess. The more you wipe away, the less old the piece will look. To remove more of the varnish, dampen the cloth with white spirit (turpentine) if oil based, or water if acrylic.

Applying button polish (shellac)

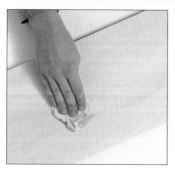 

You will need

- button polish (shellac)
- soft cloth

1 Rub on button polish (shellac) using a soft cloth. Ensure that the whole surface is covered.

2 While wet wipe off the excess to even out the effect.

OPPOSITE: The tinted varnish used to decorate this frame gives it an air of aged distinction. Use this method to soften the harsh appearance of a brand new wooden frame, or apply it to an old frame that needs a new treatment.

Applying a tinted wash

1 Mix a little burnt umber artists' oil colour paint with white spirit (turpentine) in a paint kettle (pot) until you have a very thin wash. Brush on to the surface of the piece of furniture.

2 While wet, wipe off the excess to leave a slightly stained look. To remove the wash, dampen the cloth with white spirit (turpentine). Varnish the surface when dry to protect it.

WOOD WASHING (WOOD STAINING)

Wood washing (wood staining) actually stains wood with a colour, so that the beauty of the grain shows through and is enhanced by the colour. The technique can only be used on totally bare, stripped wood once all traces of varnish, wax or previous paint have been completely removed.

Depending on the product used, the surface may or may not need varnishing, so make sure you read the manufacturer's information on the container. Usually a matt (flat) finish looks appropriate for this technique.

Colours that often work well include yellow ochre, blue, Indian red, violet, cream and pale green.

Using a specialist (specialty) wood wash (wood stain)

You will need

- specialist (specialty) wood wash (wood stain)
- paint kettle (pot)
- household paintbrush
- cloth

1 Pour the pre-mixed wash into a paint kettle (pot). Then brush the wash (stain) evenly on the wood in the direction of the grain.

2 While wet, wipe off the excess with a cloth. This will even the effect and expose slightly more of the grain. Then, leave to dry before varnishing if required.

Using satinwood paint

You will need

- satinwood paint
- white spirit (turpentine)
- paint kettle (pot)
- household paintbrush
- cloth

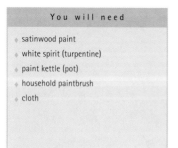

1 Dilute the satinwood paint with 50 per cent white spirit (turpentine) in a paint kettle (pot). Brush the mixture on to the wood in the direction of the grain.

2 While wet, wipe down with a cloth to remove the excess and even the effect. Leave the surface to dry before varnishing if required.

Using artists' oil colour paint

You will need

- artists' oil colour paint
- white spirit (turpentine)
- paint kettle (pot)
- household paintbrush
- cloth

1 Dilute a small blob of artists' oil colour paint with white spirit (turpentine) in a paint kettle (pot) to make a thin wash. You only need to use a small amount of colour, as the pigment is intensely strong. Brush the mixture on to the wood in the direction of the grain.

2 While wet, remove the excess with a cloth to expose a little more of the grain and even the effect. Leave to dry before varnishing if required.

ABOVE: A pale blue wood wash (stain) gives this door a nautical appearance.

WOOD WASHES (STAINS)

yellow ochre

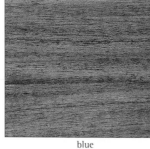

blue

Indian red

violet

cream

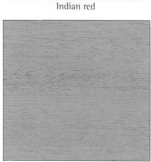

pale green

BASKET WEAVE

This is almost a controlled version of colourwashing in which you apply the paint in an overlapping, interlocking basket weave motion to create an overall pattern within the wet paint. The effect on a wall should be quite loose rather than precise, so that you quickly cover a large area. The basic technique involves brushing on the wash in wide columns, then taking a wide brush, starting at the top and pulling down in alternating strokes creating a criss-cross pattern down the length of the wall.

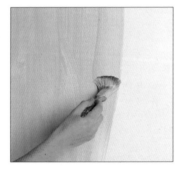

1 Mix 50 per cent emulsion (latex) paint with 50 per cent wallpaper paste (premixed to a thin solution) in a paint kettle (pot). Brush the mixture on the wall in a wide section, totally covering from the top to the bottom.

2 Working down in columns, alternate the angle of the brush from left to right in short strokes.

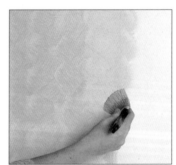

3 Continue up to the edge of each section as you go.

4 Add more paint mixture, again in a long column, slightly overlapping the previous section.

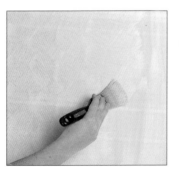

5 Redo the column that has been overlapped, using the same movement of the brush.

6 Continue until the wall is evenly covered with the effect.

RIGHT: Overlapping textured brushstrokes are applied to this wall to leave a basket weave effect. Pale sage-green paint is used over a base coat of white, which gives a subtle background colour.

BASKET WEAVE

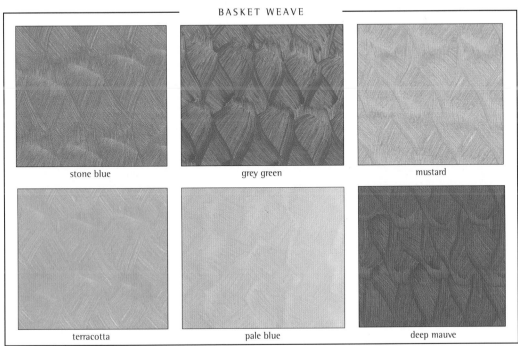

stone blue

grey green

mustard

terracotta

pale blue

deep mauve

CRACKLE GLAZE

This technique reproduces the effect of old, crackled paint, but it can only work if you use a special crackle-glaze medium. A base coat is painted first, and when dry, a layer of crackle glaze is applied. This is followed by a top coat of paint, which will not be able to grip the base coat while drying and subsequently will shrink and crack to produce a crackled effect.

You can achieve some striking colour combinations with this technique; bear in mind that the more the top coat contrasts with the base coat the more dramatic the effect will be. The size of the cracks can usually be made larger with a thicker coat of the crackle medium or by varying the thickness of the top coat of paint, depending on the product. Try a test patch beforehand.

The method of use for crackle-glaze mediums varies, so make sure you carefully follow the manufacturer's instructions. The method outlined here is a general guide.

1 Apply one coat of the base colour and leave to dry thoroughly.

2 Apply a second coat of base colour and leave to dry again.

3 Apply a good solid coat of crackle-glaze medium. The timing for applying the various coats will vary according to the manufacturer, so follow the instructions given on the container.

4 Apply the top coat. Generally, the thicker the top coat of paint, the larger the cracks in the final effect. Make sure the top coat contrasts greatly with the one underneath so that the cracks are obvious. Do not overbrush when applying the top coat, as the effect happens quite quickly and you could spoil it.

CRACKLE GLAZE

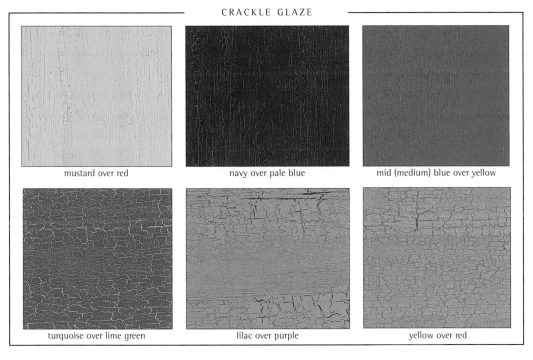

mustard over red

navy over pale blue

mid (medium) blue over yellow

turquoise over lime green

lilac over purple

yellow over red

RIGHT: This plant pot is given a crackle glaze treatment in pale blue and cream and finished with a thin border, drawn with a fine artist's brush to highlight the shape of the container.

LACQUERING

Lacquering creates a totally smooth, flat and highly polished paint finish that reflects great depth of colour. The traditional method of lacquering, as perfected by generations of Asian craftsmen, is very time consuming and consists of applying at least 16 layers of paint. The steps below describe a simulated version, though this still relies on creating a totally smooth finish using rich colours finished with a high gloss varnish. Aerosol spray paints are used for the last layers because they will create the smoothest surface possible.

This technique is still quite time consuming and it is probably wise to attempt smaller objects if you are looking for quick results. Colours that work well in a lacquered finish are turquoise, gold, red, black, deep yellow and teal green.

<table>
<tr><td>

You will need

◆ fine-grade sandpaper
◆ gloss paint
◆ household paintbrush
◆ spray gloss enamel
◆ spray gloss varnish

</td></tr>
</table>

1 Sand the surface thoroughly until totally smooth. Then wipe clean the surface, making sure that it is completely free of dust.

2 Apply a base coat of high gloss paint and leave to dry thoroughly.

3 Sand the surface again to ensure total smoothness.

4 Apply a second base coat. Leave to dry thoroughly.

5 Spray on a gloss enamel in the same colour as the base coat. Again, leave to dry thoroughly.

6 Spray a gloss varnish over the surface to protect it and provide a final finish.

LACQUERING

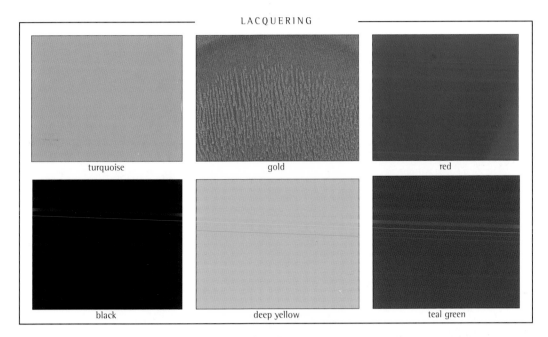

turquoise

gold

red

black

deep yellow

teal green

RIGHT: A smooth lacquered surface emphasizes the shape of this mirror sconce. Red enamel spray paint is used over a claret base coat of high gloss paint. The lacquering is protected with spray gloss varnish.

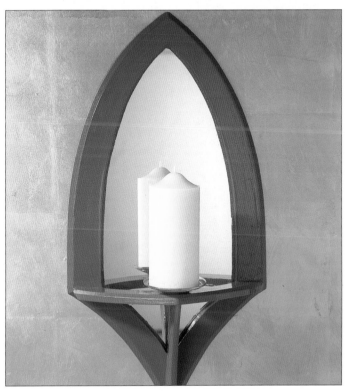

GILDING

Gilding is an attractive finish that enhances and adds a touch of luxury to furniture or smaller items and home accessories. The technique consists of placing a thin layer of gold leaf over a base coat, then burnishing and polishing it to a gloss or sheen finish. Size is used to help the gold leaf adhere, prepared by pouncing or dusting talc on to the surface first. In small areas where the gilding is rubbed away the colour of the base coat shows through and adds depth to the finished effect.

The materials needed for gilding are readily available at craft shops. As real gold leaf is expensive, you may prefer to use Dutch Metal, particularly if you are a beginner to this technique. This is an alloy that gives a similar effect, but it can become tarnished in time, so you will need to varnish it.

You will need

- paintbrushes
- acrylic primer
- grey lacquer undercoat
- dark green lacquer paint
- soft cloths or rags
- talc
- string
- water-based gilder's size
- gold leaf or Dutch Metal
- gilder's pad
- gilder's knife or sharp craft knife
- gilder's tip
- petroleum jelly
- cotton wool balls (cotton balls)
- burnishing brush or soft cloth
- wire (steel) wool
- methylated spirits (methyl alcohol)
- wadding (batting)
- liquid polish

1 Prime the wood to be gilded with acrylic primer and leave to dry for a couple of hours or so.

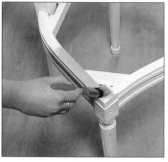

2 Paint on a coat of grey lacquer undercoat and leave to dry for at least four hours.

3 Paint on one or two coats of dark green lacquer paint and leave each coat to dry for at least six to eight hours, or overnight if possible.

4 Fill a cloth or rag with talc and close it up with string to make a pounce bag. Pounce or dust the areas to be gilded by dabbing the bag on the surface to give a thin sprinkling. Brush off any excess talc.

LEFT: Gilded plant pots make very attractive bases for colourful fresh or dried flower arrangements.

5 Paint a thin, even coat of water-based gilder's size on to the areas to be gilded and leave for 20–30 minutes, until the size becomes clear and tacky.

6 Blow a sheet of gold leaf on to a gilder's pad, cutting it into smaller pieces with a gilder's knife if required. Brush petroleum jelly on to the inside of your forearm and lightly brush the gilder's tip over the petroleum jelly. Then use the tip to pick up the leaf.

7 Lay the leaf on the sized area and gently press into place with cotton balls. Continue until the whole sized area is covered with gold leaf. Burnish with a burnishing brush or soft cloth to remove the excess leaf.

BELOW: Gilding has been used here to add decorative details to a Louis XIV chair.

8 Dip some wire (steel) wool into a little methylated spirits (methyl alcohol) and rub gently on the areas of detail to remove tiny amounts of the leaf.

9 Cover some wadding (batting) with a clean rag, leaving an opening at the top. Add a few drips of polish to soak the wadding (batting), close up and rub over the gilded areas.

STAINED GLASS

Everyone loves the bright jewel colours of stained glass, and it is an easy matter to decorate ordinary household glass containers by painting freehand with special glass paints. Choose colours and motifs to match your china or curtains, or experiment with messages and make up your own patterns. Another interesting technique is to replicate the look of etched glass, relying on the frosted design to give a subtle surface effect. Glass paints and etching paste are available at craft shops.

ETCHING GLASS

Create the pattern or motifs you require by masking the glass with self-adhesive vinyl. The etching paste (cream), will eat the surface of the glass that is not protected by vinyl to produce a frosted effect.

You will need

- self-adhesive vinyl
- scissors
- rubber gloves for protection
- etching paste (cream)
- 2.5cm/1in flat paintbrush
- clean cotton rag

1 Draw your designs on self-adhesive vinyl and cut out. Decide where you want to position them on the glass, then remove the backing paper from the vinyl and stick them down.

2 Wearing rubber gloves for protection, paint the etching paste (cream) evenly over the glass with a paintbrush. Make sure you do not spread it too thinly, or you will find the effect quite faint. Leave to dry for three minutes.

3 Wearing rubber gloves, wash the paste (cream) off under a running tap. Wipe off any residue and rinse. Peel off the shapes, and wash the glass again. Dry the glass with a clean cotton rag.

LEFT: Painted glass picture frames.

PAINTED GLASS

Use simple plain glass objects to decorate and add as much decoration and colour as you like.

You will need

- Glass salt and pepper pots
- Contour relief paint (leading) in two colours
- Glass paints in various colours
- Medium paintbrushes
- Clear varnish

1 Start by drawing a few loose circles on to the pots with black contour relief paint (leading).

2 When the lines are completely dry, colour in the background using the glass paint.

3 Fill in the circles with a different coloured paint or use a variety of different colours.

4 Apply dots of black contour paint (leading) over the background colour to add texture.

5 When completely dry, paint squares over the circles using the gold contour relief paint (leading).

6 Leave the pots to dry for at least 4 hours, then paint with clear varnish.

RIGHT: There are endless plain glass items you can decorate. Simple designs of circles and squares can look stunning outlined in black paint.

FAUX
FINISHES

Techniques that reproduce the look of a particular
surface or material are great fun and satisfying to
paint. The following pages describe a number of
wood and stone finishes for which artists' oil
colours are used, as the lengthy drying times allow
more time to work into the effect, and the colours
are intense and translucent. Enamel paints are used
for metal effects and emulsion (latex) paints for
animal prints and trompe l'oeil decorations.

BIRDSEYE MAPLE

Birdseye maple has an attractive close grain. The wood is often used for parquet flooring as well as for furniture and was popular in the 1930s. This technique is useful if you wish to re-create the look of that era. Birdseye maple has a slightly yellowish tinge, so a pale yellow paint is used for the base coat for this effect. One of the features of the patterning of maple grain is its "eyes" and these are easy to make by simply using your fingertips. Practise on small pieces, before trying a large area, such as floorboards.

You will need

- satin or gloss finish paint in pale yellow
- artists' oil colour paint in Naples yellow and flake white
- white spirit (turpentine)
- paint kettle (pot)
- household paintbrush
- large paintbrush
- varnish

1 Apply two coats of pale yellow satin or gloss finish paint as a base coat. Leave to dry thoroughly. Mix Naples yellow artists' oil colour paint with a little flake white and white spirit (turpentine) until you have a mixture the consistency of a thick cream. Brush on.

2 Drag the glaze in one direction using the same brush as in step 1.

3 To make the pattern in the wet paint push the bristles of the brush into the glaze, coming down within columns, alternating the angles in a tight zigzag.

4 To add the "eyes" to the maple, dab your finger into the wet glaze around the edges of the pattern.

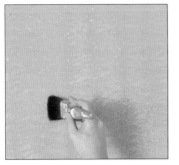

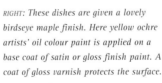

5 Leave for two hours, then soften gently using a large dry brush in a stippling motion. Varnish when dry.

RIGHT: *These dishes are given a lovely birdseye maple finish. Here yellow ochre artists' oil colour paint is applied on a base coat of satin or gloss finish paint. A coat of gloss varnish protects the surface.*

OAK

Perhaps nothing speaks more of a traditional style than solid oak wood furniture or panelling. Here is a way of disguising inexpensive white wood or modern pine and giving it the look of dark oak. If you are painting bare wood, remember to give it a coat of primer before starting the paint effect. This technique requires a heart grainer (graining roller) and a comb to recreate the details of the woodgrain, both of which can be bought quite easily at craft shops or specialist (specialty) decorating shops.

You will need

- gloss or satin finish paint in beige
- paintbrush
- artists' oil colour paint in burnt umber
- white spirit (turpentine)
- graduated comb
- paint kettle (pot)
- fine graduated comb
- heart grainer (graining roller)
- cloth
- large paintbrush
- varnish

1 Apply two coats of beige for the base coat in either gloss or satin finish and leave to dry thoroughly.

2 Mix burnt umber artists' oil colour paint with white spirit (turpentine) in a small paint kettle (pot) until it is the consistency of thick cream. Brush on and drag in a lengthways direction.

3 Using a graduated comb, pull down on the surface, not in totally straight lines, butting one up against the other.

4 Use a heart grainer (graining roller) to start making the details of the graining. Do this by pulling the tool down gently with a slight rocking motion, to create the hearts with random spacings. Butt one line straight over the other as you go.

5 Using a fine graduated comb, comb over all the previous combing.

6 Wrap a cloth around the comb and dab on to the surface to create the angled grain, pressing into the wet paint. Then soften the overall effect using a large dry brush. Varnish when dry.

BELOW: *An old junk cupboard can be picked up inexpensively and by adding an oak finish, here using burnt sienna for a warmer feel, it is instantly transformed into a beautiful piece of furniture.*

MAHOGANY

This beautiful hardwood has a rich, warm colour that seems to suit most styles of home, whether traditional or modern. It was extremely popular during the Victorian era when it was complemented by deep-toned furnishings and fabrics. Mahogany is not as easy to obtain as it once was and is an expensive wood, so all the more reason to paint some for yourself. Practise on sample pieces first to get the effect right, then progress to larger furniture when you have more confidence in the technique.

You will need

- satin or gloss finish paint in dusky pink
- artists' oil colour paint in burnt sienna
  crimson and burnt umber
- white spirit (turpentine)
- paint kettle (pot)
- 10cm/4in paintbrush
- large paintbrush
- varnish

BELOW: Achieve a deeper mahogany finish with a red base coat rather than dusky pink. The rich tones on this chair are produced by using burnt sienna and burnt umber artists' oil colours.

1 Apply two coats of dusky pink satin or gloss finish paint as a base coat and leave to dry. Tint a little burnt sienna artists' oil colour paint with a touch of crimson. Add white spirit (turpentine) until it reaches the consistency of thick cream. Brush it on in elongated sections.

2 Then mix burnt umber with a little white spirit (turpentine) until the mixture is the consistency of thick cream. Fill in the gaps, making elongated shapes.

3 Stipple the surface gently, using the tips of the bristles of a dry paintbrush to soften and blend the overall effect.

4 Starting at the bottom, with a 10cm/4in paintbrush held almost parallel to the surface, drag through the wet paint making elongated arcs. Use the burnt umber area as the middle section. Leave for several hours. Then, before completely dry, soften in one direction using a large dry brush. Varnish when dry.

BEECH

Beech is a light-coloured, straight-grained wood and its close patterning gives it a look of solidity. Beech has become popular in recent years for both furniture and home accessories such as trays, and mirror and picture frames. Its soft, warm colour and generally matt finish adds a quiet, but modern, tone to a room as well as helping to lighten it up. Like oak, beech is sometimes given a limed effect, so if this is what you require allow more of the base coat to show through when painting.

You will need

- satinwood paint in white
- artists' oil colour paint in Naples yellow and white
- white spirit (turpentine)
- paint kettle (pot)
- household paintbrush
- heart grainer (graining roller)
- fine graduated comb
- narrow comb
- varnish

1 Apply two coats of white satinwood paint and leave each to dry. Mix Naples yellow and artists' oil colour with a little white spirit (turpentine) until it reaches the consistency of thick cream, then brush it over the surface. Drag this in a single, lengthways direction.

2 Use a heart grainer (graining roller) to start making the graining. Do this by pulling the tool down gently, slightly rocking it and working in several spaced lines. Do not butt the lines up together.

3 With a graduated comb and working in the same direction, fill in the lines between the heart graining.

4 Again, working in the same direction, soften the effect with a large dry brush. Now take a narrow comb and go over the entire surface in the same direction to add detail to the effect. Varnish when dry.

RIGHT: A beech effect used on a table top.

PINE

Woodgraining and wood effects can seem difficult and daunting to the beginner, but the right choice of colours and suitable base coats can be half the battle. The only specialist (specialty) tools used are a heart grainer (graining roller) and comb, which are necessary as the patterns they create cannot be imitated in any other way. Both are relatively simple to use with a little practice and create convincing effects.

Look at pieces of real wood so that you can learn to replicate the grain accurately. Pine is readily available and you can use a pine effect surface in many locations throughout your home.

You will need

- satinwood paint in pale yellow
- artists' oil colour paint in yellow ochre and burnt umber
- white spirit (turpentine)
- household paintbrush
- paint kettle (pot)
- heart grainer (graining roller)
- large paintbrush
- varnish

1 Apply two coats of pale yellow satinwood paint to the surface and leave to dry thoroughly.

2 Mix yellow ochre artists' oil colour paint with a tiny amount of burnt umber to dirty the colour slightly. Then mix with white spirit to create a thick cream, and brush over the surface.

3 Drag the brush in a lengthways direction over the wet paint to simulate planks.

4 Following the direction of the dragging, pull the heart grainer (graining roller) down gently, rocking it as you work, to create the effect. Butt one line straight over the other.

5 Make a graduated cone shape in random areas in between the heart graining, slightly overlapping it in areas.

6 Soften the surface while wet with a large dry brush by applying only light pressure and brushing in the direction of the effect. Varnish when dry.

BELOW: Wooden floors are ever increasing in popularity and this paint technique is ideal for covering a large area very inexpensively. The chequerboard design used here adds an interesting touch to this natural-look flooring.

BURR WALNUT

Burr walnut is one of the most decorative of wood grains. It is found extensively in furniture where matching panels are used. It is even used for the dashboards of luxury motor cars and for the interior fittings of boats. It is a warm, mid-brown colour, and its graining is fun to replicate because the shapes within the wood are worked with a flowing movement. Make the burrs or "eyes" of the walnut with a piece of cloth wrapped round your index finger, so that the paint blends naturally.

You will need

- artists' oil colour paint in yellow ochre and burnt sienna
- white spirit (turpentine)
- paint kettle (pot)
- household paintbrush
- household cloth (dish cloth)
- large paintbrush
- varnish

1 Mix yellow ochre artists' oil colour paint with a little white spirit (turpentine) until you have a mixture the consistency of thick cream. Brush the mixture on in patches.

2 Then, mix burnt sienna oil colour paint with a little white spirit (turpentine) until a thick cream. Using this mixture, fill in the patches where the yellow ochre has been left.

3 Stipple the whole area with the tips of the bristles of the brush to slightly soften the paint and gently blend the colours together.

4 Fold a household cloth (dish cloth) until it is a square shape and a straight edge is achieved. Make circular ribbon shapes, gently pulling the cloth from side to side while doing this to make the pattern. Overlap the circular ribbon shapes.

5 To make the "eyes" of the burr walnut, wrap the cloth over your index finger and dab to make circular points around the ribbon shapes.

6 When nearly dry (about four hours) slightly soften with a large dry brush. Varnish when dry.

BELOW: A burr walnut effect is a suitable effect for a small treasure chest. Apply a pale yellow base coat, then paint on the effect with yellow ochre oil colour paint. This gives a lighter overall effect than burnt sienna. The edging, bands and lock are painted in gold.

MALACHITE

This green mineral is one of the most beautiful stones. It takes a high polish and is ideal for small ornaments. Malachite has circular and ribbon-like patterning and the colour within the stone ranges from pale green through viridian to a deep Prussian green. Use this effect to paint home accessories such as plain wood boxes, photograph frames and table lamps. A malachite finish is ideal for painted gifts.

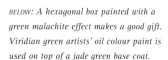

You will need

- satin or gloss finish paint in jade green
- artists' oil colour paint in Prussian green and viridian green
- household paintbrush
- card (card stock) about 10cm/4in square
- fine artist's brush
- gloss varnish

1 Apply two coats of jade-green satin or gloss finish paint and leave to dry thoroughly. Apply patches of Prussian green artists' oil colour without diluting it.

3 Stipple the whole surface with the tips of the bristles of the brush to blend the edges and even the effect.

2 Then, fill in the patches where there is no Prussian green with undiluted viridian green artists' oil.

BELOW: A hexagonal box painted with a green malachite effect makes a good gift. Viridian green artists' oil colour paint is used on top of a jade green base coat.

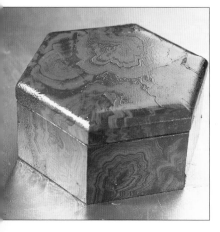

4 Hand tear a straightedge from a piece of card (card stock). Make circular ribbon shapes with it, adjusting the cardboard from side to side.

5 Using the end of an artist's brush, outline each circular shape about 1.25cm/½in from the actual edge. Varnish when dry.

AGATE

Agate is a type of silica rock. When cut and highly polished it reveals flowing ribbon-like patterns. These vary according to the type of agate, and their names, such as "moss" or "clouded", describe the form of patterning.

Although it is seen in a wide range of colours, agate is most usually found in rich brown and ochre tones. This stone was much favoured by the Victorians for jewellery, and as decorative inlay in furniture.

1 Apply two coats of white satin or gloss finish paint as a base coat. Leave to dry thoroughly. Mix Naples yellow artists' oil colour paint with a touch of burnt umber in a paint kettle (pot) until slightly brown. Add white spirit (turpentine) until you have a mixture that is the consistency of thin cream and brush on. Then drag this in one direction.

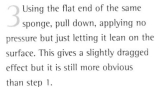

2 While it is wet gently dab over with a dry sponge in certain areas.

3 Using the flat end of the same sponge, pull down, applying no pressure but just letting it lean on the surface. This gives a slightly dragged effect but it is still more obvious than step 1.

4 Fold the sponge cloth and pull down in a slightly wobbly manner, making sure to drag to give a ribbon effect.

5 Soften the effect with a large dry brush. Varnish when dry.

RIGHT: An agate trug.

STONE BLOCKING

Paint these stone blocking effects in your home for a look of permanence and solidity that is usually associated with old traditional buildings and grand mansions. Two effects are described here. The first, stone blocking, replicates the slightly haphazard look of natural stone, and the second reproduces formal stone that has been carved into precise blocks.

NATURAL STONE BLOCKING

The charm of this technique owes much to the mottled effect used for the pieces of stone. The various indentations of the surface of the stone take on subtle changes in colour as they become weathered. Paint highlights on to the blocks to enhance the natural look.

1 Use a large brush to apply a base coat of stone yellow emulsion (latex) paint in random sweeping strokes, leaving a mottled surface. Leave to dry thoroughly.

You will need
• emulsion (latex) paint in stone yellow, off-white and beige
• large brush
• card (card stock) A3 size (29 x 42cm/11½ x 16½in)
• pencil
• 2.5cm/1in paintbrush
• swordliner (liner)

2 Repeat step 1 using off-white emulsion (latex) paint but apply this with a dry brush, scraping off the excess and applying the paint to the surface in alternating directions, not totally covering the base coat.

3 Using card (card stock), and starting round the bottom corner, draw round with a pencil to give the outline of the stone blocks.

4 Using the off-white emulsion (latex) from step 2, add a lighter patch to the left and bottom patch of each block. Blend into the middle with a dry brush.

5 With a swordliner (liner) and beige emulsion (latex) paint, outline each block, slightly curving the corners. The edges do not have to be rigidly straight.

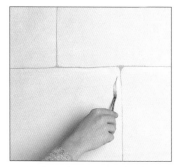

6 Again, with a swordliner (liner), using the off-white paint from step 2, add a rough highlighted edge to the top and right edge of each block. This can be far rougher than before, as it will stand as a highlight to give form to the stone instead of sectioning up the blocks.

RIGHT: *Stone blocking in a hallway.*

FORMAL STONE BLOCKING

Here the blocks of stone have been formalized so that they have precise rectangular corners like carved blocks. To ensure their regularity a grid is used as a base. Carefully painted highlighted and shadowed edges complete the effect.

1 Dip a sponge into stone yellow emulsion (latex) paint and apply to the wall in a circular motion, creating an overall mottled effect.

You will need
• sponge
• emulsion (latex) paint in stone yellow, off-white and beige
• spirit level (level)
• pencil
• paint kettle (pot)
• wallpaper paste
• 1.25cm/¹/₂in flat end paintbrush

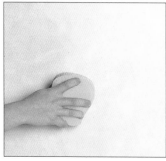

2 Add a second coat of the stone yellow emulsion (latex) paint in patches and leave to dry.

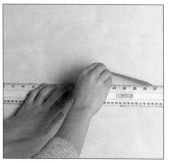

3 Using a spirit level (level), draw a grid simulating the blocks to produce an accurate grid for the stone blocking.

4 Mix 50 per cent off-white emulsion (latex) paint with 50 per cent wallpaper paste. Using a 1.25cm/$^1/_2$in flat end paintbrush, paint a stroke across the top and right hand of each block. Leave to dry.

5 Mix 50 per cent beige emulsion (latex) paint with 50 per cent wallpaper paste in a small paint kettle (pot). Use the same flat end paintbrush to paint along the bottom and left of each block, beginning each line on a mitred corner.

6 Make sure the mitred corners are painted neatly.

BELOW: The accessories and furniture in this setting perfectly complement the "church" look of the stone blocking.

GRANITE

This granite effect is great fun to paint. It allows you the pretence of living in an ancient castle with all the warmth and modern convenience that are not usually found in real buildings made of granite. If large expanses of granite wall seem too overbearing to you, however, try just painting a fire hearth.

1 Mix equal parts of mid grey emulsion (latex) paint and wallpaper paste. Brush on to the surface.

2 Stipple the whole area while it is wet. Leave to dry thoroughly.

3 Take a sponge and dip into darker grey emulsion (latex). Wipe off the excess and sponge lightly over the whole surface until an even colour is achieved – the base colour should remain visible.

4 Mix black emulsion (latex) with water until it is the consistency of thick cream. Dip a small brush into this and wipe off the excess. Then take it over the surface, tapping the handle with another brush, to achieve a spattering effect.

5 Repeat with white emulsion (latex) paint mixed with water and with a small brush spatter over the whole surface by tapping the handle of the brush with another. Then take the mid grey base coat and spatter over the whole surface until the effect is even.

BELOW: A plant pot is given the granite treatment, in white, black and grey.

TORTOISESHELL

Real tortoiseshell actually comes from the beautiful shells of turtles and has been used for many years to make small decorative personal items such as combs, hair ornaments, needlework boxes, mirrorbacks and similar treasures. Its appearance is still admired, and plastic reproductions have taken the place of real shell. This technique uses artists' oil colours worked over a metallic enamel paint base to give depth.

1 Apply a coat of gold enamel and leave to dry thoroughly.

2 Mix yellow ochre artists' oil colour paint and white spirit (turpentine) until it reaches the consistency of thin cream. Brush a very thin layer of the mixture over the whole surface.

3 Mix burnt sienna artists' oil colour paint with white spirit (turpentine) to make a mixture the consistency of thick cream. Paint the mixture on in dashes, working in one direction in a diagonal motion over the wet yellow.

4 Mix Naples yellow artists' oil colour paint with white spirit (turpentine) until you have a thick creamy consistency, and add dashes of it between the burnt sienna dashes.

5 Soften the paint in the same direction with a brush.

6 Mix burnt umber artists' oil colour paint with white spirit (turpentine) until a thick cream. Add small dashes to the surface. Spatter a small amount of this mixture over the top of the surface and soften with a brush, again working in one direction. Varnish when dry.

BELOW: To make a richer tortoiseshell effect, use a red basecoat. This makes an attractive finish for a box of paints.

LAPIS LAZULI

Lapis lazuli was favoured by the ancient Egyptians who carved it into ornaments and amulets that bore the sacred scarab beetle. Artists throughout history have ground down this stone to produce a stunning, brilliant blue pigment that formed the basis of ultramarine. This technique shows you how to paint a lapis lazuli stone effect using modern synthetic paints that closely resemble the colours of the true mineral.

You will need

- satin or gloss finish paint in mid (medium) blue
- household paintbrush
- artists' oil colour paint in ultramarine and Prussian blue
- enamel paint in silver, gold and red
- medium artist's brush
- varnish

1 Apply two coats of blue satin or gloss finish paint and leave to dry. Then apply random patches of undiluted ultramarine blue artists' oil colour.

2 Apply random patches of undiluted Prussian blue artists' oil colour paint, filling in patches where the ultramarine blue has not been put.

3 Stipple over the whole surface with the tips of the bristles of the brush to blend the colours slightly together.

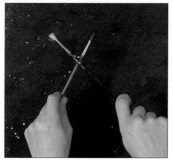

4 Spatter over the whole surface by dipping an artist's brush in silver enamel paint, wiping off the excess and tapping the handle of one brush on to the handle of another over the painting.

5 Repeat step 4 with gold enamel paint, again spattering the paint over the whole surface.

6 Similarly, spatter over the whole surface using red enamel paint. Varnish when dry.

LEFT: This amphora, bought from a garden centre, has been decorated with lapis lazuli round the base and gilding at the neck, to give it an ancient feel. The deep ultramarine base is reminiscent of the colour favoured by ancient Egyptians.

WROUGHT IRON

Here, black and silver are carefully blended to give a realistic effect of wrought iron. The light catches and enhances the shape. The technique uses the same kind of enamel paints that are used on real wrought iron to protect it from the elements. You can create the illusion on a variety of surfaces, including wood, but make sure that you key the surface by sanding down before you start.

You will need
◆ sandpaper
◆ cardboard or tape for masking
◆ enamel paint in black and silver
◆ household paintbrush
◆ cloth

1 Rub down the object with sandpaper. Mask off any areas that you do not want to get paint on.

2 Apply a base coat of black enamel paint and leave it to dry thoroughly.

3 Stipple small patches of silver enamel paint over the whole surface very lightly with the tips of a brush.

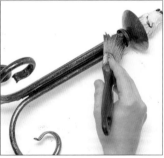

4 Lightly stipple with black enamel paint in random patches.

5 Before the black paint is dry wipe over some of it with a cloth, leaving the raised areas with a more polished look.

LEFT: Wrought iron makes an unusual effect for this box. The undercoat is dark grey, with gilt cream in old silver applied on top for a denser metallic finish.

COPPER

The warm, reddish tones of copper are extremely decorative and seem to complement decorating schemes of every period. Over time, however, real copper is susceptible to the atmosphere and can take on a dullish brown look before acquiring the greenish patina known as verdigris. Painting objects with a copper effect ensures that they remain permanently bright and glowing in appearance.

You will need

- cardboard or tape for masking
- sandpaper
- enamel paint in copper
- household paintbrush
- gilt cream in copper
- polishing cloth

1 Mask off any areas that you do not want to get paint on. Rub down the surface with sandpaper to provide a key so that the paint will adhere.

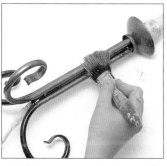

2 Stipple copper enamel paint over the whole surface using the tips of the bristles of a household paintbrush. Leave it to dry.

3 Brush copper gilt cream over the surface of the object.

4 Dab on more copper gilt cream in patches for a fairly solid effect.

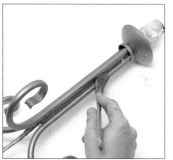

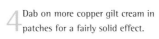

5 Use a dry cloth to buff the surface to a strong shine.

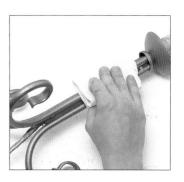

ABOVE: This shallow dish is painted with a gold enamel paint, then stippled with copper enamel and finished with gilt cream.

PEWTER

While new pewter is a shiny silver colour, old pewter takes on a deep grey patina and attractive mellow sheen when buffed. It was once much used in well-to-do households for domestic items such as tankards, flagons and plates. This technique is ideal for transforming ordinary everyday items into decorative accessories that bring a period feel to your kitchen shelves and dining area.

1 Rub down the object with sandpaper to key the surface.

2 Mask off any areas with tape that you do not want to get paint on.

3 Apply a base coat of black enamel paint and leave to dry thoroughly.

4 Lighten the black enamel paint with a little white enamel until you have a dark grey mixture. Using the tips of the bristles of a household paintbrush, stipple this over the whole surface, but in random patches, so that the base coat shows underneath.

5 Mix the dark grey mixture with a little silver enamel paint to lighten it and slightly stipple over the surface in a very patchy manner.

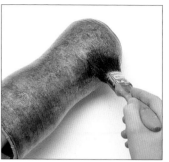

6 Taking silver enamel on its own, stipple the whole surface very lightly with an almost dry brush, just to give a gentle mottled sheen to the surface.

LEFT: Turn an ordinary vase into a deep pewter one. Apply an undercoat of black enamel paint, then stipple on enamel paint in dark grey and old silver.

STEEL

Steel is one of the brightest and shiniest of metals and a glint of steel adds a clean and clinical look to a room or object. The technique shown here will enable you to reproduce this modern-looking surface just by applying two types of silver finish and polishing well. Steel is an extremely hard metal, so it is important to achieve a solid paint effect before brushing on gilt cream.

You will need

- masking tape
- sandpaper
- enamel paint in bright aluminium silver
- gilt cream in silver
- soft brush
- polishing cloth
- gloss varnish

1 Mask off any areas that you do not want to get paint on.

2 Rub down the surface with sandpaper to provide a key so that the paint will adhere.

3 Apply a base coat of bright silver enamel paint. Leave to dry.

4 Apply a second coat of bright enamel silver until you achieve a completely solid effect.

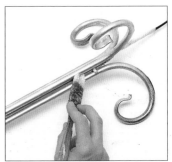

5 When the paint is dry use a soft brush to gently apply bright silver gilt cream over the surface.

6 Buff and shine with a cloth to achieve a highly polished look. Varnish with a high gloss finish.

BELOW: A wooden bowl is transformed with a steel finish. Two coats of bright aluminium enamel paint are applied over a dark grey undercoat. The surface is finished with a gloss varnish.

AGED BRONZE

Few people have authentic ancient or antique bronze items in their house. This paint effect can be used on all manner of ordinary household containers and other items to give the appearance of bronze. With this effect, you can transform simple bowls and plates into attractive pieces that look as if they are precious archaeological finds, yet can be used without undue care around the house.

You will need

- sandpaper
- masking tape
- enamel paint in black and bronze
- household paintbrush
- gilt cream in bronze
- polishing cloth

1 Rub down the object with sandpaper to key the surface so that the paint will adhere.

2 Mask off any areas that you do not want to get paint on.

3 Apply a base coat of black enamel paint to the object.

4 While wet stipple over the surface with the tips of the bristles of a household paintbrush to create an even, mottled effect. Leave to dry thoroughly.

5 Stipple over the whole surface in bronze enamel paint, being careful not to cover the base coat totally.

6 Rub over the surface with bronze gilt cream and then take a dry cloth and buff to a shiny finish.

RIGHT: Candle sconces take on a different look with an aged bronze effect, giving a room a historic feel to it. These have a red oxide primer base coat, with bronze enamel and gilt cream applied on top.

LEATHER

Surfaces covered with leather have an air of distinction and sophistication. Yet you can achieve this look of luxury quite inexpensively with an ingenious combination of satinwood paint, filler and artists' oil colours. In addition, you need have no moral reservations about the source of the material. Real leather can be dyed in any number of colours, so experiment with your own favourite hues.

1 Apply a base coat of pale pink satinwood paint. Leave to dry.

2 Mix pale pink satinwood paint with powdered interior filler (casting plaster) until you have a paste-like mixture. Dab this mixture over the whole surface until it is about 1cm/¹/₂in thick.

3 Stipple over the whole surface with the tips of the bristles of the same household brush used in step 2, texturing the surface. Leave this to dry thoroughly.

4 Brush undiluted crimson artists' oil colour over the whole surface in a fairly thick coat.

5 Stipple to even out, using the same brush as in step 4.

6 Using the flat side of a clean dry sponge, skim over the surface very gently. Apply no pressure but just let the sponge sit on the surface, removing some of the oil from the top layer and highlighting the whole texture. Varnish when dry.

BELOW: *Great for studious vegetarians, this leather-look table top is perfect for the study and has a traditional feel to it.*

BAMBOOING

If you are eager to reproduce an Asian look in your home, then this technique is ideal. A bamboo effect can be adapted to suit many different forms of decoration, from large expanses of wall to smaller pieces of furniture such as dining chairs and coffee tables. You can paint ordinary pieces of garden cane to make them look more authentic and then use them to make items such as picture frames.

You will need

- satin or gloss finish paint in pale yellow
- artists' oil colour paint in yellow ochre and burnt umber
- household paintbrush
- white spirit (turpentine)
- small paint kettle (pot)
- tape measure
- pencil
- lining brush

1 Apply two coats of pale yellow satin or gloss finish paint and leave to dry thoroughly.

2 Mix yellow ochre artists' oil colour paint with white spirit (turpentine) into a creamy consistency in a paint kettle (pot). Drag the mixture over the surface. Leave this to dry thoroughly.

3 Measure and draw pencil lines to mark the bamboo panels and then make marks within these about 1.25cm/½in apart in the direction of the dragging.

4 Once the pencil lines are complete, draw in the slightly rounded ends of the bamboo. Make sure there are not too many of these, or it will look far too complicated when finished.

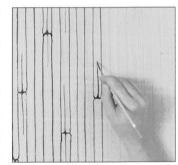

5 Mix burnt umber artists' oil colour paint with white spirit (turpentine) in a small paint kettle (pot) to make a thick cream. Using a lining brush, draw over the pencil lines, adding elongated lines from the middle of the bamboo ends about 10cm/4in long.

6 Flick tiny dots of the burnt umber and white spirit (turpentine) mixture over the surface and soften these with the edge of a brush in the direction of the dragging and the bamboo lines.

BELOW: The furniture and accessories in this room have an Oriental feel to them which is a perfect setting for the bamboo effect on the wall.

MARBLING

There are many specialist (specialty) techniques for achieving a marble effect, but here is a very simple method. Types of marble vary greatly in colour and pattern, and it may be a good idea to use a piece of real marble as a reference source. Aim for a general effect of marbled patterning that is subtle in colour, with most of the veining softened to create depth.

Always use an oil-based gloss or satin base coat to enable the paint to slide and not absorb the colour.

Try colour variations of crimson and ultramarine; raw sienna and black; Indian red, yellow ochre and black; raw sienna, yellow ochre and Prussian blue; Prussian blue and ultramarine; or Naples yellow and yellow ochre.

You will need

- satinwood paint in white
- artists' oil colour paint in ultramarine and yellow ochre
- small paint kettle (pot)
- fine artist's brush
- white spirit (turpentine)
- stippling brush
- swordliner (liner) brush
- gloss varnish

1 Paint a base coat of white satinwood paint on to the surface. Then squeeze a long blob of ultramarine artists' oil colour paint into a paint kettle (pot) and add some white spirit (turpentine) to form a thick cream. Brush on patches of this.

2 Then squeeze some yellow ochre artists' oil colour paint in to a paint kettle (pot) and dilute it with white spirit (turpentine) until you have a thick cream. Fill in the patches where the blue has not been painted with this mixture.

3 While these colours are wet, take a stippling brush and blend them gently together.

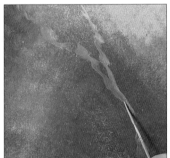

4 Dip a swordliner (liner) brush into white spirit (turpentine) and drag it through the wet surface, applying no pressure but just letting the brushstroke sit on the surface. Slightly angle the bristles while you pull the brush down.

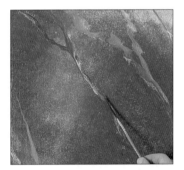

5 Dip the brush back into the white spirit (turpentine) for each line. The white spirit (turpentine) will finally separate the oil glaze surface. Make sure there are not too many lines and only add the odd fork – the less complicated the pattern, the better the effect will be.

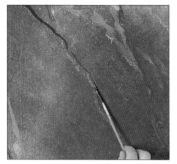

6 Dip the swordliner (liner) into the dark blue glaze remaining from step 1 and draw down the side of each line with a very fine line. Varnish with gloss when dry.

RIGHT: This wooden frame has been changed beyond recognition by using the decorating technique of marbling to give it a patterned border.

MARBLING

crimson and ultramarine

raw sienna and black

Indian red and burnt umber

raw sienna, yellow ochre and Prussian blue

Prussian blue and ultramarine

Naples yellow and yellow ochre

FLOATING MARBLE

Floating marble is also known as fossil marble, and this is one of the simplest marble effects to reproduce. The technique can only be done on a totally flat surface as the paint and white spirit (turpentine) should not be allowed to run. It relies on many drops of white spirit (turpentine) being spattered over wet oil paint, which then disperses to create tiny veining effects and distortions. The result is a complicated but realistic-looking fossil marble effect with little effort.

Interesting colour variations for this effect are ultramarine and yellow ochre; Indian red, raw sienna and black; crimson, yellow ochre and blue; violet, ultramarine and yellow ochre; burnt umber, raw sienna and Indian red; raw sienna, Prussian blue and violet.

You will need

- artists' oil colour paint in Davy's grey, yellow ochre and Prussian blue
- white spirit (turpentine)
- small paint kettle (pot)
- medium artist's brush
- stippling brush
- synthetic sponge
- gloss varnish

1 Mix Davy's grey artists' oil colour paint with some white spirit (turpentine) in a paint kettle (pot) until you have a thick creamy mixture. Brush this on your surface in random patches.

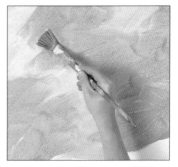

2 Then mix yellow ochre artists' oil colour paint with some white spirit (turpentine) until it is a thick creamy mixture. Use this to fill in the patches where the grey has not been painted.

3 Add smaller patches of Prussian blue artists' oil colour paint mixed into a thick cream with white spirit (turpentine).

4 While these paints are still wet stipple them together to fuse the colours and blend slightly.

5 Dip a sponge into white spirit (turpentine) and then dab over the surface. The white spirit (turpentine) will begin to disperse the artists' oil colour paint.

6 Dip a brush into white spirit (turpentine) and flick the bristles, spattering the surface. The white spirit (turpentine) will pool and create the fossil stone formation. Varnish with gloss when dry.

RIGHT: This floor is painted with a floating marble technique. The base coat is white satinwood paint, and the colours are achieved with Prussian blue, emerald green and yellow ochre artists' oil colour paint. The effect is protected with varnish.

FLOATING MARBLE

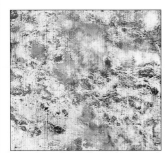

ultramarine, yellow ochre and burnt umber

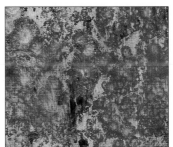

Indian red, raw sienna and black

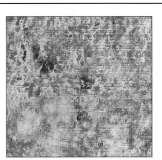

crimson, yellow ochre and blue

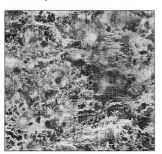

violet, ultramarine and yellow ochre

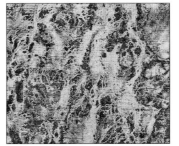

burnt umber, raw sienna and Indian red

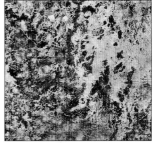

raw sienna, Prussian blue and violet

VERDIGRIS

Verdigris is the beautiful green crust or patina that develops on copper, bronze or brass when it is exposed to the elements. Thus, this effect is suitable for objects both inside and outside the house. It is ideal for disguising and enhancing planters, pots and statuary to add a finishing touch to a conservatory. If the surface is polished with gilt cream it gives a hint of the original bright metal that hides beneath.

You will need

- sandpaper
- satin or gloss finish paint in jade green
- enamel paint in bronze and gold
- household paintbrush
- gilt cream in copper
- polishing cloth

1 Rub down the surface with sandpaper to provide a key so that the paint will adhere to it.

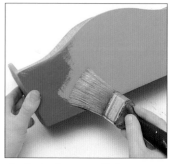

2 Apply a base coat of jade green satin or gloss finish paint and leave to dry thoroughly.

3 Lightly stipple bronze enamel paint over the surface using the tips of the bristles of the brush. Make sure that you keep a little of the base coat exposed.

4 Stipple gold enamel paint over the whole surface even more lightly than the bronze layer and in random patches.

5 With a dry brush dab over the surface of the jade green base coat, blending slightly. Leave to dry.

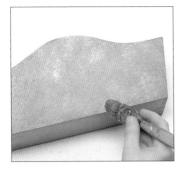

6 Brush a little copper gilt cream over the whole surface with the tips of the brush. Then buff to a strong shine with a dry cloth.

BELOW: *The clever use of paint to create a verdigris effect transforms this mirror, as well as helping to hide any imperfections on the original frame.*

FAUX PLASTER

The soft texture of new plaster has a warm welcoming feel that is usually lost when covered in many layers of paint. However, this technique shows you how to re-create the look of bare plaster, whether new or old. Two finishes are shown – freshly applied in a textured manner or a distressed, layered surface that looks as if it has seen centuries of wear. Emulsion (latex) paint is used for both effects.

TEXTURED PLASTER

The textured finish of this effect is easily achieved by adding powdered interior filler (casting plaster) to the paint mixture.

You will need

- 10cm/4in household paintbrush
- emulsion (latex) paint in white, dark beige and old white
- interior filler powder (casting plaster)
- wide paintbrush
- paint kettle (pot)

1 Apply a base coat of white emulsion (latex) paint to the surface. Then, using a large brush in random strokes, add dark beige emulsion (latex) to the surface in a roughly painted dry-brush motion, leaving the white base coat showing through beneath.

2 Mix some old white emulsion (latex) in a paint kettle (pot) with powdered interior filler (casting plaster) to make a thick paste. Using a wide brush, apply this to the surface in a roughly painted dry-brush motion as in step 1, alternating the angle of the brush and holding it almost flat to the surface.

3 Continue to apply the paint mixture, making sure that the beige layer of paint is still visible.

4 Using the flat side of the brush, add thicker areas of mixture for a more textured effect.

LEFT: A crisp white finish is added to the textured faux plaster effect to give it the look of a whitewashed cottage.

5 Once dry, dry-brush white paint over the entire surface, picking up the top layer.

6 Without adding any more paint to the surface, gently soften the paint you have added in step 5 with the edge of the brush to complete the textured plaster effect.

FLAT PLASTER EFFECT

This flat plaster effect, reminiscent of ancient Mediterranean walls, is produced by using methylated spirits (methyl alcohol), which eats into the layers of paint without building up texture on the walls.

You will need

- 10cm/4in household paintbrush
- emulsion (latex) paint in dark beige, old white and off-white
- methylated spirits (methyl alcohol)
- cloth/sponge

1 Using a large brush, apply dark beige to the surface with random strokes. Do this by dipping the bristles of a 7.5cm/3in household paintbrush into the paint, scraping off the excess and then loosely applying it to the wall.

2 Using old white emulsion (latex) paint and a large brush, dry brush over the dark beige, leaving some of the base coat exposed. Continue to keep the angle of the strokes random so that the effect looks quite rough.

3 Using off-white emulsion (latex) paint, dry brush over the previous layer in patches.

4 Soften this down with the edge of the brush, hardly adding any paint to the surface. Leave to dry.

5 Soak a sponge in methylated spirits (methyl alcohol) and work it in random patches to wear down the layers of the paint, giving a softer effect.

ANIMAL PRINTS

Animal prints are amazingly versatile as a decoration and are popular with all ages. Of course, they are particularly colourful for children's rooms, but they can be a fun addition to even the most sophisticated of adult decorating schemes. Large expanses of these animal prints can add a touch of the exotic, and there are many other animal patterns that you can try after practising with these techniques for giraffe, zebra and cowhide, such as the leopard print skirting illustrated opposite.

GIRAFFE

It is a good idea to look at some real animals first to check that you are reproducing their patterns correctly. The markings on a giraffe are fairly regular.

1 Apply a base coat of white emulsion (latex) paint and allow to dry. Dry brush yellow emulsion (latex) over the surface, leaving some of the white base showing.

2 Once this is dry, repeat with pale yellow emulsion (latex) paint to mottle and soften the effect.

3 Draw random giraffe shapes, leaving about 2.5cm/1in gap between them. Fill in the shapes with dark brown emulsion (latex) paint and leave to dry.

4 Apply a second coat of dark brown emulsion (latex) paint to the shapes so that the colour is solid.

5 Dip a large brush into the pale yellow emulsion (latex) paint and wipe off the excess until the minimum amount of paint is left on the bristles. Holding the brush almost parallel to the surface and applying hardly any pressure, gently wisp over the shapes to knock the slight edge off the dark brown emulsion (latex).

ZEBRA

The distinctive stripes of the zebra needed to be carefully observed to note the way in which they sometimes join together. Black is used over brown to prevent the stripes from looking harsh and add texture to the zebra's coat.

1 Dry brush cream emulsion (latex) paint over the whole surface, leaving a patchy finish. Use a large brush for this.

2 Draw the stripes from a rough central line in an outwards direction, making sure you keep these lines quite wobbly and arched.

3 Dry brush off-white emulsion (latex) paint in between the stripes and working in the direction of the stripes. Leave some of the base coat exposed to give the look of a textured coat.

4 Paint in the stripes with dark brown emulsion (latex). Once dry, roughly paint over the brown stripes with black.

5 Soften the top edge of the stripes with off-white emulsion (latex), flicking the brush inwards from outside.

RIGHT: Create a leopard print on a skirting board by using a foam stamp to print the black shapes over a yellow gloss paint.

COWHIDE

The markings on cowhide can be placed quite randomly and the more varied the shapes you paint, the more realistic will be the overall effect.

You will need
◆ emulsion (latex) paint in pale beige, pale cream, black and dark brown
◆ household paintbrush
◆ pencil

BELOW: *This frame is decorated with a traditional folk art animal print. The paw prints are made using a dry stencil brush dipped in paint and the effect is finished with a tinted varnish.*

1 Dry brush vertical strokes of pale beige emulsion (latex) paint over the surface.

2 Allow the first layer of paint to dry, then dry brush vertical strokes of pale cream emulsion (latex) paint over the surface. Leave to dry.

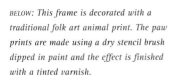

3 Draw the shapes of the cowhide in pencil, keeping them random and making sure that plenty of the background remains.

4 Fill in these shapes with black emulsion (latex) paint. Leave to dry.

5 Dry brush a little dark brown emulsion (latex) paint over the black to soften the look slightly, following in the direction of the dry brushing in step 1.

6 When dry, flick along one side from the outside inwards into the shapes with pale cream emulsion (latex) paint to achieve an overlapped fur effect.

TROMPE L'OEIL DOORWAY

Here is a design for a trompe l'oeil doorway that you can follow exactly or use as a guide for your own design. Colours are suggested for you to use, but you may prefer to choose others. The basic techniques used for this doorway could also be used to paint a window or smaller cupboard door. Final details are drawn in with a coloured pencil. By starting with a simple design like this you will soon find that your confidence builds up and you will be able to tackle more complicated designs.

You will need

- paint roller
- emulsion (latex) paint in cream, warm yellow, terracotta and green
- large household paintbrush
- pencil
- set (T) square
- paper
- spirit level (level)
- straightedge
- string
- masking tape
- medium household paintbrush
- medium artist's brush
- hand sander
- brown pencil

1 Experiment with mixing the colours. You can use quite strong shades as they will soften once they have been sanded back.

2 Using a paint roller, paint the wall surface with a base coat of cream emulsion (latex) paint.

3 Wash over the base colour with warm yellow emulsion (latex) paint, using a large paintbrush.

LEFT: *This effect is simpler to achieve than it looks; its basic shape can be pencilled in with the help of a piece of string used as a pair of compasses and a ruler.*

4 Draw your design to scale on paper, using a set (T) square.

5 Draw the straight lines that will represent the doorway and border design on the wall, using a spirit level (level) and straightedge.

6 Draw the upper curve of the doorway, using a pencil tied to a piece of string.

7 Mask off the areas of the design that will be painted in terracotta with masking tape.

8 Paint these areas with the terracotta emulsion (latex) paint, then remove the masking tape. Any smudging can be wiped off immediately.

9 Using a medium paintbrush, paint the green areas of the doorway. Use masking tape, if necessary, to mask off each area.

10 Using an artist's brush, paint a thin yellow outline around all the edges of the doorway. Leave to dry.

11 Lightly sand over the design, using a hand sander. Sand down to the base coat in some areas and leave other sections untouched.

12 Wash over the whole design again using warm yellow emulsion (latex) paint.

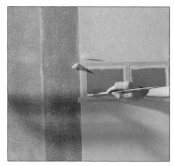

13 Mask off squares in the border area with masking tape. Using an artist's brush, outline each square in yellow, and then immediately remove the masking tape.

14 Using a brown pencil, draw fine lines in the semicircular fanlight.

RIGHT: The look of frescoes, faded over the centuries by the hot Italian sun, can be recreated in your own home. The secret is to build up colours in layers and rub them back to different levels.

TROMPE L'OEIL PANELLING

Using simple trompe l'oeil techniques you can transform your room into any style or period you wish. This simple effect shows you how to paint panels with planked sides and mitred corners. Using lighter and darker tones for the narrow inner panel creates the illusion of light and shadow and gives depth to the frame. You can vary the size of the panels to suit the design of your room.

1 Apply two coats of white emulsion (latex) to make a base coat. Leave to dry between coats. When dry, use a ruler, spirit level (level) and pencil to draw up a central panel with planked sides.

2 Mask off the central panel, running the masking tape all the way up the sides and then across the top and along the bottom of the central panel.

3 Mix 50 per cent beige emulsion (latex) paint with 50 per cent wallpaper paste in a paint kettle (pot). Paint over the central panel and then drag downwards with the brush.

4 Remove the tape from the top and bottom then paint and drag the top and bottom sections horizontally with the same mixture from step 3. Then remove the side tape and drag the panels in a downwards motion.

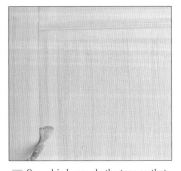

5 Once dried, reapply the tape so that a band of about 2.5cm/1in is created around the central panel, masking the surrounding area off. Mix white emulsion (latex) paint with some of the mixture from step 3 and apply to the sides closest to the light source, mitring the corners with masking tape.

6 Once this is dry, apply tape to mitre the corners in the opposite direction. Mix brown emulsion (latex) paint with some of the mixture from step 3 and apply it to the top and right sides to give the shadows. Remove the tape.

RIGHT: *This technique is particularly good for large, bare expanses of wall. The deep red colour used here gives an air of formality which is enhanced by the addition of faux panelling.*

TROMPE L'OEIL SKY

This lovely effect is suitable for any room in which you wish to create a sense of calm and imagine yourself floating away among the clouds. Draw the outline shapes of the clouds, but do not feel you have to follow them rigidly. Allow yourself the freedom to paint loose shapes with merging edges for a realistic look. Adding wallpaper paste to the paint gives texture and depth to the whole effect.

1 Apply two coats of white emulsion (latex) as a base coat, allowing to dry between coats. Dip a sponge into sky blue emulsion (latex) paint and rub over the whole surface in a circular motion, leaving a mottled effect.

2 Apply a second coat of sky blue with a sponge in the same way as step 1. The second coat will leave the whole effect almost solid but with a slightly mottled look.

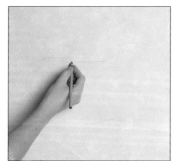

3 Using a light pencil, carefully outline rough cloud shapes to give a guide to painting.

4 Dilute white silk emulsion (latex) paint with 50 per cent wallpaper paste in a paint kettle (pot) and stipple this onto the surface, starting along the top edge of the pencil line. Continue to stipple downwards without applying any more paint to the brush and this will gradate the colour.

5 Build up the depth of the clouds in layers when each has dried. Go over the first layer along the top side and then stipple downwards as before. This will strengthen the effect.

6 Finally, add a sharper edge to define the white.

BELOW: Add to the sense of light by hanging a mirrored candle holder on the wall that acts as a window into the sky beyond it.

TARTAN (PLAID)

Painting a tartan (plaid) surface is a fun technique to create an interesting patterned fabric effect. By overlapping different coloured grids of colour, using varying widths of lines, endless combinations can be achieved. Replicating a colour scheme from an actual piece of checked or tartan (plaid) fabric, for instance on a cushion or a throw, can save a lot of trial and error and can be a good way of continuing a theme in a room scheme. When planning the technique and drawing the grid, take the width of bands into account. If they are too close the whole effect will look busy, but if too spaced they will look weak.

Traditional tartan (plaid) colours work well, as do the following: a jade base with mid (medium) greens; a navy base with pale blue and pale yellow; a red base with dark green and yellow; a grey base with lilac and white; a pale yellow base with pale blue and navy; or a grey-green base with mint green and dark red.

You will need

- emulsion (latex) paint in three colours
- household paintbrush
- paint tray
- pencil
- plumb line
- ruler
- paint roller
- lining brush

1 Apply the base coat of paint. Make sure the colour is completely solid – two coats may be needed.

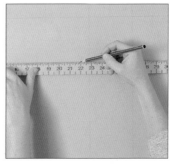

2 Draw on the grid, using a pencil, plumb line and ruler. Bear in mind the width of the paint roller you are going to use while drawing the grid.

3 Apply the second colour on to the roller and roller down one side of the drawn lines. Leave to dry.

4 Draw the grid for the fine lines using a ruler and pencil.

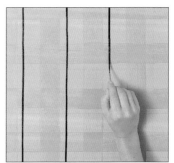

5 Mix the third colour with a little water until a thin cream. Add the fine line in one direction using a lining brush. Leave to dry.

6 Complete the pattern by adding in the cross strokes.

RIGHT: If you do not want to decorate a whole wall, simply add a couple of bands of tartan (plaid) at dado (chair) rail height, beneath the level of the window.

— TARTAN (PLAID) —

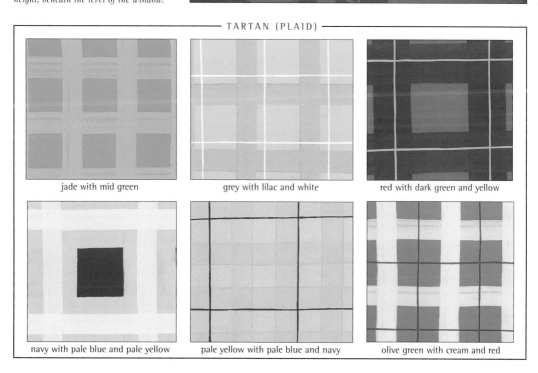

| jade with mid green | grey with lilac and white | red with dark green and yellow |
| navy with pale blue and pale yellow | pale yellow with pale blue and navy | olive green with cream and red |

PAINT EFFECTS PROJECTS

Many people find the thought of painting their homes rather daunting, but a room can be completely transformed by just a single layer of well-chosen paint. If you use some of the decorative paint effects described in this first section of the book, such as trompe l'oeil three-dimensional panels, frescoes, crackle glazing, sponging and graining, the room is guaranteed to look unusual, stylish and highly professional. Today there is an ever-increasing range of beautiful paints to choose from as well as helpful facilities in many shops for mixing your own paints to create a highly individual scheme. You may find yourself getting carried away with colour!

ABOVE: Distress a piece of furniture by rubbing back thin layers of paint. Decorate with a simple hand-painted leaf design.

LEFT: This textured paint effect is achieved by pressing tissue paper over the wet surface.

ROUGH PLASTER COLOURWASH

This sunny yellow wall was given a rough-textured look by trowelling on a ready-mixed medium (joint compound), available from do-it-yourself stores, which is normally used for smoothing walls and ceilings that have unwanted texture. Colourwashing in two shades of yellow gives added depth and tone. The absorbent wall surface picks up varying degrees of paint, and there will be some areas which are not coloured at all, but this is all part of the attractive rural effect.

You will need

- medium (joint compound) for coating walls
- plasterer's trowel or large scraper
- large decorator's paintbrush
- emulsion (latex) paint in white
- emulsion (latex) paint, in two different shades of bright yellow
- household sponge

1 Apply the coating medium (joint compound) to the wall, using a plasterer's trowel or large scraper. You can decide whether to have a very rough effect or a smoother finish. Leave to dry overnight.

2 Using a large decorator's paintbrush, paint the wall with two coats of white emulsion (latex), leaving each coat of paint to dry thoroughly.

3 Dilute one shade of yellow paint with about 75 per cent water. Dip a damp sponge into the paint and wipe it over the wall, using plenty of arm movement as though you were cleaning it.

4 Leave the first shade of yellow paint to dry. Dilute the second shade of yellow paint with about 75 per cent water and wipe it over the first colour in the same way.

DIAMOND-STENCILLED WALL

Here a stunning colour scheme is created by dragging a deep green glaze over a lime green base. The surface is then stencilled with shiny aluminium leaf diamonds, which stand out against the strong background. This paint finish would look very dramatic in a dining room, with muted lighting used to catch the metallic diamond highlights.

You will need

- 2 large decorator's paintbrushes
- emulsion (latex) paint in lime green
- artist's acrylic paint in monestial green and emerald green
- acrylic scumble
- pencil
- stencil card (stock)
- craft knife
- cutting mat or thick card (stock)
- 2 artist's paintbrushes
- acrylic size
- aluminium leaf
- make-up brush
- clear shellac and brush

1 Using one of the large decorator's brushes, paint the wall with lime green emulsion (latex) paint. Leave to dry.

2 Mix a glaze from 1 part monestial green acrylic paint, 1 part emerald green acrylic paint and 6 parts acrylic scumble. Paint the glaze on to the wall with random brushstrokes.

3 Working quickly with a dry large decorator's brush, go over the surface using long, downward strokes. Overlap the strokes and don't stop mid-stroke. Leave to dry.

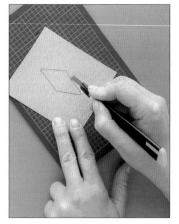

4 Draw a small diamond shape in pencil on to stencil card (stock). Cut out the shape, using a craft knife and cutting mat or thick card.

5 Using an artist's paintbrush, apply a thin, even coat of acrylic size through the stencil card on to the wall. Repeat the diamond motif as many times as desired to make a decorative pattern.

6 After about 20 minutes, touch the size lightly with a finger to check that it has become tacky. If not, wait a little longer. Press a piece of aluminium leaf gently on to the size.

7 Working carefully, peel off the aluminium leaf, then brush off the excess with the make-up brush.

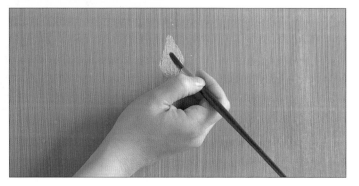

8 Using the second artist's paintbrush, apply clear shellac over the diamond motifs. Leave to dry.

LIMEWASHED WALL

For an instant limewashed effect, apply white emulsion (latex) paint over a darker base with a dry brush, then remove some of the paint with a cloth soaked in methylated spirits (methyl alcohol). This is a good way to decorate uneven or damaged walls, and gives a pleasing rustic effect.

You will need

- matt emulsion (flat latex) paint in cream and white
- 2 large decorator's paintbrushes
- clean cotton cloths
- methylated spirits (methyl alcohol)
- neutral wax

1 Paint the wall with a coat of cream matt emulsion (flat latex) paint, using one of the large decorator's brushes. Leave to dry.

2 Using the second decorator's brush, dip the tip of the dry paintbrush into the white emulsion paint. Using random strokes, dry brush the paint on to the wall. Leave to dry.

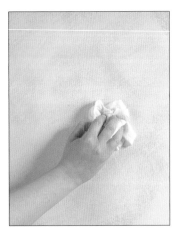

3 Using a cloth, rub methylated spirits (methyl alcohol) into the wall in some areas. This will remove some of the paint, giving a natural weathered effect. Leave to dry.

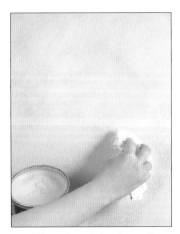

4 Using a clean cloth, rub wax all over the wall to seal the paint and protect the surface.

FRESCO EFFECT

A dry brush and cloth are used here to soften rough brushstrokes and give the faded effect of Italian fresco painting. This wall treatment is the ideal background for a mural, so if you are feeling artistic you could paint a scene on top.

You will need

- emulsion (latex) paint in pale pink and ultramarine
- acrylic scumble
- 2 large decorator's paintbrushes
- clean cotton cloth

1 Begin by mixing a glaze of 1 part pale pink emulsion (latex) paint to 6 parts acrylic scumble. Paint the glaze on to the top half of the wall with random brushstrokes.

2 Using a dry brush, go over the top half of the wall while the glaze is still wet to even out the brushstrokes.

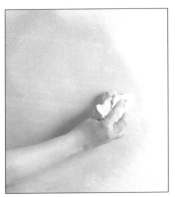

3 Rub a clean cotton cloth into the glaze with circular motions, to produce the faded effect of Italian fresco painting.

4 Repeat steps 1–3 on the bottom half of the wall, using ultramarine paint. Softly blend the two colours together with a dry brush.

EGYPTIAN BATHROOM

Here, a roller fidgeting technique is ideal for establishing the impression of a slightly textured surface and disguising any small imperfections in the plaster. This bathroom is decorated with Egyptian fan motifs that are carefully measured and drawn before being painted in. The shapes are masked to make painting them in easier and then outlined with paint to make them stand out clearly. Decoration within the motifs is made with a comb while the paint is still wet.

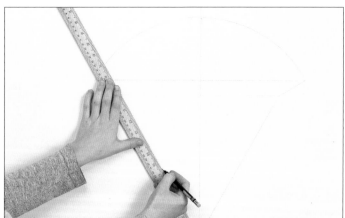

1 Roller fidget the background using pale yellow and off-white in the same way. When dry, mark out the fan shapes in pencil. Do this with the aid of a long ruler, measuring and marking either side of a centre vertical line. Secure a piece of string to the centre line with a drawing pin and attach the pencil to the other end to draw an arc for the top of the fan. Similarly measure and mark the smaller half fans.

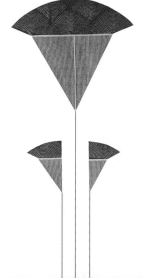

2 Carefully mask off the lower part of each fan (the triangular shape) with masking tape and brush over the enclosed area with a layer of orange emulsion (latex) paint.

3 Immediately, and before the paint has dried, comb over the orange colour in a downwards vertical direction, keeping your hand steady so that the lines are straight. Leave to dry.

4 Mask off the top part of each fan and brush over with turquoise emulsion (latex) paint, until the enclosed area is completely covered.

5 Again, comb immediately. To achieve the semi-circle patterns, start by angling the comb and your wrist on the left and arc with the top, without moving the bottom of the comb. Leave to dry.

6 Mix some off-white emulsion (latex) paint with a little water until you have a thin creamy mixture. Use this mixture with a lining brush to paint a thin line around all the coloured shapes to clean up any untidy edges. Finally, paint in the centre line of the large fans and the supporting lines of the half fans.

RIGHT: These Egyptian fan motifs are painted in the typical colours of orange and turquoise used by the ancient Pharaohs. These colours were originally made from natural clays and minerals, and their earthy tones are complemented by the pale yellow colourwashed wall. The vibrant look is completed with the addition of colourful shutters and bright accessories.

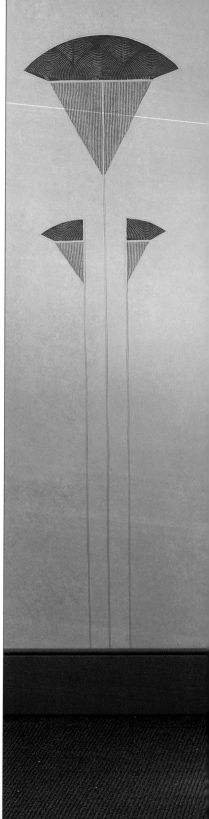

NEO-CLASSICAL BATHROOM

After a hard day's work, transport yourself to the relaxing atmosphere of the ancient Roman baths but with all the conveniences of modern living. This old cast-iron bath (bath tub) is painted with a marble effect on the outside that is easy to achieve, with enamel paint used as a base coat. Use a swordliner (liner) or feather to paint in veins, then soften them off for a realistic subtle look. The wall panels are given a light trompe l'oeil sky effect, so that you have the impression of looking through columns or open window spaces to the exhilarating fresh air outside.

You will need

- cast-iron bath (bath tub)
- suitable enamel paint in white
- household paintbrush
- artists' oil colour paint in Davy's grey (medium gray)
- white spirit (turpentine)
- paint kettle (pot)
- swordliner (liner) or feather
- large softener (blending) brush
- varnish in gloss finish
- emulsion (latex) paint in white and sky blue
- silk finish emulsion (latex) paint in white
- sponge and pencil
- wallpaper paste

1 To decorate the bath tub, apply two coats of white enamel paint to the outer surface of it.

2 Mix a little Davy's grey (medium gray) artists' oil colour paint with white spirit (turpentine) in a small paint kettle (pot) until it has a thin creamy consistency. Use this mixture to paint in the fine veins of the marble with a swordliner (liner) or a feather.

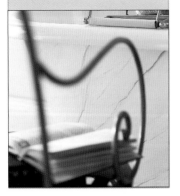

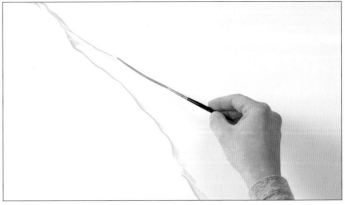

3 Soften the veins using a large soft brush to sweep over the lines.

4 Add more veins, disregarding the positions of the first ones but working in the same general direction.

5 Soften these new veins with the large soft brush using only a little pressure this time, to give these ones a slightly stronger edge.

6 Using the swordliner (liner), add a defining line along the side of the second set of veins. Pull the softening brush along these once if slightly heavy. Leave to dry. Varnish in a gloss finish.

7 To paint the walls, apply two coats of white emulsion (latex) as a base coat, allowing to dry between coats. Measure, draw and mask off the panels. Dip a sponge into sky blue emulsion (latex) paint and rub over the panel in a circular motion, leaving a mottled effect. Once dry, apply a second coat of sky blue with a sponge in the same way. The second coat will leave the whole effect almost solid but slightly mottled in appearance.

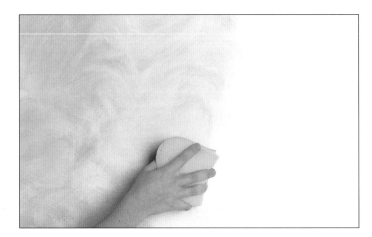

8 Using a light pencil, carefully outline rough cloud shapes to give a guide for painting.

9 Dilute white silk emulsion (latex) paint with 50 per cent wallpaper paste in a paint kettle (pot) and stipple this on to the surface, starting along the top edge of the pencil line. Continue to stipple downwards without applying any more paint to the brush and this will gradate the colour. Build up the depth of the clouds in layers when each has dried: go over the first layer along the top side and again stipple downwards. This will strengthen the effect.

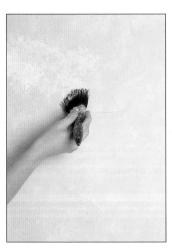

10 Finally add a sharper edge to define the white.

RIGHT: This wonderful trompe l'oeil sky is glimpsed through window shapes and adds the illusion of space to the bathroom. Try it also on ceilings. The luminous quality is achieved by working down the surface several times, gradating the colour as you progress without adding more paint to the brush.

MISTY LILAC STRIPES

Here, wide stripes are painted and the wet paint dabbed with mutton cloth (stockinet) to soften the effect and blend in brushmarks. As an extra touch, paint a triangle at the top of each stripe. If you do not have a picture rail, take the stripes up to the top of the wall and place the triangles along the skirting (base) board.

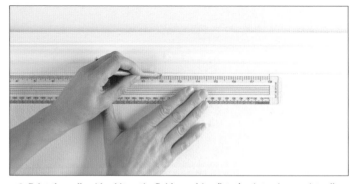

1 Paint the walls with white satin-finish emulsion (latex) paint, using a paint roller and tray. Mark the centre of the most important wall, below the picture rail (if you have one), with a pencil. Make marks 7.5cm/3in either side of this, then every 15cm/6in. Continue making 15cm/6in marks around the room until the marks meet at the least noticeable corner.

2 Hang a short length of plumbline from one of the marks, and mark with a dot where it rests. Hang the plumbline from this dot and mark where it rests. Continue down the wall. Repeat for each mark below the picture rail.

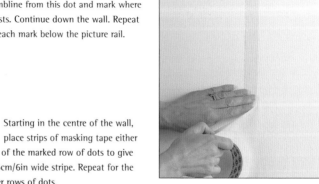

3 Starting in the centre of the wall, place strips of masking tape either side of the marked row of dots to give a 15cm/6in wide stripe. Repeat for the other rows of dots.

4 Dilute some of the lilac paint with about 25 per cent water and 25 per cent acrylic scumble. Brush on to a section of the first stripe. Complete each stripe in two or three stages, depending on the height of the room, blending the joins to get an even result.

5 Dab the wet paint lightly with a mutton cloth (stockinet) to smooth out the brushmarks. Complete all the stripes, then carefully peel away the masking tape and leave the paint to dry.

6 Cut a card (stock) triangle with a 15cm/6in base and measuring 10cm/4in from the base to the tip. Use this as a template to mark the centre of each of the stripes, lilac and white, 10cm/4in below the picture rail.

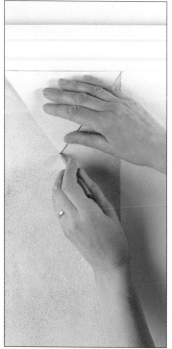

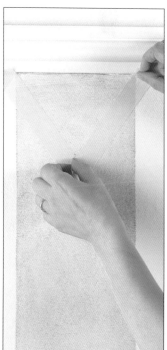

7 Working on one stripe at a time, place strips of masking tape between the top corners of the stripe and the marked dot, as shown.

8 Brush on the lilac paint mix, then dab the mutton cloth over the wet paint as before. Leave the paint to dry. Repeat for all the stripes.

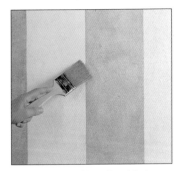

9 Dilute some lilac paint with about 20 parts water. Brush over the wall in all directions to give a hint of colour to the white stripes.

10 Add a little paint to the remaining diluted mixture to strengthen the colour. Using a paint guard or strip of card to protect the painted wall, brush the paint on to the picture rail.

RED-PANELLED WALL

This bright red wall has been beautifully toned down with a translucent glaze of deep maroon acrylic paint mixed with scumble. The panel has been given a very simple trompe l'oeil treatment, using dark and light shades of paint to create a 3-D effect.

You will need

- satin-finish emulsion (latex) paint in bright red
- medium and small decorator's paintbrushes
- ruler and pencil
- spirit level
- plumbline
- masking tape
- craft knife
- artist's acrylic paint in deep maroon, black and white
- acrylic scumble
- mutton cloth (stockinet)
- clean cotton cloth
- coarse-grade abrasive paper

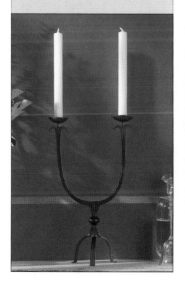

1 Paint the wall with two coats of bright red paint, leaving each coat to dry. Mark the centre top of the panel. Draw a horizontal line 30cm/12in either side of this mark.

2 Drop a plumbline 90cm/36in down from each end of the drawn line and make a mark. Draw a line between all the marked points to give a 60 × 90cm/24 × 36in panel.

3 Place strips of masking tape around the outer edge of the panel. Neaten the corners where the strips of tape meet with a craft knife.

4 Mix the maroon paint with acrylic scumble to the required colour. Brush this on to the panel.

5 Immediately dab a mutton cloth (stockinet) over the wet glaze to even out the texture. Leave the glaze to dry.

6 Starting in a corner, brush the maroon glaze on to a section of the wall, roughly the same size as the panel. Dab it with the mutton cloth to blend the brushmarks as before, stopping just short of the edge of the panel. Roll up the cotton cloth into a sausage shape and then immediately roll it over the wet glaze, changing direction to give a more random effect. Leave the glaze to dry. Repeat all over the rest of the wall.

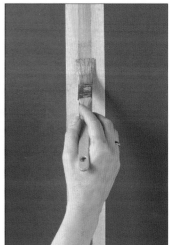

7 Remove the masking tape. Place new strips of tape either side of the bright red line now revealed and trim the corners with the craft knife. Mix a small amount of black acrylic paint with some of the maroon glaze. Brush this between the masking tape down one side of the panel, on the side where the light source is. Place a piece of coarse-grade abrasive paper diagonally at the top and clean off the glaze that extends beyond. Keeping the abrasive paper in the same position, repeat on the top border of the panel.

8 Add a small amount of white acrylic paint to the maroon glaze and apply to the remaining two borders in the same way. Leave to dry, then carefully remove the masking tape.

TWO-TONE ROLLERED WALL

For this quick, ingenious paint effect, two shades of emulsion (latex) are placed next to each other in a paint tray and then rollered on to the wall together. Moving the roller in different directions blends the paint very effectively.

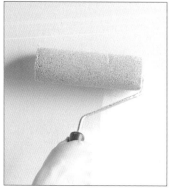

1 Using a paint roller, paint the wall with a base coat of cream emulsion (latex). Leave to dry.

2 Pour the yellow and the terracotta emulsion into the paint tray together, half on each side. The two colours of paint will sit side by side without mixing.

3 Paint the wall, applying the roller at a variety of different angles to blend the two colours.

4 When complete, roller over the wall a few times to blend the paint further, but don't overwork.

OTHER COLOURS

ABOVE: Alternative colours – yellow and cream emulsion (latex) over a dark turquoise base coat.

ABOVE: Complementary colours – light and mid-blue emulsion (latex) over a pale green base coat.

STONE WALL

A subtle stone effect is created using several different techniques. Layers of paint are built up by stippling, sponging and rubbing colours on and off, and a hog softening brush is used to blend the wet glazes to look like stone. The wall is divided by a trompe l'oeil dado (chair) rail.

You will need

- large decorator's paintbrush
- emulsion (latex) paint in cream
- spirit level
- ruler
- pencil
- masking tape
- acrylic paint in raw umber, white and yellow ochre
- acrylic scumble
- decorator's block brush or stippling brush
- natural sponge
- hog softening brush
- clean cotton cloths
- fine artist's paintbrush

1 Using a large decorator's paintbrush, paint the wall with cream emulsion (latex). Leave to dry.

2 Using a level and ruler, draw pencil lines 6.5cm/2½in apart at dado (chair) rail height.

3 Place masking tape inside the two pencil lines, smoothing it in place with your fingers.

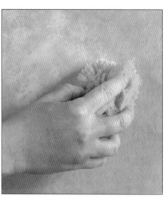

4 Mix a glaze of 1 part raw umber acrylic paint to 6 parts scumble. Stipple this on to the wall, using the tip of the decorator's block brush or stippling brush. Do not stipple over the masked area. Leave to dry.

5 Mix a glaze with the white acrylic paint in the same way. Dampen a sponge and apply the glaze over the stippling, varying your hand position to avoid a uniform effect.

6 Using a hog softening brush, skim gently over the surface of the white glaze while it is still wet.

7 Mix a glaze with the yellow ochre paint as in step 4, but this time rub it into the wall with a cloth. Leave some areas of white glaze showing.

8 Using another dampened cloth, rub some areas to disperse the paint. Leave to dry.

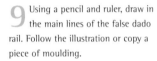

9 Using a pencil and ruler, draw in the main lines of the false dado rail. Follow the illustration or copy a piece of moulding.

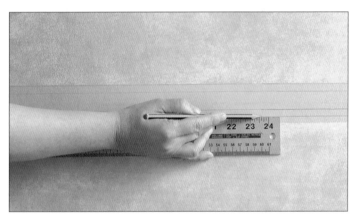

10 Highlight the pencil lines in white acrylic paint, using a fine artist's paintbrush. Leave to dry.

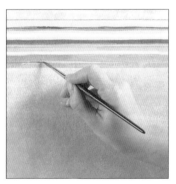

11 Paint the darker areas of the trompe l'oeil dado rail in raw umber acrylic paint. Leave to dry. Mix a little white acrylic paint into the raw umber and then add the softer, shadowed areas.

JAPANESE LIVING ROOM

Roller fidgeting is used to create the warm-looking walls of this traditional Japanese-style living room. Two paint colours mix and merge on the wall as they are applied, providing an ideal ground for a simple freehand leaf design. Painted bamboo panels worked in richer artists' oil colours add an air of authenticity and are fun to paint. Finally the furniture is given a smooth lacquered finish to complement the setting.

You will need

- emulsion (latex) paint in off-white, sand yellow, pale cream and plum
- wide household paintbrush
- masonry paint roller
- roller tray
- pencil
- fine artist's brush
- satin or gloss finish paint in pale yellow
- artists' oil colour paint in yellow ochre and burnt umber
- white spirit (turpentine)
- small paint kettle (pot)
- tape measure
- fine lining brush
- coffee table
- fine-grade sandpaper
- gloss finish paint in plum
- spray gloss enamel in plum
- spray gloss varnish

1 Apply a coat of off-white emulsion (latex) paint to the wall and leave to dry thoroughly.

2 Pour sand yellow and pale cream emulsion (latex) paint into each side of a roller tray. Coat a masonry roller with the paint and apply it to the wall at random angles, making sure that you do not totally cover the base coat.

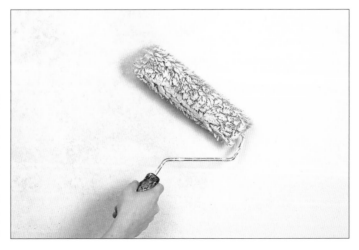

3 When the wall is dry mark with a pencil the height and position of the leaf spray border design. Take into account the width of the bamboo panels which will alternate between the leaves. Draw these in at the same time. Draw the centre lines, making sure they are equally spaced around the room, then draw in the leaves freehand.

4 Use an artist's brush to paint in the main stalk in plum emulsion (latex).

5 Paint in the leaves in plum emulsion (latex) paint. Some parts of the leaf spray design may need a second coat.

6 Mask off each of the panels. Apply two coats of pale yellow satin or gloss finish paint and leave to dry thoroughly. Mix yellow ochre artists' oil colour paint with white spirit (turpentine) into a creamy consistency in a small paint kettle (pot). Drag the mixture over the surface. Leave this to dry thoroughly.

7 Measure and draw pencil lines about 1.25cm/½in apart in the direction of the dragging. Once the pencil lines are complete, draw in the slightly rounded ends of the bamboo. Make sure there are not too many of these or it will look far too complicated when finished.

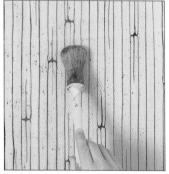

8 Mix burnt umber artists' oil colour paint with white spirit (turpentine) in a paint kettle (pot) to make a thick cream. Using a fine lining brush, draw over the pencil lines adding elongated lines from the middle of the bamboo ends about 12.5cm/5in long. Flick tiny dots of the paint over the surface, and soften with the edge of a brush, moving downwards.

9 To prepare the surface of the table, first sand it thoroughly until totally smooth. Clean the surface, making sure that it is completely free of dust. Apply a base coat of high gloss paint and leave to dry thoroughly. Sand the surface again to ensure total smoothness.

10 Apply a second base coat. Leave to dry thoroughly.

11 Spray on a gloss enamel in the same colour as the base coat. Again, leave to dry thoroughly. Spray a gloss varnish over the surface to protect it and provide a final finish.

RIGHT: The table is lacquered in plum-coloured paint to match the leaf design on the walls. This colour provides a sophisticated contrast to the warm creamy yellow of the walls and darker ochre tones of the bamboo panel without looking too overpowering.

CHURCH HALLWAY

Turn your hallway into a welcoming area of serenity by decorating the walls with a dressed-stone effect reminiscent of an old country church. This easy technique relies on precision in drawing a grid to mark out the individual blocks before painting them in. Consistent edges of highlight and shadow define the blocks. To emphasize the church-like look, the cupboard is painted with a dark oak effect. The rich depth of colour of solid oak is achieved by using burnt umber artists' oil colour paint.

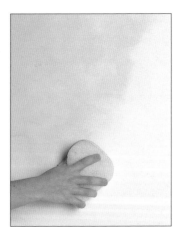

1 Dip a sponge into stone yellow emulsion (latex) and apply to the wall in a circular motion, creating an overall mottled effect.

2 Add a second coat of the stone yellow emulsion (latex) in patches and leave to dry. This will create a slight movement in the overall effect but will look almost solid.

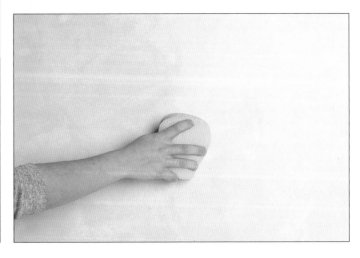

3 Using a spirit level (level), draw a grid simulating the blocks to achieve a straight and accurate grid for the stone blocking effect.

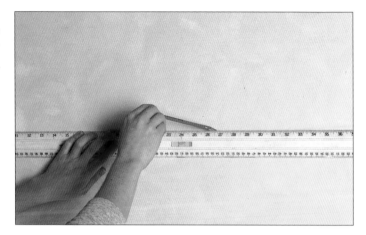

4 Mix off-white emulsion (latex) paint with 50 per cent wallpaper paste in a small paint kettle (pot). Using a 1.25cm/½in flat end paintbrush, paint a stroke across the top and right side of each block. Leave to dry.

5 Make sure the mitred corners are painted crisply.

6 Mix beige emulsion paint with 50 per cent wallpaper paste in a small paint kettle (pot). Use the same flat end paintbrush to paint along the bottom and left of each block. Mitre each corner which joins the highlight.

▶

7 To paint the cupboard, apply two coats of beige for the base coat in either gloss or satin finish and leave to dry thoroughly. Mix burnt umber artists' oil colour paint with white spirit (turpentine) in a paint kettle (pot) until it is the consistency of thick cream. Brush on and drag in a lengthways direction.

8 Using a graduated comb, pull down on the surface, not in totally straight lines, butting one up against the other.

9 Use a heart grainer (graining roller) to start making the details of the graining. Do this by pulling the tool down gently with a slight rocking motion, to create the hearts with random spacings. Butt one line straight over the other. Using a fine graduated comb, comb over all the previous combing.

10 Wrap a cloth around the comb and dab on to the surface to create the angled grain, pressing into the wet paint. Then, soften the overall effect using a large dry brush. Varnish when dry.

RIGHT: *Enhance the church-like effect of the dressed-stone blocking by adding a formal flower arrangement and accessories such as old leather-bound books. Plain church candles are readily available and give a gentle glow at night when lit.*

COLONIAL LIVING ROOM

One of the easiest methods for creating a wood panel effect is to use the technique of dragging. Simply pull the wet paint with the tips of the bristles of a dry brush in the direction of the wood grain. The technique creates maximum impact in rooms where large areas of panelling are required, such as this Colonial-style living room. It is important to keep the lines in each vertical or horizontal section clean and unbroken, so make sure you plan panels that can be covered with a comfortable stroke of the brush.

You will need

- emulsion (latex) paint in off-white and mid (medium) brown
- household paintbrush
- long ruler
- pencil
- masking tape
- wallpaper paste
- paint kettle (pot)
- soft artist's brush
- cloth

1 Apply two coats of off-white emulsion (latex) paint over the whole wall. Leave to dry. Measure and mark the height and size of the panelling you require with the ruler and pencil. Make sure the proportions balance well across the length of the wall.

2 Mask off the dado (chair) rail. Mix mid brown emulsion (latex) paint with 50 per cent wallpaper paste in a paint kettle (pot). Brush the paint mixture over the dado (chair) rail area. Using a dry brush, drag along the middle of the rail in a horizontal direction to remove some of the paint and create a highlight effect. Apply masking tape to the borders of the main panels, mitring the corners, then paint and drag the centre panel in a vertical direction.

3 Mask off the top and bottom sections, and paint and then drag them in a horizontal direction.

4 Remove the tape except from the centre panel border. Brush the brown paint mixture on to the side panels and drag down in a vertical direction. Leave the paint to dry.

LEFT: Masking with mitred edges enables you to drag right up to the corners with precision. The highlights and shadows give the illusion of depth. You can achieve the effect easily by mitring the masking tape before applying it, then removing it length by length as you paint each edge.

5 Remove the tape from the bottom of the centre panels and paint in a second coat of the brown mixture to give a darker shadow effect, using a soft artist's brush. Repeat the process for the right-hand side (assuming the light source is from the left).

6 Remove the tape from the left of the centre panels and paint in a coat of the brown mixture, dragging the brush along the inner edge. To create a highlight, take a cloth, while the paint is still damp, wrap it over your index finger and run this along the band removing most of the paint. Repeat the process for the top side (assuming the light source is coming in from the left).

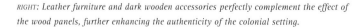

RIGHT: *Leather furniture and dark wooden accessories perfectly complement the effect of the wood panels, further enhancing the authenticity of the colonial setting.*

MANHATTAN DINING ROOM

This minimalist, yet striking, striped wall provides an interesting backdrop to a room that is a haven away from the hubbub of city life. The impact of these wide stripes is maximized by taking them right over the skirting (base) board to floor level. A plain beech effect is used to paint the table top, and the surface pattern and texture is achieved by using a heart grainer (graining roller) and comb. The techniques are easy to master. Finally, remember to varnish the table to protect your handiwork.

You will need

- emulsion (latex) paint in off-white and taupe
- household paintbrush
- long ruler
- spirit level (level)
- pencil
- wide paint pad
- table
- satinwood paint in white
- artists' oil colour paint in Naples yellow
- white spirit (turpentine)
- paint kettle (pot)
- heart grainer (graining roller)
- graduated comb and narrow comb
- varnish

1 Apply two coats of off-white emulsion (latex) paint to the wall. Leave the paint to dry completely.

2 Using a long ruler and spirit level (level), measure 30cm/12in wide stripes, marking them out with a pencil.

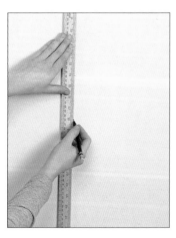

3 Paint in alternate bands using a wide paint pad and taupe emulsion (latex) paint. Concentrate on the edges before filling the inside of the bands. The paint pad should be well coated, but not over loaded. Press firmly whle pulling down the pencil line to achieve an accurate line.

4 To paint the beech-effect table, apply two coats of white satinwood paint as a base coat. Leave each to dry before applying the next. Mix Naples yellow artists' oil colour paint with white spirit (turpentine) until you have a mixture the consistency of thick cream, then brush it evenly over the surface.

5 Drag the surface in a single, lengthways direction.

6 Use a heart grainer (graining roller) to start making the graining. Do this by pulling the tool down gently, slightly rocking it and working in several spaced lines. Do not butt the lines up together.

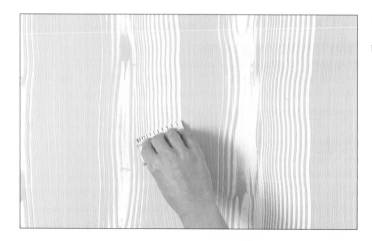

7 With a graduated comb, work in the same direction and fill in the lines between the heart graining.

8 Again, working in the same direction, soften the effect with a large dry brush.

9 Now take a narrow comb and go over the entire surface in the same direction to add detail to the effect. Repeat this until fine lines are achieved. Varnish when dry.

RIGHT: Beech is a light-coloured wood much used for modern furniture and this effect tones well with the stripes on the wall. Although all the colours are neutral in this room, they are varied and warm looking. Choose simple shapes for accessories to enhance the overall contemporary look.

SEASIDE KITCHEN

Bring the look of happy seaside vacations into your kitchen throughout the year. The wall is colourwashed using two layers of the same colour to produce an effective backdrop of movement and depth. Simple beach flag motifs are stamped on the wall in a casual manner to reflect the coastal theme, and details painted in with a small brush. The flaking paint on the cupboard is the result of applying a crackle-glaze medium between the two layers of colour on the panels and dry brushing.

You will need

- emulsion (latex) paint in white, mid (medium) blue and yellow
- decorator's brush
- wallpaper paste
- paint kettle (pot)
- mini roller
- flag stamp
- artist's brush
- cupboard
- household paintbrush
- crackle-glaze medium

1 Apply a base coat of white emulsion (latex) paint to the wall. Leave to dry. Mix mid (medium) blue emulsion (latex) paint with 50 per cent wallpaper paste in a paint kettle (pot). Apply the mixture to the wall at random angles using a broad decorator's brush and allowing the base coat to show through.

2 When the first layer of blue colourwash is dry, apply a second coat, again in random directions.

3 Using a mini roller, apply a good coat of white emulsion (latex) paint to the raised surface of the stamp.

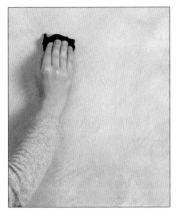

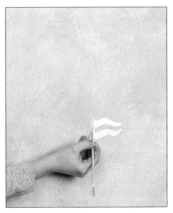

4 Decide where you are going to place the stamp, position it and then press firmly on the wall.

5 Continue to apply stamps to the wall, placing them randomly and making sure that one motif is not directly positioned directly in line with another.

6 When you have completed the stamping use an artist's brush to paint the flagpoles in yellow emulsion (latex) paint to complete the motifs.

7 To decorate the cupboard, apply two base coats of mid (medium) blue emulsion (latex) paint to the outside. Leave to dry.

RIGHT: Cupboards and other small items of furniture are easy to treat with a crackle-glaze effect. Use it to reproduce surfaces that are reminiscent of beach huts exposed to salt and the extremes of the elements through rain and shine.

8 When the blue paint is dry, apply a good coat of crackle-glaze medium to the centre panel, following the manufacturer's instructions.

9 Paint a good coat of white emulsion (latex) over the area where you applied the crackle-glaze medium. Do not overbrush, since the medium will react with the paint fairly quickly to produce the crackle effect. Leave to dry upright to achieve a dramatic cracking effect.

10 Complete the surround to the cupboard panel by scraping the excess white paint from the brush and dry brushing along the edging in the direction of the grain of the wood.

RIGHT: The seaside theme is continued in the accessories in the kitchen, with bright striped china and wooden boats. Plain white shelving can be given an antiqued effect or made from leftover pieces of wood that have been washed up on the shore.

TARTAN (PLAID) STUDY

A warm-looking and well-ordered study is an encouragement to settle down to some writing, reading or serious contemplation! Time-honoured plaids exude a feeling of comforting reliability and a tartan border is much less complicated to paint than you might think. Again, careful measuring is the secret to success and you can use this technique to design any number of combinations of colours and checks. Antique office furniture is expensive, but it is a simple matter to paint an inexpensive desk with a dark wood effect and an attractive leather inset.

You will need

- emulsion (latex) paint in claret red and dark green
- household paintbrush
- long ruler and pencil
- low tack masking tape
- mini paint roller
- acrylic paint in gold
- swordliner (liner) brush
- desk or table
- satinwood paint in pale pink
- interior filler powder (casting plaster)
- artists' oil colour paint in crimson
- synthetic sponge
- varnish

1 Apply two coats of claret red emulsion (latex) paint to the walls that you wish to decorate. Leave to dry.

2 Decide how wide and deep you wish the tartan (plaid) border to be. Then measure and mark it out with a pencil. Taking into account the widths of the roller, mask off the horizontal edges with low-tack masking tape.

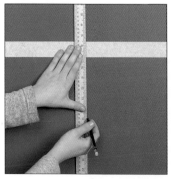

3 Measure and mark out a grid for the main check by drawing in the vertical lines, again taking into account the width of roller you will be using.

4 Coat the mini roller with dark green emulsion (latex) paint and pull along the horizontal pencil lines. Leave to dry.

5 Add the vertical lines in dark green using the mini roller.

6 Dilute gold acrylic paint with water until you have a thin creamy mixture. Using this mixture with a lining brush, paint a thin line about 2.5cm/1in to the right of each vertical green line. Leave to dry.

7 Using the same thin mixture of gold acrylic paint and the swordliner (liner) brush, paint a thin line 2.5cm/1in below each horizontal green line.

8 Paint the whole desk in a dark oak effect and leave to dry. Draw a large rectangle on the top and mask off. Apply a base coat of pale pink satinwood paint and leave to dry. Mix pale pink satinwood paint with powdered interior filler (casting plaster) until you have a paste-like mixture. Dab this mixture over the whole surface until it is about 1cm/½in thick.

9 Stipple over the whole surface with the tips of the bristles of the same household brush used in step 8, texturing the surface. Leave this to dry thoroughly.

10 Brush undiluted crimson artists' oil colour paint over the surface in a fairly thick coat. Stipple to even out, using the same brush as in step 9.

11 Using the flat side of a clean dry sponge, skim over the surface very gently. Apply no pressure but just let the sponge sit on the surface, removing some of the oil from the top layer and highlighting the whole texture. Varnish when dry.

RIGHT: The deep colours chosen for the tartan (plaid) border complement and provide a contrast for the walls of the study, creating a co-ordinated scheme. Borders and bands of checks can define the shape of a room. Placing a horizontal border immediately under the window helps to emphasize the width of the room.

POTTING SHED

Create the relaxing atmosphere of a rural potting shed in a hallway where you keep all the clutter needed for use in the garden. Here, broken-colour techniques are used, adding layers of paint to produce a gentle, muted look to the surroundings. The wall is dry brushed in a downward dragging motion to give a softly textured effect. Four layers of colours are used to give depth to the effect as each coat is allowed to show through. The window box and the individual plant pots are given a verdigris finish to make them stylish for decorative use.

1 Apply a base coat of white emulsion (latex) paint to the wall and leave to dry. Dip the tip of a large household paintbrush into cream emulsion (latex) paint, scrape off the excess and apply to the wall in long vertical strokes. Vary the starting point with each stroke and allow the base coat to show through. Leave to dry thoroughly.

2 Then, dip the tip of the paintbrush into moss green emulsion (latex) paint and scrape off the excess. Dry brush the paint on to the wall using long vertical strokes. Make sure that the layer of colour underneath shows through. Leave to dry.

3 Similarly, dry brush a layer of sage green emulsion (latex) paint using vertical strokes and allowing the underlayers to show through. Leave to dry thoroughly.

4 Finally, when dry, dry brush a layer of cream emulsion (latex) paint in a similar manner to steps 2 and 3.

▶

RIGHT: Dry-brushed layers of soft greens and cream produce a gentle background that exudes calmness and tranquillity. Use this effect to turn an area of your home into a retreat away from the stresses of everyday life and a place to get in touch with nature by caring for plants.

5 To prepare the window box for decorating, rub down the surface with sandpaper to provide a key so that the paint will adhere. Apply a base coat of jade green satin or gloss finish paint and leave to dry thoroughly.

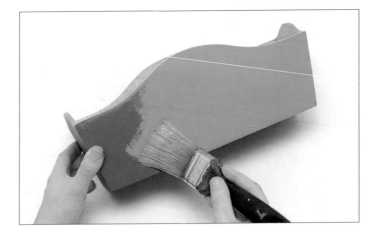

6 Lightly stipple bronze enamel paint over the surface using the tips of the bristles of the brush, making sure that you keep the base coat exposed.

7 Stipple gold enamel paint over the whole surface even more lightly than the bronze layer and in random patches.

8 With a dry brush, dab over the surface of the jade green base coat, blending slightly. Leave to dry. Rub a little copper gilt cream over the whole surface with the tips of the brush. Then, buff to a strong shine with a dry cloth.

RIGHT: The colours used in this arrangement are kept light and are enhanced by the harmoniously painted furniture and accessories.

WAX-RESIST SHUTTERS

Give new wooden shutters or doors a weatherworn look by applying wax between two layers of different-coloured paint. Two colourways are shown – creamy yellow beneath bright blue, and pastel blue over candy pink for a sunny Caribbean feel.

You will need

- acrylic primer in white
- medium and small decorator's paintbrushes
- matt emulsion (flat latex) paint in soft yellow and bright blue or candy pink and pale blue
- neutral wax
- medium-grade abrasive paper

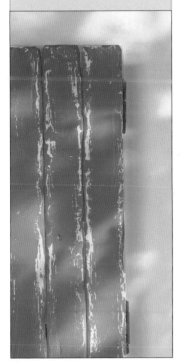

1 Paint the shutters with a coat of white primer and leave to dry. Then paint with soft yellow emulsion (latex). Leave to dry.

2 Using a small decorator's paintbrush, apply wax in areas that would naturally receive wear and tear such as the edges of the boards. Leave to dry.

3 Paint all over the shutters with bright blue emulsion, covering the waxed areas. Leave to dry.

4 Sand over the waxed areas to reveal the yellow base colour and create the "worn" effect.

ALTERNATIVE COLOURWAY

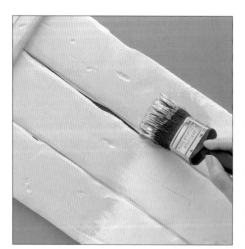

ABOVE: For an alternative colourway, apply candy pink matt emulsion (flat latex) paint over the primer.

ABOVE: Apply wax as described in step 2, then paint with a pale blue top coat. Rub back with abrasive paper to reveal pink areas.

KITCHEN TILES

These clever "tiles" are, in fact, simple squares painted using three different techniques. Fine tape separates the tiles and is removed at the end to give the illusion of grouting. You can experiment with other paint effects (see Painting Techniques) and colours to create your own design, or leave some of the squares white as a contrast.

1 Paint the wall white, using a paint roller for an even texture. Decide on the width of your tiled panel. Mark the wall 45cm/18in above your work surface and in the centre of the width measurement.

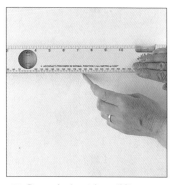

2 Draw a horizontal pencil line across the width of the panel at this height, using a spirit level to make sure that it is straight. Place a strip of masking tape to sit above this line.

3 Mark dots along the tape at 15cm/6in intervals either side of the centre mark. Use the spirit level to draw vertical lines down the wall. Mark vertical dots at 15cm/6in intervals and draw horizontal lines.

4 Place fine line or car striping tape over the lines in both directions. Smooth the tape into place with your fingers, pressing it down well to ensure that as little paint as possible will be able to seep underneath it.

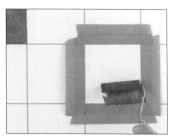

5 Place easy-mask tape around one square. Pour blue paint into a small paint tray and add 25 per cent water. Apply an even coat of paint to the roller, then roll it over the square. Repeat for all the plain blue squares.

6 Mask off a square to be sponged. Dampen the sponge in water, dip it into the blue paint and dab the excess on to some kitchen paper. Sponge the paint on the square. Repeat the same process for all the sponged squares.

7 Mask off a square to be dabbed with the mutton cloth (stockinet). Using a brush, apply the paint and then use the cloth to blend it. Continue other dabbed squares as before.

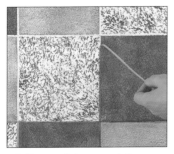

8 Remove all the tape and clean off the pencil marks. If any paint has seeped under the tape in places, use a craft knife to scrape it off, leaving a clean finish.

FROTTAGE HALLWAY

The technique of texturing paint by pressing tissue paper over the wet surface is known as "frottage". Here, tone-on-tone in soft green creates a delicate effect at the top of the hallway. The pattern in the textured wallpaper below the dado (chair) rail has been highlighted by stippling on a darker green glaze, then wiping it off with a cloth.

You will need

- satin-finish emulsion (latex) paint in light, medium and dark shades of soft green and white (buy a dark shade of the green paint and mix it with white to make the medium and light shades)
- large and medium decorator's paintbrushes
- matt emulsion (flat latex) paint in medium shade of soft green
- tissue paper
- acrylic scumble
- stippling brush
- clean cotton cloth

1 Paint the upper part of the wall with two coats of light green satin-finish paint, leaving each to dry.

2 Dilute the matt (flat) green paint with about 20 per cent water. Brush this on to a section of the wall.

3 Immediately press a sheet of tissue paper over the entire surface except for a narrow band adjacent to the next section you will be working. Work on a manageable area at a time so that you can keep the edge wet. Better still, ask someone to assist you – one brushing, one following with the tissue paper.

4 Carefully peel back the tissue paper to reveal most of the base colour underneath. Repeat over the rest of the upper part of the wall, using a fresh sheet of tissue paper on each section of your work.

5 Brush on two coats of medium green silk finish paint over the textured wallpaper below the dado (chair) rail, leaving each to dry. If the wallpaper is new, it may bubble, but it will shrink back when dry.

6 Mix the dark green silk finish paint with acrylic scumble in a ratio of 1 part paint to 6 parts scumble. Brush this glaze on to a section of the wallpaper.

7 Immediately dab over the wet glaze with a stippling brush to eliminate the brushmarks and even out the texture.

8 Wipe a cotton cloth gently over the stippled glaze to remove the glaze from the raised areas of the wallpaper. Complete the lower part of the wall section by section. Leave to dry. Paint the dado rail with white paint, leave to dry and then brush over the dark green glaze.

VINEGAR-GLAZED FLOORCLOTH

Painted floorcloths were fashionable with the early American settlers, and they remain popular as inexpensive, handmade alternatives to carpets. This one is painted with vinegar glaze and decorated with patterns, using a cork and other simple objects as stamps. Dark shellac gives the finished floorcloth an antique finish.

You will need

- heavyweight cotton duck canvas (from artist's suppliers), 7.5cm/3in larger all round than the finished floorcloth
- staple gun or hammer and tacks
- acrylic wood primer in white
- large and medium decorator's paintbrushes
- fine-grade abrasive paper
- set square (T square)
- pencil
- large scissors
- PVA (white) glue and brush
- 2.5cm/1in masking tape
- dessertspoon
- emulsion (latex) paint in bright red
- gloss acrylic floor varnish and brush – use matt (flat) acrylic varnish if preferred
- 1cm/¹/₂in masking tape
- malt vinegar
- sugar
- bowl and spoon
- powder pigment in dark ultramarine
- reusable putty adhesive
- clean cotton cloth
- craft knife
- cork
- dark shellac and brush
- floor varnish and brush

PREPARATION

Before beginning this project, stretch the canvas across an old door or table top and staple or tack it in place. Paint the surface with three or four coats of primer, leaving to dry between coats, then sand to give a completely smooth surface. Using a set square (T square), check that the canvas is square – if not, trim it down. Mark a pencil border 2.5cm/ 1in from the edge. Cut diagonally across each corner, through the point where the pencil lines cross.

1 Fold over each edge to the pencil line. Glue and then secure with masking tape until dry. Rub the edges firmly with a dessertspoon. Sand the edges where the primer has cracked.

2 Turn the canvas to the right side. Using masking tape, mark a wide border. Paint with bright red emulsion (latex), carrying the paint over the outer edges. When dry, apply a coat of floor varnish. Leave to dry.

3 Remove the masking tape and tidy any ragged edges with extra paint. When dry, place 1cm/¹/₂in masking tape around the outer edge to a depth of 1cm/¹/₂in. Repeat around the inner edge of the border.

4 Mix 150 ml/¼ pint/⅝ cup malt vinegar with 1 teaspoon sugar. Add up to 2 tablespoons of dark ultramarine powder pigment and stir well – the glaze should be of a consistency to flow on smoothly. Paint the glaze over the top of the red border.

5 While the dark ultramarine glaze is still wet, make patterns by pressing the reusable putty adhesive on top and then removing it.

6 Copy the patterns shown in the illustrations or experiment with your own. Wipe the glaze with a damp cotton cloth if you make a mistake. The glaze will take about 15 minutes to dry.

7 Using a craft knife, cut a hole in one end of the cork. Paint the dark ultramarine vinegar glaze over the centre panel. While the glaze is still wet, stamp a pattern of circles and lines.

8 Cut a square at the other end of the cork to make a different stamp. Experiment with other objects. Use the reusable putty adhesive to make additional lines and curves.

9 When the glaze is dry, remove the masking tape. Tidy the edges with a damp cloth wound around your finger. Apply a coat of dark shellac, then several coats of floor varnish, allowing the canvas to dry between coats. Leave the floorcloth for at least 4 days before walking on it.

COMBED CHECK FLOOR

A simple combing technique has been used to decorate this warm, sunny floor. You can experiment with other patterns instead of the traditional wave pattern shown here. Using a hardboard template to draw the squares saves the chore of measuring and marking out the floor before you start.

You will need

- emulsion (latex) paint in yellow ochre, orange and red
- medium decorator's paintbrush
- 30cm/12in wide piece of hardboard
- pencil
- masking tape
- acrylic scumble
- rubber comb
- acrylic floor varnish and brush

1 Paint the floor with two coats of yellow ochre emulsion (latex), leaving each to dry thoroughly.

2 Starting in the corner most on view, place the piece of hardboard against the side of the wall. Draw pencil lines widthways across the room. Return to the same corner and draw lines lengthways to form a grid.

3 Place masking tape on the outside of alternate lines, both horizontally and vertically, to prepare for the first colour of squares.

4 Mix some scumble into the orange emulsion. Paint this mixture on to one square (you will need to work on one at a time so that the paint remains wet).

5 Run the rubber comb through the wet paint, twisting your hand slightly to form a wave pattern. Repeat the process with the orange squares on alternate rows. Leave to dry, then remove the masking tape.

6 Place masking tape the other side of those squares previously marked. Paint these, one at a time, with red emulsion mixed with scumble.

7 Run the comb through the wet paint, this time in the opposite direction. Half the squares on the floor will now be painted.

8 To complete the remaining squares, simply mask each square individually and then paint in the appropriate colour.

9 Comb each of the squares as you go, while the paint is still wet. While combing, vary the direction of the wave pattern as before.

10 When the paint is dry, seal the floor with three coats of acrylic floor varnish. Leave to dry thoroughly before walking on the floor.

DISTRESSED TABLE TOP

A second-hand buy can be transformed with a fashionably distressed look in shades of blue paint. Petroleum jelly and candle wax resist the paint in different ways. The petroleum jelly is applied to the table top in the main areas of natural wear and tear; the candle wax is then used, giving a more subtle effect.

You will need

- sanding block and medium-grade abrasive paper
- emulsion (latex) paint in navy blue, pale blue and mid-blue
- small decorator's paintbrush
- petroleum jelly and brush
- clean cotton cloth
- candle
- matt (flat) acrylic varnish and brush

1 Sand the table top to provide a key for the paint.

2 Paint with the navy blue emulsion (latex). Leave to dry.

3 Brush blobs of petroleum jelly on to the table top, working inwards from the edges of the table.

4 Paint the table top with pale blue emulsion, applying the brushstrokes in the same direction – don't cover the surface completely. Leave to dry.

5 Wipe over with a cloth and soapy water. In the areas where the petroleum jelly has been applied, the pale blue paint will come away, revealing the navy blue base coat.

6 Rub over the surface of the table with candle wax, concentrating on the edges of the table top and areas where there would be natural wear and tear.

7 Paint the table with mid-blue emulsion, again applying the brushstrokes in the same direction. Leave to dry.

8 Rub over the surface with abrasive paper. Where the candle wax has been applied, the mid-blue paint will be removed. Seal the table with two coats of varnish.

DRY-BRUSHED CHAIR

A soft, distressed look is achieved by dry brushing off-white paint over a light brown base painted to imitate wood. This is another excellent technique for making a tired old piece of furniture look desirably aged.

You will need

- clean cotton cloth
- sanding block and medium-grade abrasive paper
- emulsion (latex) paint in pale terracotta and off-white
- small decorator's paintbrush
- sponge
- matt (flat) acrylic varnish and brush

1 Wipe over the chair with a damp cloth, then sand it in the direction of the grain.

2 Mix the pale terracotta emulsion (latex) 50/50 with water. Paint the whole chair.

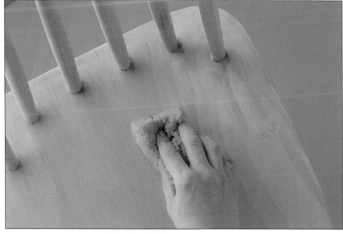

3 While the paint is still wet, use a sponge dampened with water to remove the excess paint mixture carefully.

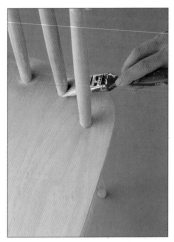

4 Using a dry brush, apply the off-white emulsion over the chair. At the angles, flick the paint from the base upwards.

5 For the flat surfaces, hold the brush at an angle and apply the paint with minimal pressure. Leave to dry then seal with two coats of varnish, leaving to dry between coats.

GRAINED DOOR

This strongly textured combed graining is achieved by mixing wall filler with sky blue emulsion (latex). Lime green paint is then brushed over the blue and sanded off when dry to give a surprisingly subtle effect.

You will need

- medium-grade abrasive paper
- emulsion (latex) paint in sky blue and lime green
- medium decorator's paintbrush
- wall filler
- rubber comb
- matt (flat) acrylic varnish and brush

1 Using medium-grade abrasive paper, sand the door to provide a key for the paint. Paint the surface with a base coat of sky blue emulsion (latex). Leave to dry.

2 Mix 25 per cent filler with 75 per cent sky blue paint. Paint on, working on a small section at a time. While still wet, comb lines, following the grain. Leave to dry.

3 Paint the door with a thin coat of lime green emulsion, applying the paint in the same direction as the combing to follow the grain of the wood. Leave to dry.

4 Sand the door, revealing lines of sky blue paint beneath the lime green top coat. Seal with two coats of acrylic varnish.

SCANDINAVIAN DOOR PANELS

Painted furniture and fittings are very popular in Scandinavia, especially designs that celebrate nature. These beautiful panels are painted freehand, with flowing brushstrokes. Do not worry too much about making the doors symmetrical – it is more important that the painting should look natural. Practise the strokes with art brushes first on a piece of paper until you feel confident. Any cupboard or dresser doors would be suitable for this design. You could even decorate modern kitchen units.

You will need

- pale yellow emulsion (latex) paint – ochre rather than lemon
- medium decorator's paintbrush
- plant and flowerpot design
- pencil
- artist's acrylic paint in yellow ochre, ultramarine and antique white
- old white plates
- lining brush
- rounded artist's brush
- clear matt varnish and brush

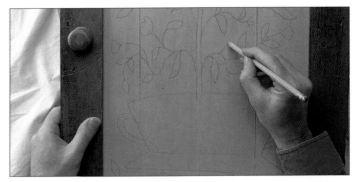

1 Paint the door panels with pale yellow emulsion (latex). Leave to dry. Draw the design on each panel in pencil, using the template at the back of the book.

2 Put some yellow ochre artist's acrylic paint on to a plate. Mix in ultramarine to make grey-green. Using a lining brush, begin painting the design at the top of the first panel.

3 Work your way down the panel, resting your painting hand on your other hand to keep it steady.

4 Put some antique white artist's acrylic paint on to a plate. Using an artist's brush, paint the flowerpot and swirls below. Add the flowers, applying pressure to the brush. Darken the paint with more yellow ochre, then add the soil colouring in the pot.

5 Paint the other panel and leave to dry. Apply a protective coat of clear matt varnish.

RIGHT: Use this design on a cupboard to create a country theme in a kitchen.

INDIAN BEDHEAD

The inspiration for this arch-shaped bedhead (head board) comes from Indian temple wall paintings. The bedroom feels as if it has been magically transported thousands of miles, but the real magic here comes in a simple pot of paint. Before painting the bedhead (head board), set the mood with a deep rust-coloured wash on the walls. If you can, use a water-based distemper (tempera) for an authentic powdery bloom. If you are using emulsion (latex) paint, thin it with water and use random brushstrokes for a patchy, mottled look. The arch is simply chalked on to the wall using a paper template.

You will need

- large roll of brown parcel wrap (packing paper)
- felt-tipped pen
- masking tape (optional)
- scissors
- spray adhesive
- chalk
- water-based paint in dark blue, bright blue and red
- plate and kitchen sponge
- emulsion (latex) paint in sandy cream
- medium and fine paintbrushes
- fine-grade sandpaper

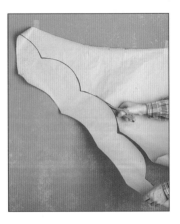

1 Tape a sheet of brown parcel wrap (packing paper) on the wall and draw the half-arch directly on to it, following the pattern shape. Cut out the half-arch shape using a pair of scissors.

2 Position the paper pattern on the wall with spray adhesive and draw around the edges with chalk.

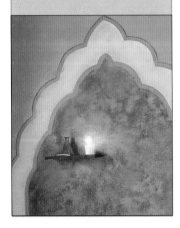

3 Remove the pattern from the wall, flip it over and position it on the opposite side to produce the shape for the second half of the arch. Draw around the edges as before.

4 Spread some dark blue paint on to a plate and use a damp sponge to dab it on to the central panel. Do not cover the background completely but leave some of the wall colour showing through. When the paint is dry, apply the bright blue paint over the dark blue in the same way.

5 When the paint is dry, paint the arch in sandy cream emulsion, using a medium-size paintbrush.

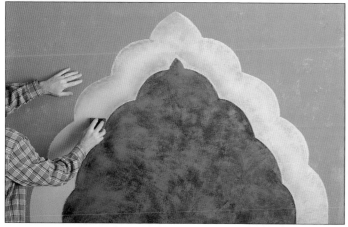

6 When the sandy cream paint is dry, rub it back in places with fine-grade sandpaper, to give a faded effect.

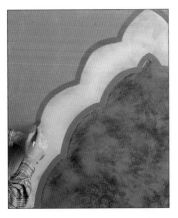

7 Outline the inside and outside of the arch with red paint, using a fine paintbrush. Support your painting hand with your other hand. Use the width of the brush to make a single line.

8 Outline the outer red stripe with a thinner dark blue line. Work as described in the previous step, keeping the line as clean as possible.

9 Leave to dry, then use fine-grade sandpaper to soften any hard edges so that the arch has the naturally faded appearance of an old temple wall.

RIGHT: *A painted head board instantly tranforms the simplest of beds into an item of furniture with a definite style.*

HARLEQUIN SCREEN

Two simple paint techniques – stippling and rag rolling – are used here to great effect. Choose bright shades of paint as the colours will be softened by the white-tinted scumble glaze.

PREPARATION

It is best to remove the hinges before sanding the surfaces to be decorated. Apply cream emulsion (latex) and leave to dry, then sand to give a smooth surface. Refer to the artwork at the back of the book for templates of how to mark up the screen.

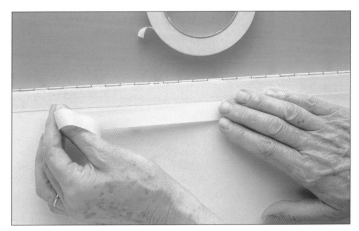

1 Place masking tape close to the edge of the screen along the outer borders of the two outer panels, and along the base of all three panels. Place a second line of tape next to the first.

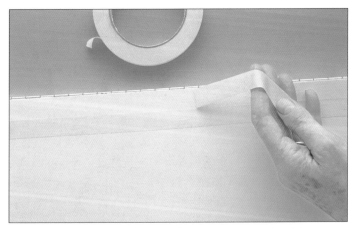

2 Remove the outer tape, leaving a 1cm/¹/₂in border along the edge of the screen. Smooth down the remaining tape. Using flexible masking tape, repeat steps 1 and 2 along the top of all three panels.

3 Measure the height of the screen at the longest point and divide by six. Draw a vertical line halfway across the panel. Mark the centre point and two equally spaced points either side. Return to the centre point and divide the panel horizontally into four equal points, one each side of the central line. Draw a grid of equal-sized oblongs, four across and six down. Repeat for the other panels.

4 Lay fine line tape or car striping tape from the centre point at the top of each panel diagonally to the far right-hand corner of the next space. Continue from the far right-hand corner through the centre point until all the lines are marked with tape. Repeat in the opposite direction to make a diamond pattern. Secure the tape at the sides of the panel with a small piece of masking tape.

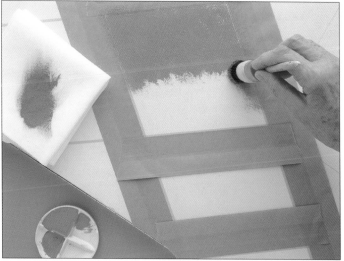

5 Using wide easy-mask decorator's tape, mask off the diamonds that are to be painted in the first colour. Follow the picture of the finished screen for colour reference.

6 Bind 2.5cm/1in at the base of the stencil brush with masking tape. Dip the brush into the first colour, wipe the surplus on kitchen paper until the brush is fairly dry, then stipple the masked diamonds. Work out to the masking tape, using a firm pouncing motion. Leave to dry. Using the other colours, stipple all the diamonds in the same way.

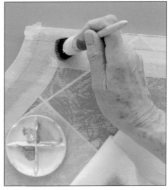

8 Holding a crumpled cloth between both hands, roll it down each panel while the glaze is still wet, moving your hands in different directions. Leave the glaze to dry.

7 When all the paint is dry, remove the fine line or car striping tape. Apply a coat of matt (flat) varnish and leave to dry. Mix a little white acrylic paint into the scumble to make a glaze. Paint this over the diamonds.

10 Mix both gold paints together. Lay masking tape either side of the cream borders. Stipple the gold paint on with a small stencil brush. Leave to dry, then remove the masking tape. Apply a final coat of varnish. When dry, replace the screen hinges.

9 Apply another coat of varnish. When this is dry, remove the masking tape from the borders of the diamonds.

GRAINED WINDOW FRAME

ere, extra interest is added to a window frame by decorating it with a subtle imitation wood pattern. The same treatment would work well on a wide picture frame. To hide a boring view, stencil the panes of glass with frosted stars.

1 Sand the window frame with medium-grade abrasive paper, then paint with pale blue-green vinyl silk paint and leave to dry. For the glaze, mix 1 part deep blue-green emulsion (latex) to 6 parts scumble. Paint the glaze over the main surfaces.

2 While the glaze is wet, draw the heart grainer (rocker) across the glazed surface, rocking it backwards and forwards. Wipe the corners with a damp cloth to make a mitre. As you work, protect the wet graining with a piece of abrasive paper. Leave to dry.

3 Apply a coat of varnish only over the glazed areas and leave to dry. Paint the inner edges of the frame and the glazing bars across the window with glaze. While still wet, draw down each piece of wood with a rubber comb. Leave to dry, then apply another coat of varnish over the whole window frame.

4 Make sure that the glass is clean, then attach the stencil with masking tape. Using a stencil brush, apply the frosting varnish evenly through the stencil. Remove the stencil before the varnish dries completely.

CRACKLE-GLAZE PICTURE FRAME

This simple picture frame – which could also be used to hold a small mirror – is made from a piece of plywood. Simply cut a square from the centre and edge with beading. As well as being treated with crackle glaze, the brightly coloured paintwork is distressed slightly with abrasive paper to give a very attractive finish.

1 Paint the frame with two coats of yellow ochre emulsion (latex), allowing each to dry. Brush on a coat of crackle glaze. Leave to dry according to the manufacturer's instructions.

2 Place strips of masking tape in a pattern on either side of the frame, as shown.

3 Where the ends of the masking tape overlap, carefully trim off the excess tape with a craft knife.

4 Brush turquoise paint on the unmasked sections of the frame, working in one direction. The crackle effect will appear almost immediately. Take care not to overbrush an area (see Painting Techniques).

5 Brush orange paint on alternate sections of the pattern in the same way. Paint the remaining sections lime green. Leave to dry.

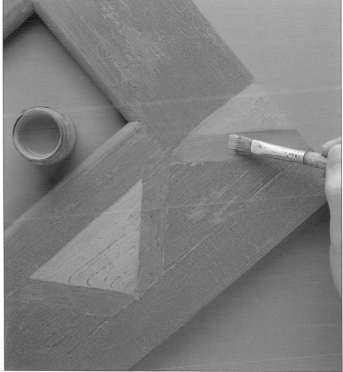

6 Carefully peel away the masking tape, revealing the yellow ochre base coat.

7 Using a flat artist's paintbrush, apply bright pink paint to the areas where the masking tape had been. Do this freehand to give the frame a handpainted look. Leave to dry.

8 Rub coarse-grade abrasive paper over the whole of the picture frame to show some of the yellow ochre paint beneath the brightly coloured surface.

9 Seal the frame with two coats of acrylic varnish. Apply the first coat quickly, taking care not to overbrush and reactivate the crackle glaze.

SPONGED LAMP BASE

hree shades of green paint are sponged on to this inexpensive lamp base to give a very attractive dappled surface. If you prefer, you can practise the sponging technique first on a piece of white paper until you are confident. You will quickly discover that it is not at all difficult, despite the very professional-looking result.

You will need

- wooden lamp base with electric cord and bulb fitting
- masking tape
- scissors
- rubber gloves
- fine wire (steel) wool
- acrylic primer
- flat artist's paintbrush
- emulsion (latex) paint in off-white, jade green and emerald green
- bowl
- natural sponge
- white paper
- clear acrylic varnish and brush

1 Cover the electric cord and bulb fitting with layers of masking tape to protect them while you work.

2 Wearing rubber gloves, rub down the existing varnish or paint with wire (steel) wool.

3 Using a flat artist's paintbrush, paint the lamp base with two coats of acrylic primer, leaving each to dry.

Paint with two coats of off-white emulsion (latex), leaving the paint to dry between coats.

5 Mix a 50/50 solution of jade green emulsion paint and water. Dampen the sponge and squeeze it until nearly dry, then dip it into the paint. Practise by dabbing the sponge on to a piece of white paper.

6 Cover the lamp base with a dappled layer of paint, applying it just a little at a time in order to build up the texture gradually.

7 Add some off-white paint to lighten the jade green colour. Sponge this lightly over the first layer of colour. Break off a small piece of sponge and use this to work the colour into the moulding to ensure that the whole lamp base is evenly covered.

8 Mix a little emerald green paint 50/50 with water. Apply this mixture sparingly over the surface of the lamp base to add extra depth and texture. When dry, seal with three coats of varnish, allowing the varnish to dry thoroughly between coats. Finally, remove the protective masking tape from the electric cord and bulb fitting.

CRACKLE-GLAZE PLANTER

Here, crackle glaze is sandwiched between dark and pale layers of emulsion (latex) paint to give a modern planter an authentic antique look. The handpainted line is easier to do than you might think, and gives a smart finishing touch.

You will need

- MDF (medium-density fiberboard) planter
- fine-grade abrasive paper (optional)
- emulsion (latex) paint in mid-blue and dark cream
- small decorator's paintbrush
- acrylic crackle glaze
- fine artist's paintbrush
- clear acrylic varnish and brush

1 You do not need to prime MDF (medium-density fiberboard), but it may need sanding. Paint the inside and outside with mid-blue emulsion (latex).

2 When the paint is completely dry, apply a layer of crackle glaze to the outside of the planter. Leave to dry.

3 Paint the outside of the planter with dark cream emulsion. The crackled effect will start to appear almost immediately, so work quickly, with regular brushstrokes. Leave to dry.

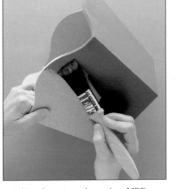

4 Holding your finger against the edge for support, paint a thin mid-blue line 1.5cm/⅝in from the edge on each side of the planter. Leave to dry, then seal with two coats of varnish.

SCANDINAVIAN TABLE

This pretty little table has been distressed by rubbing back thin layers of colour with fine wire (steel) wool. Focusing on the areas that would normally suffer most from general wear and tear gives an authentic aged look. The simple leaf design is painted freehand and picked out with paler highlights.

You will need

- MDF (medium-density fiberboard) or wooden table with drawer
- rubber gloves
- fine wire (steel) wool
- emulsion (latex) paint in dark yellow, grey-green, white, mid-green and pale green
- flat artist's paintbrush
- small decorator's paintbrushes
- acrylic scumble
- fine artist's paintbrush
- clear matt (flat) acrylic varnish and brush

1 Rub down the table with fine wire (steel) wool, wearing a pair of rubber gloves. Pay particular attention to the bevelled edges.

2 Using dark yellow emulsion (latex) and a flat artist's paintbrush, paint the mouldings (if any) around the edge of the drawer and the table top.

3 Paint the rest of the table and the drawer front with two coats of grey-green emulsion, allowing the paint to dry between coats.

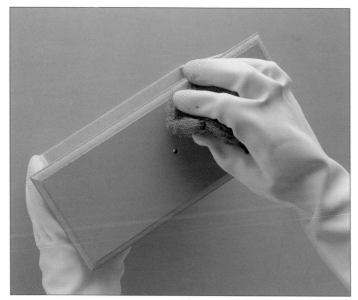

4 Wearing rubber gloves once again, rub down the entire surface of the table with wire wool. Concentrate on the areas that would naturally suffer from wear and tear.

5 Mix 50/50 white emulsion and scumble. Apply sparsely to the grey-green areas with a dry brush, using light diagonal strokes and varying the angle of the brush to give an even coverage over the surface.

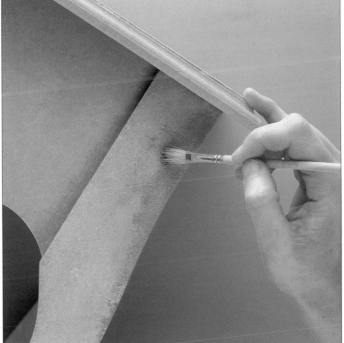

6 Mix 50/50 dark yellow emulsion and scumble. Paint this over the mouldings.

7 Apply light dabs of mid-green paint to the parts of the table that would receive the most wear: the top corners of the legs and underneath. Leave to dry, then rub back with wire wool.

8 Using a fine artist's paintbrush, paint a scrolling leaf design around the edge of the drawer front in pale green. Pick out the stalks and leaf veins with fine brushstrokes in mid-green.

9 Still using the fine artist's paintbrush, add white and dark yellow highlights to the leaf design. Leave to dry.

10 Seal the drawer and table with a coat of clear matt (flat) acrylic varnish for protection.

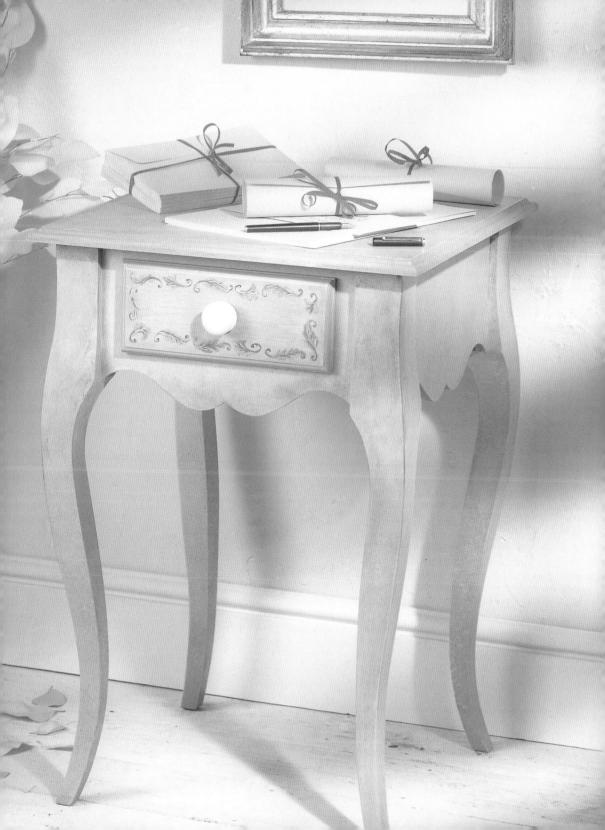

STENCILLING
PROJECTS

S tencilling is often the first paint effect that people try and it is one of the most enduring and popular of home decorating techniques. Whether you use it boldly in place of wallpaper or simply to add decorative details to walls, furniture and other household objects, you can be sure of achieving an eye-catching effect. You will be surprised at how quickly you can transform even a very large surface with a striking pattern. The joy of stencils is that they can be applied to almost any surface, from fabrics and floors to glass and walls. Although you can buy stencils from do-it-yourself stores and other specialist shops, it is much more rewarding and fun to make your own.

ABOVE: A simple sandcastle stencil is given extra vitality with hand-painted flagpoles.

LEFT: A richly ornate wall design is echoed on a matching cushion stencilled with gold fabric paint.

PENNSYLVANIA-DUTCH TULIPS

This American folk-art inspired idea uses the rich colours and simple motifs beloved by the German and Dutch immigrants to Pennsylvania. Create the effect of hand-painted wallpaper or, for a beginner's project, take a single motif and use it to decorate a small cabinet.

You will need

- emulsion (latex) paint in dark ochre
- large and small decorator's paintbrushes
- woodwash in indigo blue and mulberry
- stencil card (stock)
- craft knife and self-healing cutting mat
- pencil
- ruler
- stencil brushes
- stencil paint in red, light green, dark green and pale brown
- saucer or cloth
- artist's paintbrush

1 Dilute 1 part dark ochre emulsion (latex) with 1 part water. Using a large paintbrush, cover the top half of the wall with the diluted paint. Use vertical brushstrokes for an even texture.

2 Paint the lower half of the wall with indigo blue woodwash. Finish off with a curving line using a dry brush to suggest woodgrain.

3 Paint the dado (chair) rail or a strip at dado rail height in mulberry woodwash, using a narrow brush to give a clean edge.

4 Trace the tulip and heart templates at the back of the book and cut the stencils from stencil card (stock) as described in Stencilling Techniques. Mark the centre of each edge of the stencil. Measure the wall and divide it into equal sections, so that the repeats will fall at about 20cm/8in intervals. Mark the positions with pencil, so that they can be rubbed out later.

5 Dip a stencil brush into red stencil paint. Rub the brush on a saucer or cloth until it is almost dry before stencilling in the tulip flowers. Leave to dry.

6 Paint the leaves in light green stencil paint with dark green shading, using an artist's paintbrush. Paint the stems in dark green. Leave to dry.

7 Stencil the basket in pale brown stencil paint using a chunky stencil brush to give texture.

8 Stencil a single heart between each two baskets of tulips using red stencil paint. Judge the positioning of the hearts by eye to give a natural handpainted look.

ABOVE: Decorate a matching key cabinet following the same method and using a single motif.

ABOVE: A simple tulip motif stencilled kitchen storage tin gives instant folk-art style.

THROUGH THE GRAPEVINE

T his classic grape stencil will bring back holiday memories of sipping wine under a canopy of vines. The stencilled grapes are all the more effective set against the purple and green dry-brushed walls. Practise your paint effects on small pieces of board before tackling full-scale walls.

You will need

- large decorator's paintbrush
- emulsion (latex) paint in purple and green
- pencil
- ruler
- spirit level
- acetate
- craft knife and self-healing cutting mat
- masking tape
- stencil paint in purple and lilac
- stencil brush
- silver gilt cream
- soft cotton cloth

1 Dip the end of a large paintbrush in purple emulsion (latex), scrape off the excess and apply to the wall, brushing in varying directions and not completely covering the wall. This process is known as dry-brushing.

2 Repeat the dry-brushing process with green emulsion, filling in some of the bare areas and going over the purple paint.

3 Draw a horizontal pencil line at the desired height on the wall using a ruler and spirit level.

4 Trace the grape stencil at the back of the book and cut the stencil from acetate. Tape the stencil in place with its top edge on the pencil line. Apply purple stencil paint over the whole stencil.

5 Add lilac stencil paint at the bottom of each window in the stencil to create the effect of highlights on the grapes. Repeat the stencil along the wall to create a frieze.

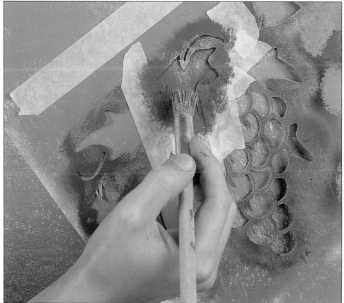

6 Dip the stencil brush in the silver gilt cream, brush off any excess and brush over the stencils using an up and down movement.

7 Select a few leaf shapes from the stencil and mask them off. Position the leaves randomly over the wall and stencil in purple. Brush over with the gilt cream using the same technique as before.

8 Leave the stencilling to dry
overnight. With a soft cotton cloth,
buff up the silver gilt cream to a shine. A
single stencil would also work well on a
cabinet panel or table top.

RENAISSANCE ART

Turn your hallway into a dramatic entrance with ornate stencils and rich colours. Combine them with gold accessories, antique furniture and velvets and braids to complete the theatrical setting. This design would also be ideal for creating an intimate dining room for candlelit dinners.

1 Using a ruler and spirit level, divide the wall in half horizontally with a pencil line, then draw a second line 15cm/6in above the first. Stick a line of masking tape just below this top line. Dilute 1 part slate-blue emulsion (latex) with 1 part water and colour the top half of the wall using a sponge.

2 Stick masking tape above the bottom pencil line. Dilute 1 part terracotta emulsion with 1 part water. Sponge over the lower half of the wall.

3 Sponge lightly over the terracotta sponging with pale slate-blue to add a textural effect. Remove the strips of masking tape.

4 Colour the centre band with diluted peach emulsion using a stencil brush. Trace the templates at the back of the book and cut out the stencils from stencil card (stock) using a craft knife and self-healing cutting mat.

5 Stencil the wall motifs at roughly regular intervals over the upper part of the wall, using dark grey-blue stencil paint. Rotate the stencil with every alternate motif to give movement to the design.

6 Starting at the right-hand side of the peach band, stencil the border motif with terracotta stencil paint. Add details in emerald and turquoise. Continue along the wall, positioning the stencil beside the previous motif so that the spaces are equal.

OPPOSITE: *Make a matching patchwork cushion cover with pieces of fabric stencilled with gold fabric paint. Add offcuts of velvet and cover all the seams with ornate trimmings.*

ROPE AND SHELLS

The chunky rope cleverly linking the seashells is echoed by individual stencilled knots. Shells are always popular motifs for a bathroom design and look good in many colour combinations, from nautical blue and white to greens and aquas or pinks and corals.

You will need

- large household sponges
- emulsion (latex) paint in nautical blue and white
- ruler
- spirit level
- pencil
- acetate
- craft knife and self-healing cutting mat
- masking tape
- stencil paint in dark blue, light blue and camel
- stencil brush
- eraser
- clean cotton cloth

1 Using a household sponge rub nautical blue emulsion (latex) paint over the wall to create a very rough and patchy finish. Leave to dry.

2 Using a clean sponge, rub a generous amount of white emulsion over the wall so that it almost covers the blue, giving a slightly mottled effect.

3 Using a ruler and spirit level, draw a horizontal pencil line at the desired height of the border. Trace the templates at the back of the book and cut the stencils from acetate. Position the seashore stencil with its top edge on the pencil line and secure with masking tape. Stencil dark blue stencil paint around the edges of the shells and seaweed, using a stencil brush.

4 Using light blue stencil paint, shade in the centre of the shells, the seaweed and the recesses of the rope.

5 Using camel stencil paint, fill in the remainder of the rope and then lightly highlight the shells and seaweed. Continue to stencil the shell and rope border right around the room.

6 Draw a vertical line from each loop of rope to the skirting (base) board. Starting 30cm/12in from the stencilled border, make pencil marks at 30cm/ 12in intervals down the line to mark the positions of the rope knots. Start every alternate line of marks 15cm/6in below the border so that the knots will be staggered.

8 Stencil the remainder of the rope in camel. Leave to dry. Remove any visible pencil marks with an eraser and wipe over with a slightly damp cloth.

7 Tape the knotted rope stencil on to the first pencil mark. Stencil dark blue stencil paint in the recesses of the rope.

LEFT: Create a variation on the sea theme by stencilling a simple row of starfish at dado (chair) rail height. The starfish motif is repeated on the chair seat to give a pleasing coordinated look.

HERALDIC DINING ROOM

Lend an atmosphere of medieval luxury to your dining room with richly coloured walls and heraldic motifs stencilled in the same deep tones. Gilt accessories, heavy fabrics and a profusion of candles team well with this decor. All that remains is to prepare a sumptuous banquet.

1 Using a large household sponge, rub camel emulsion (latex) all over the wall. Leave to dry.

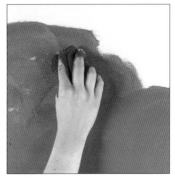

2 Repeat using a generous amount of deep red emulsion so that it almost covers the camel, giving a slightly mottled effect. Leave to dry.

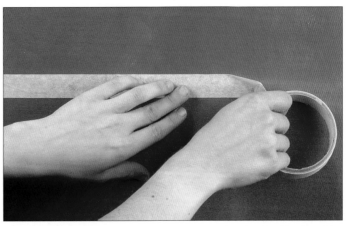

3 Using a ruler and spirit level, draw a pencil line at dado (chair) rail height. Stick a line of masking tape just above it.

4 Sponge deep purple emulsion all over the wall below the masking tape to give a slightly mottled effect. Leave to dry, then remove the masking tape.

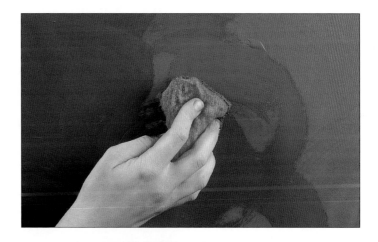

5 Trace the heraldic templates at the back of the book and cut the stencils from acetate. Secure the rose stencil above the dividing line with strips of masking tape. Stencil in purple emulsion, using the stencil brush. When dry, position the fleur-de-lys stencil next to the rose and stencil in camel emulsion. Continue to alternate the stencils around the room.

6 Place the highlight stencils over the painted motifs and, with a stencil brush, add purple details to the camel fleurs-de-lys and camel details to the purple roses as shown.

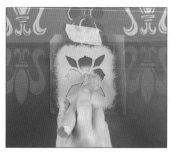

7 Flip the stencils over and position as mirror images below the previously stencilled motifs. Stencil the roses in camel, and the fleurs-de-lys in red.

8 Add highlights as before, using camel on the red fleurs-de-lys, and purple on the camel roses.

9 Using a fine lining brush and camel paint, paint a narrow line where the red and purple paints meet. If you do not have the confidence to do this freehand, position two rows of masking tape on the wall, leaving a small gap in between. When the line of paint is dry, carefully remove the masking tape.

CELESTIAL CHERUBS

This exuberant baroque decoration is perfect for a sumptuous bedroom. The cherubs are stencilled in metallic shades of bronze, gold and copper, but you could use plain colours for a simpler result that would be suitable for a child's room.

You will need

- emulsion (latex) paint in white, blue and grey
- large decorator's paintbrush
- sponge
- stencil card (stock)
- craft knife and self-healing cutting mat
- masking tape
- stencil paint in gold, copper, bronze and white
- stencil brush
- scrap paper

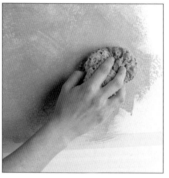

1 Paint the wall with white emulsion (latex). Dilute 1 part blue emulsion with 1 part water, and, using a sponge, lightly apply it to the wall.

2 Sponge in a few areas of grey to give the impression of a cloudy sky. Sponge in a few pale areas by mixing a little white into the grey paint to suggest the edges of clouds.

3 Trace the cherub and heart templates at the back of the book and cut the stencils from stencil card (stock). Secure the cherub stencil to the wall with masking tape. Stencil the body of the cherub in gold stencil paint.

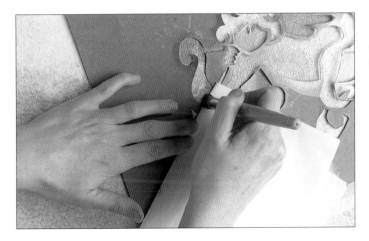

4 Stencil the cherub's wings and bow in copper stencil paint, covering the adjacent parts of the stencil with a piece of scrap paper.

5 Stencil the cherub's hair and arrow in bronze stencil paint, again protecting the adjacent areas with scrap paper.

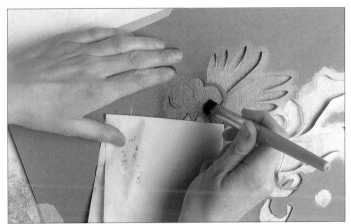

6 Stencil the drape in white stencil paint. Add some bronze shadows to the folds of the drape.

7 To give a three-dimensional effect to the whole design, add bronze shadows at the edges of various parts of the cherub motif. Follow the shading shown in the photograph below.

8 Stencil more cherubs, varying the design by reversing the card sometimes. Stencil the interlinked hearts in the spaces using bronze stencil paint.

LEFT: Try to position the stencils so that the cupids are aiming their arrows at the interlinked hearts – a perfect theme for a romantic bedroom.

FOLK ART WALL

This combination of border patterns and larger single motifs is typical of the stencil designs used by the itinerant painters who worked in the American colonies in the early 19th century. There was little anxiety about whether patterns turned the corners accurately, it was the harmonious colour schemes that made the result so successful.

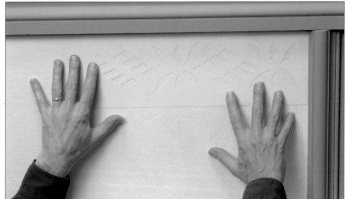

1 Enlarge the templates at the back of the book on a photocopier. Cut out from acetate sheet using a craft knife and cutting mat. Spray the border stencil lightly with spray mount and align it with either the picture or the dado (chair) rail.

ABOVE: This door was painted but you could easily stencil heart motifs instead.

2 Begin stencilling the border design, using a separate stencil brush for each colour.

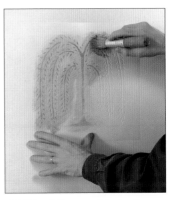

3 If your stencil is an acetate sheet you will be able to see where the second stencil meets the first; if you are using stencil card place it above the first and lift the bottom corner to check that it is in position.

4 Turn the stencil to make the border panels, using a plumbline from the ceiling in order to check the borders are aligned. Repeat this process to frame the room with as many stencilled panels as you need.

5 Using dull green paint, stencil the willow trees in the centre of the panels, one above the other, keeping the stencil brush upright and moving it in a circular motion. The tree looks best with a bit of space all around it.

STAR BATHROOM

This misty blue colour scheme is ideal for a bathroom or staircase because the lower part of the wall is varnished to provide a practical wipe-clean surface. The tinted varnish deepens the colour and gives it a sheen that contrasts well with the chalky distemper (tempera) above. The stencil is a traditional quilting motif.

You will need

- tracing paper and pencil
- scissors
- spray adhesive
- stencil card (card stock)
- sharp craft knife and cutting mat
- soft blue distemper (tempera) or chalk-based paint
- large decorator's paintbrushes
- straightedge
- spirit level (level)
- clear satin water-based varnish
- Prussian blue artist's acrylic paint

1 Trace the star from the back of the book and cut out. Spray the back with adhesive and stick to the card.

2 Using a craft knife, cut out the star. Cut inwards from the points towards the centre so that the points stay crisp.

3 Taking a corner first, carefully peel away the paper template on the top to reveal the stencil underneath.

4 Dilute the paint, if necessary, according to the manufacturer's instructions. Brush it on to the wall with sweeping, random strokes to give a colourwashed effect.

5 Using a straightedge and spirit level (level), draw a pencil line across the wall at the height you want to end the darker varnished surface.

6 Tint the varnish with a squeeze of Prussian blue acrylic paint. Using a separate brush, apply this on the lower part of the wall up to the marked line.

7 Spray the back of the stencil with adhesive and position at one end of the wall, 5cm/2in above the marked line. Stencil with the tinted varnish, using a broad sweep of the brush. Repeat along the wall, spacing the stars evenly.

RIGHT: *A classic geometric eight-pointed star is a beautifully simple decoration.*

SEASHORE BATHROOM SET

Seaside themes are always popular for a bathroom and these stencils in fresh blue and white link the different elements of the room. For best results, choose paints to suit the surface you are planning to stencil: enamel paint for plastic and glass, and fabric paint for the towels.

You will need

- acetate
- craft knife and self-healing cutting mat
- clear plastic shower curtain
- stencil brush
- enamel (latex) paint in white and blue
- cotton hand towel with a smooth border
- fabric paint in dark blue
- iron
- 2 glass tumblers
- masking tape (optional)

1 Trace the shell, starfish and fish templates at the back of the book. Cut the stencils from acetate as described in Stencilling Techniques. Lay the shower curtain on a flat surface. Lightly dab the stencil brush in the white enamel paint and begin to stencil the shapes on the curtain.

2 Continue to stencil the shell, starfish and fish shapes randomly over the whole shower curtain, taking care not to overload the brush with paint. Leave to dry.

3 Reposition the stencils on the painted shapes and dab on the blue paint. Leave some of the shapes white. Leave the shower curtain to dry before hanging it up in place.

4 Lay the hand towel on a flat surface. Using the fish stencil and dark blue fabric paint, stencil fish along the towel border. Position the fish one behind the other, varying the angle slightly.

5 Stencil the opposite end of the towel, arranging the fish in pairs facing each other. Iron the towel to fix the fabric paint, following the manufacturer's instructions.

6 To decorate the first glass tumbler, hold or tape the fish stencil in place and gently dab on white enamel paint. Leave to dry, then reposition the stencil and continue to stencil fish all over the glass tumbler, placing the fish at different angles.

7 Decorate the second tumbler with blue fish in the same way. The tumblers should only be used for decoration; do not apply enamel paints to surfaces that will be drunk or eaten from.

ABOVE: Blue and white stencils work well in a plain white bathroom. You can also choose colours to coordinate with your existing decor.

GREEK URNS

Classic Greek urns softly outlined under a warm terracotta colourwash have a very Mediterranean feel. The stencilling is worked in clear varnish so that the top colour slides over without adhering, leaving subtly coloured motifs. Arrange the urns randomly over the wall for an informal effect.

1 Working in rough, sweeping strokes, rub a base coat of cream emulsion (latex) over the wall using a sponge. Trace the urn template at the back of the book and cut a stencil from acetate as described in Stencilling Techniques. Tape it to the wall and stencil with clear acrylic varnish. Reposition the stencil and cover the wall with randomly placed urns. Wash the sponge.

2 Make up the wallpaper paste following the pack instructions. Mix 1 part terracotta emulsion with 1 part paste. This will make the colourwash slimy and slow down the drying time to prevent "joins" in the finished colourwash. Using the sponge, dab lumps of the mixture over about 1m/3ft square of the wall.

3 Immediately rub the wall with the sponge in a circular motion to blur the original sponge marks.

4 Continue dabbing on the paint mixture and blurring it with the sponge to cover the whole wall. The varnished urns should be revealed underneath the colourwash.

5 If the urns are not clear enough, use a slightly damp cloth and your index finger to rub off a little more of the colourwash from the varnished shapes. This can be done even after the wall has dried.

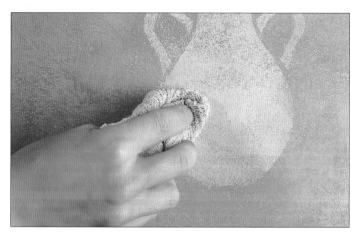

LEFT: Experiment with other colour combinations. This wall is colourwashed with duck-egg blue emulsion (latex) over a beige emulsion background. See the Working with Colour section at the beginning of the book for other ideas.

MAKING SANDCASTLES

Evocative of childhood summers spent on the beach, sandcastles are simple, colourful shapes to stencil. Perfect for a child's room or for a family bathroom, they will bring a touch of humour to your walls. Paint the flags in different colours or glue on paper flags for added interest.

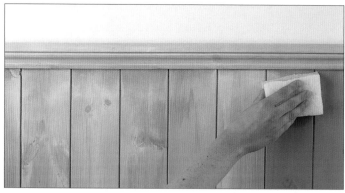

1 Paint below dado (chair) rail height in blue emulsion (latex). When dry, rub on white emulsion with a sponge. Trace the template at the back of the book. Cut the stencils from acetate as described in Stencilling Techniques.

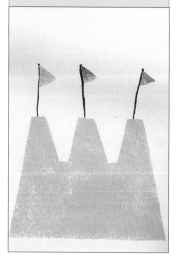

2 Using a tape measure, measure the wall to calculate how many sandcastles you can fit on and make light pencil marks at regular intervals. Hold the stencil above the dado rail centred on one of the marked points and secure the corners with masking tape.

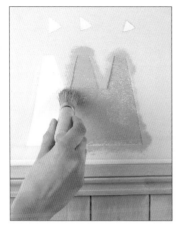

3 Using yellow stencil paint and a stencil brush, stencil in the base of the first sandcastle.

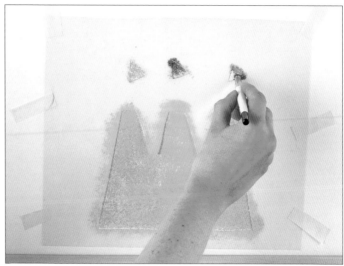

4 Using a smaller stencil brush, paint each of the three flags in a different colour of your choice. Carefully remove the stencil from the wall.

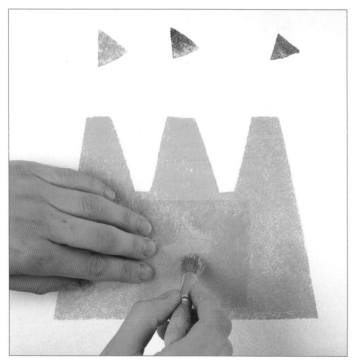

5 When the paint has dried, stencil a star on the sandcastle in a contrasting colour of paint. Try to alternate the colour of the star for each sandcastle on the wall.

6 Using a fine artist's paintbrush and black stencil paint, paint in the flagpoles. The lines do not need to be straight: wavy lines will add to the quality of the finished project.

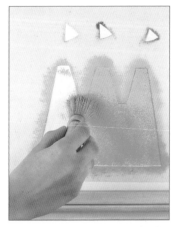

7 Continue stencilling the sandcastles along the wall using your pencil marks to position them.

8 As an alternative to stencilling the flags, cut out triangles of coloured paper and glue them to the wall with PVA (white) glue, then paint in the flagpoles.

ABOVE: Don't be too exacting when hand painting the flagpoles. Wobbly lines and erratic angles add to the childlike and spontaneous quality of the sandcastle frieze.

LEFT: As a variation on the holiday theme, you could cover the wall above the dado (chair) rail with tropical shapes in Caribbean colours. Paint the wall first in a strong background colour.

FLAG STENCILS

This strong graphic design will add colour and fun to a child's room or a study. The easiest way to make a stencil is to photocopy a simple motif on to acetate sheet. Here, two complementary flag motifs are combined. Use the stencils as a border at picture or dado (chair) rail height, randomly around the room or in straight lines to make a feature of, for example, an alcove on one wall.

You will need

- acetate sheet
- craft knife and self-healing cutting mat
- masking tape
- emulsion (latex) paint in black and several bright colours
- stencil brush or small decorator's paintbrush

1 Photocopy the designs from the back of the book at various sizes until you are happy with the size. Photocopy them directly on to the acetate sheet.

2 Cut out the stencils using a craft knife and cutting mat.

OPPOSITE: Bold and primary colours have been used here and work well on a plain white background. You could soften the effect by using pastels if you wish.

3 Tape the stencils to the wall using masking tape, alternating the flags and the direction they are facing. Stencil a bold outline in black.

4 Use a medium stencil brush to apply the colour inside the outlines, or paint it freehand for a looser, more childlike effect.

CHILD'S SEASIDE ROOM

This pretty frieze shows a jaunty crab, a starfish and a scallop shell riding on the crest of a wave stencilled along a practical peg rail. A small co-ordinating mirror bordered with little fishes and a wave completes the effect. Use sea-inspired colours such as blue, aquamarine or pale coral as here or choose your own colour palette.

You will need

- tracing paper and pen
- masking tape
- stencil card
- craft knife and self-healing cutting mat
- small decorator's paintbrush
- wooden peg rail
- pale blue emulsion (latex) paint
- flat paintbrush
- acrylic paints in aquamarine, turquoise, dark coral and pale coral
- ceramic tile
- stencil brush
- spirit level
- soft pencil
- eraser
- wooden framed mirror
- fine-grade abrasive paper (optional)
- damp rag (optional)
- sheet of paper

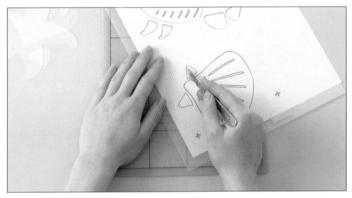

1 Trace the templates at the back of the book. Tape a piece of stencil card to the tracings. Using a craft knife and cutting mat, cut out the stencils. You will need two stencils for the frieze – the starfish, crab and shell, and the details.

2 Remove the pegs from the peg rail. Paint the peg rail with pale blue emulsion (latex) paint. Leave to dry. Tape the waves stencil to the top of the peg rail at one end. Using a flat paintbrush, spread a thin coat of aquamarine and turquoise acrylic paints on to a ceramic tile. Dab at the paints with a stencil brush and stencil the wave, blending the colours together at random.

3 Leave to dry completely then remove the stencil. Move the stencil along the peg rail, matching the valley of the waves so the stencil appears to "flow" seamlessly, and continue stencilling.

4 Use the stencil brush to paint the ends and lower edge of the peg rail to match the waves using a flat paintbrush blending the colours together at random as before. Fix the pegs in place. Paint the pegs with dark coral paint.

5 Using a spirit level, lightly mark the position of the peg rail on the wall with a soft pencil. Tape the starfish, crab and shell stencil to the wall above the peg rail position. Stencil the cut-outs with dark coral paint and leave to dry.

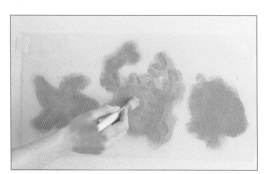

6 Stencil the centre of the starfish, crab and shell with pale coral acrylic paint.

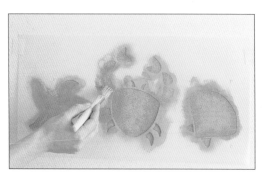

7 Lightly shade the edges of the crab stencil with aquamarine acrylic paint. Leave to dry completely then carefully remove the stencil.

8 Tape the stencils of the details to the wall, matching up the registration marks. Stencil the details with turquoise paint. Leave them to dry then erase the pencil marks. Fix the peg rail to the wall matching the top edge of the peg rail to the drawn pencil line.

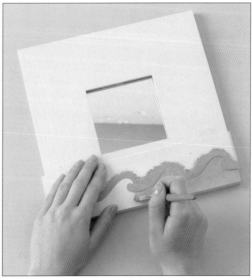

9 If your wooden mirror frame is varnished or already painted, sand it first with fine-grade abrasive paper then wipe it clean with a damp rag. Slip pieces of paper under the edges framing the mirror to protect it from any splashes of paint. Paint the frame with pale blue emulsion paint. Leave to dry.

10 Tape the waves stencil across the bottom of the frame. Using the flat paintbrush, spread a thin coat of aquamarine and turquoise paint on the ceramic tile. Dab at the paints with the stencil brush and stencil the wave, blending the colours together on the frame. Use the stencil brush to paint the lower edges of the frame to match the waves.

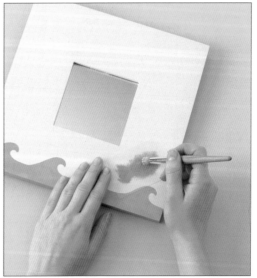

11 Tape the fish stencil to the frame above the waves. Stencil the fish with dark coral paint. Leave to dry.

12 Lightly shade the fish with aquamarine paint. Stencil more fish at random on the frame.

PAINTED DRAWERS

Jazz up plain drawers with bright paintbox colours and simple daisy stencils. The stencils could also be used to decorate larger pieces of furniture such as a chest of drawers for a child's room or kitchen units. Sample pots of emulsion (latex) paint are ideal to use on small projects.

You will need

- set of wooden drawers
- fine-grade abrasive paper
- emulsion (latex) paints in various bright colours
- medium and small decorator's paintbrushes
- screwdriver
- acetate sheet
- craft knife and self-healing cutting mat
- stencil brushes
- matt (flat) acrylic varnish
- wood glue (optional)

1 Remove the drawers and sand down the frame and drawers to remove any rough areas or patches of old paint.

2 Paint the drawer frame with emulsion (latex) paint. Leave to dry, then apply a second coat of paint.

3 Unscrew the drawer knobs and paint each drawer in a different-coloured emulsion paint. Leave to dry and apply a second coat. Trace the flower template at the back of the book and cut a stencil from acetate sheet using a craft knife and cutting mat.

OPPOSITE: If you use more muted colours such as pale green or cream, you can create a much subtler effect.

♦ 329 ♦

4 When the drawers are dry, position the flower stencil in the centre of a drawer and, using a stencil brush and paint in a contrasting colour, stencil on the flower. Leave to dry.

5 Stencil a daisy flower in the centre of each drawer, using a different colour paint for each one.

6 Paint the drawer knobs with two coats of paint, leaving them to dry between coats. Leave to dry.

7 Screw or glue a painted knob to the centre of each drawer. Varnish the drawers with matt acrylic varnish. Leave to dry before reassembling.

TRAIN TOY BOX

This chugging train stencil will fit any child's toy box. Simply add or decrease the number of wagons to suit your requirements. You could add more wagons to extend the train around the entire box.

You will need

- masking tape
- toy box, painted sky blue
- flat paintbrush
- acrylic paints in grey, red, aquamarine, pink, white, yellow, blue, black and purple
- ceramic tile
- stencil brush
- tracing paper and pen
- acetate sheet
- craft knife and self-healing cutting mat
- metal ruler
- soft pencil
- eraser
- clear matt (flat) varnish and brush

1 Stick a length of masking tape around the toy box immediately below the intended position of the rails. Stick another length of tape 5mm/¼in above the first. Keep the tape parallel with the base of the toy box.

2 Using a flat paintbrush, spread a thin coat of grey paint on to a ceramic tile. Dab at the paint with a stencil brush and stencil the rails. Leave the paint to dry then carefully pull off the tape.

3 Trace the toy box and clouds templates at the back of the book. Tape a piece of acetate to the tracings. Using a craft knife and cutting mat cut out the stencils, cutting straight lines against a metal ruler. You will need two toy box stencils – the train engine, wagons and smoke, then the wheels and the details. Also cut out the registration marks to help guide your positioning.

4 Tape the engine, wagons and smoke stencil to the front of the box, placing the lower registration marks on the upper edge of the rails. Mark the top registration marks and the top strut of the lower registration marks with a soft pencil. Using the flat paintbrush, spread a thin coat of red paint on to the tile. Dab at the paint with a stencil brush and stencil the engine. Leave to dry.

5 Using the flat paintbrush, spread a thin coat of aquamarine and pink paint on to the tile. Stencil the wagons with the aquamarine and pink paint. Spread grey and white paint on to the tile. Dab at one paint then the other and stencil the steam to create a mottled effect. Leave to dry completely then remove the stencil.

6 Tape the wheels and details stencil in place, matching the registration marks. Stencil the chimneys using yellow paint. Stencil the wheels and couplings with blue paint. Stencil the coal with black paint. Hold the stencil brush upright when stencilling and move the brush in a circular motion. Leave to dry. Remove the stencil.

7 Move the wagon stencil along the box, matching the right-hand registration marks of the previous wagon with the left-hand registration marks of the next. Stencil the wheels and couplings with blue paint. Leave to dry. Replace the stencil with a wagon stencil, matching the registration marks. Stencil the wagon with purple paint.

8 Leave to dry then erase the registration marks. Tape the clouds stencil centrally to the lid of the box. Use the flat paintbrush to spread a thin coat of white paint on to the tile. Stencil the clouds with the white paint. Leave to dry. To make the toy box hardwearing paint it with two or three coats of clear matt (flat) varnish.

GEOMETRIC FLOOR TILES

This repeating pattern is derived from an ancient Greek mosaic floor. Cork floor tiles take colour well – only use a small amount of paint and build it up in layers if necessary. Make two stencils, one for each colour, so that the colours do not get mixed.

You will need

- graph paper
- ruler
- pencil
- pair of compasses
- stencil card (stock)
- craft knife and self-healing cutting mat
- masking tape
- 30cm/12in cork tiles
- spray adhesive
- stencil paint in terracotta and blue
- stencil brushes
- acrylic sealer

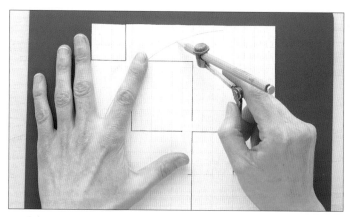

1 Enlarge the quarter section template at the back of the book so that it will fit within a 15cm/6in square. Using graph paper will make the design more accurate. Rule the three squares and draw the curves with a pair of compasses. Rub over all the pencil lines on the back with a pencil.

2 Using a craft knife and self-healing cutting mat, cut two 30cm/12in squares from stencil card (stock). Draw four lines, from corner to corner and edge to edge, to divide each card into eight equal segments. For the first stencil, tape the paper face up to one corner of the first card and draw around the corner and centre square to transfer the design. Repeat on each corner, turning the paper 90 degrees each time. Cut out the five squares. For the second stencil, draw along the curves and around the remaining square. Cut out these eight shapes.

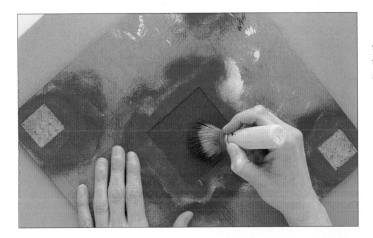

3 Wipe the tile to remove any cork dust. Coat the back of the first stencil with spray adhesive. Stencil the squares using terracotta stencil paint and a stencil brush.

4 Leave to dry, then use the second stencil and blue stencil paint to complete the design. Stencil the remaining tiles in the same way. If you wish, stencil half the tiles in different colours (see below).

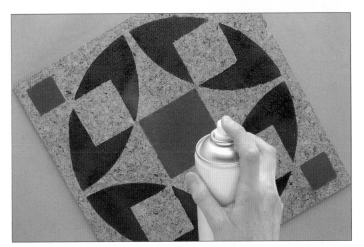

5 When all the tiles have been stencilled, spray them with acrylic sealer to make them waterproof. Fix them to the floor following the manufacturer's instructions.

ABOVE: *Stencil half the tiles in different colours to make a chequerboard-patterned design on the floor.*

ABOVE: *A gentle shading of blue has been added to the terracotta shapes and terracotta been added to the blue shapes to give a softer outline to the strong geometric design.*

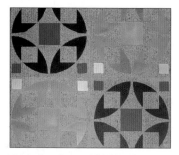

ABOVE: *Experiment with other colours to suit your decor. Different colour combinations create quite different effects. When using more than two colours, you will need to cut more stencils. Alternatively, mask out the area that is to be stencilled in a different colour.*

TROMPE L'OEIL PLATES

A shelf full of trompe l'oeil stencilled plates adds a witty touch to a kitchen wall. Follow this plate design or translate your own patterned china into stencils to give a coordinated look. You could add some individual plates to the wall as well.

You will need

- stencil card (stock)
- pencil
- ruler
- craft knife and self-healing cutting mat
- 23cm/9in diameter plates
- pair of compasses
- spray adhesive
- newspaper or brown paper
- masking tape
- spray paint in white, cream, a range of pinks and mauves, light green, dark green, red, blue and grey

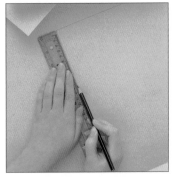

1 Cut three pieces of stencil card (stock) 30cm/12in square. Mark the centre by measuring the centre of each edge and ruling a horizontal and a vertical line across each card to join the marks.

2 Draw a line 3.5cm/1¼in in from all four edges of each card. Place the plate in the centre and draw around the edge. Cut out the plate shape from the first piece of stencil card. This will be stencil 1.

3 Using a pair of compasses, draw a circle about 4cm/1½in from the edge of the plate on the two remaining pieces of card.

4 Trace or photocopy the plate template at the back of the book to the desired size and transfer to the second stencil card.

5 Cut out the design with a craft knife on a self-healing cutting mat. Cut out the smaller areas first and the larger ones last. This will be stencil 2. On the third piece of stencil card, cut out the inner circle. This will be stencil 3.

6 Draw a faint horizontal pencil line on the wall above a shelf. Add two marks 30cm/12in apart on the line to act as a guide for positioning the stencils. Spray the back of the plate stencil (1) with adhesive and place in position on the wall. Press down firmly to ensure a good contact. Mask off the surrounding area with paper and masking tape, leaving no gaps. Spray white and cream spray paint on to the stencil. Remove the masks and stencil.

7 Attach the flower stencil (2) to the wall with spray adhesive, lining it up with the marks on the wall. Mask off the surrounding area. Stick small pieces of masking tape over the leaves on the stencil. Spray the flowers with pinks and mauves, applying a fine layer of paint in short sharp puffs. Try each paint colour on the mask surrounding the stencil first to test the colour and to make sure that the nozzle is clear.

8 Remove the masking tape from the leaves. Fold a small piece of card in half and use it to shield the rest of the stencil from paint. Spray the leaves using light and dark green paints. Take care to avoid spraying paint over the flowers.

9 Cut a small hole in a piece of card and use to spray the centres of the flowers green. Use light green or dark green paint, or vary the two colours.

10 Hold the card shield around the dot designs on the border, and spray each one with red paint. Spray blue paint over the wavy lines on the border. Again, do not apply too much paint. Remove the masks and carefully remove the stencil.

11 Spray the back of the last stencil (3) with adhesive and position it on the wall. Mask off the surrounding area as before. Spray an extremely fine mist of grey paint over the top left-hand side and bottom right-hand side of the plate design to create a shadow. Aim the nozzle slightly away from the stencil to ensure that hardly any paint hits the wall. Remove the masks and stencil.

12 Reposition stencil 1 on the wall and spray a very fine mist of blue paint around the edge of the plate. Repeat for the other plates, spacing them evenly along the shelf.

FRENCH COUNTRY KITCHEN

This curtain (drape) design is adapted from the pattern on a French Art Deco soup bowl found in a fleamarket in Brussels. The flower design is echoed in the hand-stencilled tiles and teams perfectly with the simple chequerboard border for a country look.

MEASURING UP

To calculate the amount of muslin (cheesecloth), allow 1.5 times the width of the window plus 2.5cm/1in for each side hem, and add 7.5cm/3in to the length for hems.

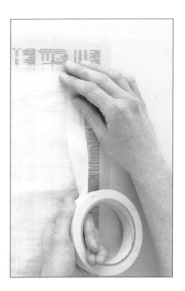

1 Press the muslin (cheesecloth) to remove any creases, then fold it lengthways in accordion-style folds. Press lightly to mark creases, then fold it widthways in accordion-style folds and press again. These squares will act as a guide for positioning the motifs. Cover the work surface with newspaper and tape down the muslin so that it is taut.

2 Trace the three floral templates and the border template at the back of the book and cut out the stencils from stencil card (stock) as described in Stencilling Techniques. Spray the back of one stencil with adhesive and, starting at the top right, lightly stencil the first motif.

3 Alternating the three floral stencils as you work, lightly stencil flowers in every other square over the whole curtain (drape), leaving 15cm/6in free at the lower edge for the border.

4 Stencil the blue chequerboard border along the bottom, lining up the stencil each time by matching the last two squares of the previous motif with the first two of the next stencil. Press the fabric well using a pressing cloth and iron.

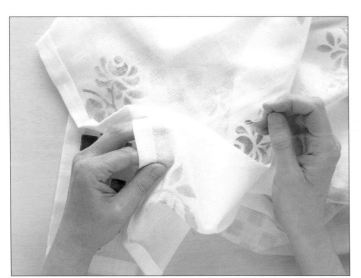

5 Press under and slip-stitch a 1.25cm/$^{1}/_{2}$in double hem around the sides and lower edge of the curtain. Make a 2.5cm/1in double hem along the top edge.

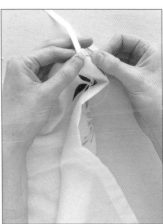

6 Measure the top edge of the curtain and, using dressmaker's chalk, mark it into sections about 20cm/8in apart. Cut a 25cm/10in piece of white cotton tape for each mark. Fold the first piece of tape in half and stitch to the back of the first mark. Sew a button on to the front of the curtain to anchor the tape. Repeat all the way along the edge and then tie the finished curtain on to the curtain pole in bows.

7 For the tiles, cut a piece of stencil card to fit the tile. Cut out the three floral stencils as before, using a craft knife and a self-healing cutting mat.

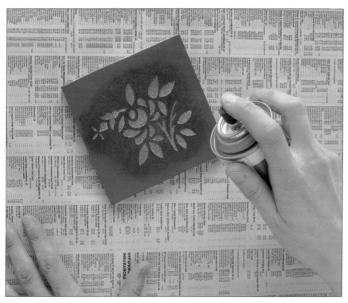

8 Wash the tiles in warm soapy water. Cover the work surface with newspaper. Using red spray paint, spray over the first floral stencil lightly and evenly. Leave to dry, then remove the stencil. Repeat with the other tiles, using all three stencils.

FIFTIES ROSE CUSHIONS

Reminiscent of the stylized designs of the 1950s, these rose print cushions would look at home in a classic or contemporary setting. Use your imagination to create more variations on the theme and alter the number of roses on each cushion.

You will need

- two 45cm/18in squares of cream furnishing fabric
- iron
- newspaper
- two A4 sheets of acetate
- sheet of glass
- heat knife or craft knife
- spray paint
- fabric paints in coral, aubergine and dark green
- stencil brushes
- two 30 x 45cm/12 x 18in rectangles of dark green fabric
- sewing machine
- matching sewing thread
- dressmaker's pins
- sewing needle
- 2 x 40cm/16in square cushion pads

1 Wash the fabric to remove any dressing and press to remove any creases before cutting out the panels. Place the first panel on a pad of newspaper to absorb paint, then check the position of the stencil (traced from the back of the book) by placing it over the square.

2 Cut out the stalk and four flower head stencils from acetate using a heat knife or an ordinary craft knife. Spray the reverse of the large rose background stencil with spray mount, then position it towards the top left corner. Block it in with coral paint, using a dry stencil brush.

3 Leave the paint to dry completely, then line up the large petal stencil over the background. Fill it in with a small amount of aubergine paint to complete the rose.

4 Spray the back of the stalk stencil and place it diagonally across the fabric. Fill it in with dark green fabric paint, again loading the brush with the minimum amount to prevent seepage.

5 The design on the second cushion cover consists of one large and two small roses. Stencil in the rose backgrounds first using coral paint, positioning them so that they point towards the centre of the cushion.

6 Using aubergine paint, add the second layer (the petal stencil) to each of the roses. Line the stencils up by eye so that they fit within the area already painted, and secure in place with spray mount.

7 Stencil in the stalks, allowing the lower part of each one to overlap the edge of the fabric. Leave to dry, then iron both covers on the back to fix (set) the paint, following the instructions supplied by the manufacturer.

8 To make up each cushion cover, stitch a narrow seam along one long edge of the two back panels. With right sides facing and the three raw edges lined up, place one at each side of the front panel so that the seams overlap. Pin and tack (baste) in place, then machine stitch 1cm/$\frac{1}{2}$in from the outside edge. Clip the surplus fabric from the corners and ease the corners into shape with the point of a pencil. Turn through and press using a cloth to protect the stencilled side of the cover, then insert the square cushion pad through the opening.

RIGHT: Vary the number of roses on each of the cushions to make them different.

ORGANZA CUSHION

If you always thought stencilling had a simple country look, then think again. This brilliant organza cushion with gold stencilling takes the craft into the luxury class. Use the sharpest dressmaker's pins when handling organza to avoid marking the fabric.

1 Copy the border template at the back of the book on to dressmaker's graph paper and cut it out with scissors. In addition, cut out a 53cm/21in square and a 53 × 40cm/21 × 16in rectangle from graph paper.

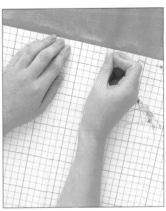

2 Pin the square and rectangle to the main colour of organza. Cut two 53cm/21in squares, and two rectangles measuring 53 × 40cm/21 × 16in. Cut four border pieces from the contrasting colour of organza.

3 Cut a piece of stencil card (stock) 18 × 53cm/7 × 21in. Trace the template and transfer to the card, 8cm/3in from the bottom edge and with 6cm/2½in to spare at each end. Cut out the stencil.

4 Spray the back of the stencil with adhesive and position it along the edge of one organza square. Cut two 45 degree mitres from stencil card, spray with adhesive and press in place. Mask off the surrounding areas with scrap paper.

5 Spray with gold paint. Leave to
dry and spray again. Remove
the masking paper and stencil. Place
the stencil along the next edge, put the
mitres in place and continue as before.
Stencil the remaining two sides. Hem
one long edge of each fabric rectangle
by folding over 1cm/³⁄₈in, then 1.5cm/
⁵⁄₈in. Pin, tack (baste) and machine stitch
the hem, then press.

6 Lay the stencilled fabric square face down and the second square on top. Lay the
two rectangles on top, overlapping the stitched edges so that the raw edges line
up with the squares. Pin, tack and machine stitch 1cm/³⁄₈in from the raw edge. Trim
the seam allowance to 7mm/¹⁄₄in. Pin, tack and stitch the border pieces together at the
mitred corners 1.3cm/¹⁄₂in from the raw edges. Trim the corners and turn the right way
out. Press. Continue until the border pieces make a ring.

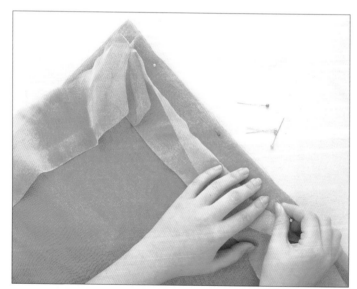

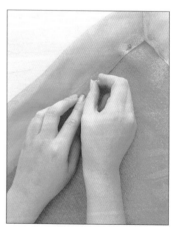

7 Press one of the raw edges under by 1.3cm/¹⁄₂in. Lay the pressed edge of
the border fabric along the edge of the main fabric square and pin, tack and
machine stitch in place.

8 Turn the cushion over and pull
the border over. Turn under the
border's raw edge by 1.3cm/¹⁄₂in and pin
in place along the front of the cushion.
Tack and machine stitch in place. Press.
Insert the cushion pad.

TABLECLOTH AND NAPKINS

Inspiration for stencil designs can be all around you, waiting to be discovered. Cutlery and kitchen utensils are wonderful graphic shapes, ideal for stencilling. Arrange them as borders around the edge of a tablecloth and matching napkins or place the knives and forks formally on each side of imaginary place settings.

You will need

- acetate
- craft knife and self-healing cutting mat
- plain-coloured cotton napkins and tablecloth
- fabric paints in various colours
- stencil brush
- fine artist's paintbrush
- medium artist's paintbrush (optional)
- iron

1 Trace the cutlery, heart and utensils templates at the back of the book and cut the stencils from acetate. Lay one of the napkins on a flat surface. Plan your design and start to stencil the cutlery around the edge.

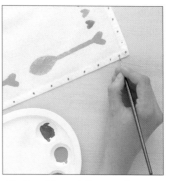

2 Stencil hearts in between the cutlery stencils. Using a fine artist's paintbrush, paint small dots around the hem of the napkins. Use different colours of fabric paint.

3 Using the stencil brush again, stencil hearts on the handles of some of the cutlery.

4 Stencil each napkin with a different pattern, varying the arrangement of the stencils and the colours.

5 Lay the tablecloth on a flat surface and begin to stencil a border of cutlery and hearts.

6 Stencil the larger utensil shapes in the middle of the tablecloth. Stencil the handles first. Stencil the top of the utensils, for example the whisk, in a contrasting colour.

7 Stencil the draining spoons and then add the draining holes in a different colour. Use a medium artist's paintbrush if you prefer to paint the holes.

8 Fill in the blank areas around the utensils with more cutlery stencils. Leave the fabric paint to dry and then iron the reverse of the fabric to fix the paint. Fabric paints are washable so you will have no trouble laundering the tablecloth and napkins.

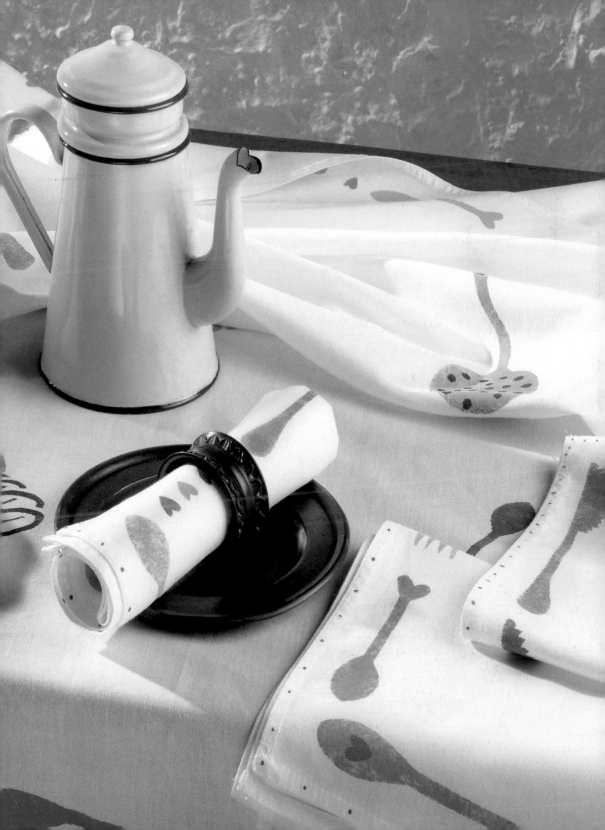

DRAGONFLY CURTAIN

Beautiful, fragile dragonflies hover on this delicate muslin (cheesecloth) curtain. The wing tips of the dragonflies are shaded in a contrasting colour and the insects are stencilled singly and in groups of three.

You will need

- tracing paper and pen
- masking tape
- acetate
- craft knife and self-healing cutting mat
- sheer curtain
- iron
- plastic carrier bag
- ceramic tile
- flat paintbrush
- stencil brush
- fabric paints in lilac and aquamarine

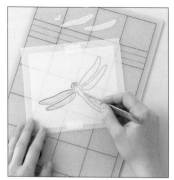

1 Trace the template at the back of the book. Attach a piece of acetate to the tracing with masking tape. Cut out the stencil using a craft knife and self-healing cutting mat, cutting carefully around the acute curved edges.

2 Iron the curtain to remove creases. Lay a section of the curtain out flat on a plastic carrier bag, to protect the work surface. Tape the stencil smoothly to the fabric with masking tape. Stencil the dragonfly with lilac fabric paint. Leave to dry.

3 Stencil the tips of the dragonfly wings with aquamarine paint. Leave to dry then remove the stencil.

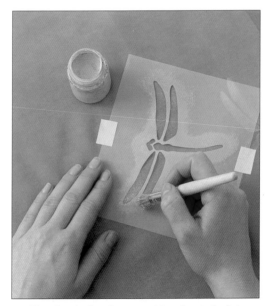

4 Move the stencil to the next position, close to the first dragonfly but not touching it. Tape it in place and stencil as before.

5 When the paint is dry, move the stencil again so that the dragonflies are positioned to "hover" in a group of three. Stencil the third dragonfly.

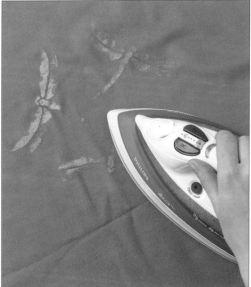

6 Move the stencil and place it at random on the curtain. Stencil a single dragonfly. Continue stencilling dragonflies all over the curtain in groups of three and singly.

7 Leave the paint to dry overnight then iron the curtain on the wrong side to fix (set) the paint, following the manufacturer's instructions.

RAINFOREST CURTAINS

Both the positive and negative parts of this stencil are used to create a sophisticated pattern from a single, almost abstract motif. Light streaming through the unlined cotton enhances the hothouse look of this design.

1 Cut the cotton fabric to required size for the curtains, allowing 5cm/2in seam allowances at the sides and lower edge and 2cm/³/₄in at the top. Press under, pin and machine-stitch 2.5cm/1in double hems down each side, then repeat the process for the hem at the bottom of the curtain.

2 Calculate the number of tabs you will need, spacing them about 20cm/8in apart. Cut a rectangle of fabric for each tab, using the template at the back of the book. Fold each rectangle in half lengthways and stitch, with a 1cm/¹/₂in seam allowance. Open out the seam allowance and pin and stitch across one end of the tab so that the seam lies at the centre.

3 Turn each tab to the right side and press. Pin the raw ends of the material to the right side of each curtain, spacing the tabs evenly along the top. For the facing, cut a 7.5cm/3in strip of fabric the width of the curtain plus 4cm/1¹/₂in for seam allowances. Pin the strip to the curtain with right sides together and then machine-stitch the top edge.

4 Fold the facing to the wrong side, fold in the seam allowances at each end and along the raw edge and then pin in place.

5 Machine-stitch the facing close to the folded edge.

6 Fold the tabs over on to the front side of the curtain and then hand-stitch one of the buttons to hold each tab in place.

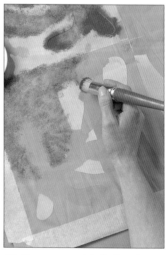

7 Enlarge the stencil template at the back of the book on a photocopier to your desired size. Cut a square of acetate sheet the size of the design and fasten it to the design with tabs of masking tape. Cut out using a craft knife and cutting mat. Retain the cut-out part of the stencil for the negative images.

8 Using tailor's chalk, mark the curtains into squares the same size as the stencil. Protect the work surface. Using spray mount, attach the stencil in place in the first marked square. Apply fabric paint with the stencil brush to create a mottled effect. Leave the stencil in place. To make the negative image, mask off the areas around the square with tape.

9 Use spray mount to fix the cut-out motif in the centre, then apply green fabric paint all around it. Remove the stencil and move it to the next marked square. Repeat this pattern all over the curtain. Leave to dry completely then iron the curtain on the wrong side to fix (set) the paint following the manufacturer's instructions.

SEASHELL BEACH BAG

Crisp cream and navy give this smart beach bag a nautical look. Much of the charm of the stencilling lies in combining colours to give a three-dimensional look to the seashell shapes, so it's worth practising on spare fabric or lining paper first.

You will need

- iron
- 55 x 75cm/21½ x 30in cream cotton drill fabric
- scissors
- tracing paper and pen
- stencil card
- craft knife and self-healing cutting mat
- spray mount
- 2 lengths of blue cotton drill fabric or denim, each 15 x 38cm/6 x 15in
- fabric paints in dark yellow, dark red and navy blue
- stencil brushes
- sewing machine
- white, dark orange and blue sewing threads
- dressmaking pins
- 2m/6ft cream cotton cord
- masking tape

1 Wash and iron the cream fabric then cut in two lengthways. Trace the stencil from the back of the book or enlarge it on a photocopier. Transfer the outline to stencil card and cut out using a craft knife and cutting mat. Coat the back lightly with spray mount, and stencil five shells on each piece of fabric, using two or three colours. Leave to dry then iron on the reverse side to fix (set) the paint according to the manufacturer's instructions.

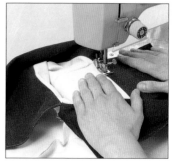

2 With the fabric right sides together, stitch a blue strip to the top edge of each cream piece, leaving a 1cm/½in seam allowance. Press the seam upward. Pin the rectangles right sides together, and stitch around the main bag. Press under the seam allowances on the open sides of the blue fabric, and topstitch in orange sewing thread. Fold in half lengthways. Machine-stitch parallel to the topstitch.

3 Cut the cord in half, and bind the ends with masking tape. Thread both pieces through the bag. Remove the tape, and bind the ends with blue thread, 5cm/2in from the ends. Fringe and comb the cord to make tassels. Trim neatly.

OPPOSITE: The choice of navy blue and red gives this beach bag a nautical look.

ELIZABETHAN LAMPSHADE

Here, an Elizabethan border design is applied to a lampshade using a combination of sponge and stencil techniques. The pattern would also look sumptuous using deep blue or red with gold. For a larger lampshade, enlarge the template on a photocopier.

You will need

- tracing paper and pen
- acetate sheet
- craft knife and self-healing cutting mat
- white paper
- stencil brush
- fabric paints in black, gold and white
- cotton lampshade
- small piece of sponge, preferably natural
- masking tape
- hairdryer (optional)

1 Trace the template at the back of the book on to the acetate sheet. Cut out using a craft knife and cutting mat or a heat knife.

2 Lay the design on a sheet of white paper and, using a stencil brush, apply undiluted black paint to the paper around the acetate. Keep the brush upright and dab, rather than brush, the paint on.

3 Apply the base colours of gold and white to the lampshade using a sponge. Take up only a small amount of paint each time, so that the texture of the sponge is transferred to the shade. Leave to dry.

4 Using strips of low-tack masking tape, attach the stencil to the lampshade. Use small curls of tape on the underside of the stencil to attach parts that do not lay flat.

5 Using the stencil brush, apply small amounts of black paint to the lampshade, gradually building up the density of colour. Remove the stencil and allow the paint to dry. To speed up the drying process, you can use a hairdryer.

6 Tape the stencil to the next position and apply paint as before until the whole lampshade has been patterned. Leave to dry.

7 Retape the stencil to the lampshade, taking care to position the stencil over the previous work. Use a small piece of sponge to apply gold highlights.

LEAFY PICTURE FRAMES

The stylish raised leaf patterns around these frames are simple to create using ordinary white interior filler instead of paint to fill in the stencilled leaf shapes. The simple shapes can be cut out with scissors.

You will need

- 2 wooden frames
- dark green acrylic paint
- medium decorator's paintbrush
- fine-grade abrasive paper
- stencil card
- scissors
- ready-mixed interior filler
- stencil brush

1 Paint the frames dark green. When dry, gently rub them down with abrasive paper to create a subtle distressed effect.

2 Enlarge the templates at the back of the book to fit the frames. Transfer the designs to stencil card and cut them out using scissors.

3 Position a stencil on the first frame and stipple ready-mixed filler through the stencil. Reposition the stencil and continue all around the frame. Leave to dry.

4 Repeat with a different combination of motifs on the second frame. When the filler is completely hard, gently smooth over the leaves with abrasive paper. ▶

OPPOSITE: You can also use textured gel combined with acrylic paint and stippled on to the frame to achieve a similar effect.

CITRUS FRUIT TRAY

This bamboo tray has been given a tropical look with juicy orange and lime stencils, perfect for summer drinks on a sunny day. You could also transform an old tray by painting over the existing surface.

You will need

- fine-grade abrasive paper
- tray
- tracing paper and pen or carbon paper and sharp pencil
- masking tape
- stencil card
- craft knife and self-healing cutting mat
- acrylic paints in pale orange, dark orange, pale green, dark green, dark brown and white
- stencil brush
- gloss or matt (flat) varnish and brush

1 Sand the tray lightly to remove any existing varnish. Trace the templates at the back of the book and tape on to stencil card. Using a craft knife and cutting mat cut them out, leaving a narrow margin round each motif.

2 Stipple a couple of pale orange circles using a small to medium-size stencil brush, as the background for the orange slices, protecting the surface of the rest of the tray with masking tape.

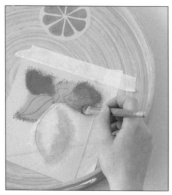

3 Fix the circle stencil back in place over the oranges and slot the segment stencil within it. Using dark orange, fill in the segments, adding some light and dark stippling to create texture within the shapes.

4 Stipple the lime and leaves in two shades of green. Give the fruit a more three-dimensional look by stippling light green in the centre and dark green around the outside edge. Stipple the stalk in dark brown.

5 Stencil the "rind" of the lime segments in dark green and the main part in light green. Add light white stippling across the "pips". Leave to dry completely then apply three coats of gloss or matt (flat) varnish.

TRAY OF AUTUMN LEAVES

The rich colours of autumn leaves are captured here on a simple wooden tray. Keep to warm natural paint colours to suit the country style and simple lines of the tray. Use the templates provided or draw around your own pressed leaves.

You will need

- wooden tray
- fine-grade abrasive paper
- water-based primer (if bare wood)
- emulsion (latex) paint in blue-grey and ochre
- small decorator's paintbrush
- household candle
- clean cotton clothes
- craft knife and self-healing cutting mat
- stencil card (stock)
- spray adhesive
- stencil brush
- stencil paint in rust and terracotta
- saucer
- matt (flat) acrylic varnish and brush

1 Sand down the tray with fine-grade abrasive paper to ensure a smooth surface. If the wood is bare, paint with a water-based primer. Apply two coats of blue-grey emulsion (latex), leaving it to dry between coats.

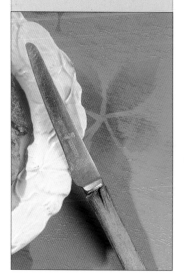

2 Rub the candle over the edges of the tray and over the base until there is a build-up of wax. Think about which areas of the tray would become worn naturally and apply wax there.

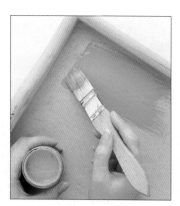

3 Wipe away any loose bits of wax with a clean cloth. Paint the whole tray with ochre emulsion. Leave to dry completely.

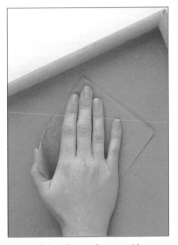

4 Lightly rub over the tray with abrasive paper to reveal some of the blue-grey paint underneath.

5 Trace the templates at the back of the book or draw around pressed leaves. Using a craft knife and self-healing cutting mat, cut out the stencils from stencil card (stock) as described in Stencilling Techniques.

ABOVE: Building up layers of paint and rubbing back the top layer in places gives the tray a pleasing distressed look.

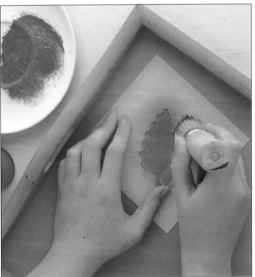

6 Lightly spray the back of the stencils with adhesive. Arrange the stencils on the tray and smooth down. Dip the stencil brush into the rust stencil paint and rub it on a saucer or cloth so that the brush is dry. Using circular movements, apply the colour evenly over the stencils, working more on one side of each motif. Apply terracotta stencil paint to the other side of the leaves to give shadow. Continue stencilling all over the tray. To give the tray a tough finish, apply two or three coats of varnish, leaving each to dry before applying the next.

GILDED CANDLES

Plain church candles look extra special when adorned with simple gold stars and stripes. Always associated with Christmas, candles are popular all year round for their soft romantic lighting. Cutting the stencils may be fiddly but it is then a quick job to spray on the gold paint.

1 Wrap a piece of acetate around the candle. Mark with a felt-tipped pen and cut it to fit exactly. Do not overlap the edges. Cut it a few millimetres shorter than the candle.

2 Trace the star templates at the back of the book. Lay the piece of acetate over the stars, choosing a pattern of stars to suit the candle. Trace over them with the felt-tipped pen.

3 Cut out the stars using a craft knife and self-healing cutting mat. Be careful not to tear the acetate.

4 Spray one side of the stencil with adhesive and wrap it around the candle, centring it so that there is a small gap at either end. Secure the acetate join with masking tape. Mask the top of the candle with tape, ensuring there are no gaps.

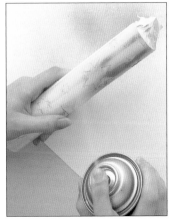

5 Spray a fine mist of metallic spray paint over the candle, holding the can about 30cm/12in from the surface. If too much paint is applied, it will drip underneath the stencil. Keep checking that the stencil is well stuck down to avoid any fuzzy lines around the stars. Leave the paint to dry for a couple of minutes, then carefully remove the masking tape and acetate.

6 For a stars and stripes candle, cut strips of acetate and trace a row of small stars along each strip. Cut out with a craft knife as before. Spray one side of the acetate strips with adhesive. Stick the strips on to the candle, measuring the gaps in between to ensure equal spacing. Secure them with small pieces of masking tape at the join.

7 Mask off the top of the candle with masking tape, ensuring there are no gaps. Spray the candle with a fine mist of metallic spray paint as in step 5. Carefully remove the masking tape and stencil when dry.

ABOVE: A basketful of gilded candles makes a pretty gift. Use a different star design on each candle.

8 For a reverse stencil design, cut out individual star shapes from acetate. Apply spray adhesive to one side, stick on to the candle and mask off the top of the candle as before. Spray with metallic spray paint and carefully remove the acetate stars when the paint is dry.

FROSTED VASES

Give coloured or clear glass vases the designer touch using glass etching cream and reverse stencilling. The shapes are cut from sticky-back plastic and removed after stencilling to reveal the clear outlines. Choose flowers and leaves, stripes or spots – the choice is yours. The same technique could be used to transform windows.

You will need

- glass vases
- sticky-back plastic
- scissors
- rubber gloves
- glass etching cream
- soft paintbrush

1 Wash the vase with hot soapy water to remove any grease. Leave the vase to dry. Trace the flower and leaf templates at the back of the book and transfer them on to the back of a piece of sticky-back plastic. Cut out the shapes with scissors.

2 Decide where you want to position the shapes on the vase. Remove the backing paper and stick the flower and leaf shapes in place, smoothing them down.

3 Wearing rubber gloves, paint the etching cream evenly over the outside of the vase with a soft paintbrush. Leave to dry in a warm, dust-free area for about 30 minutes.

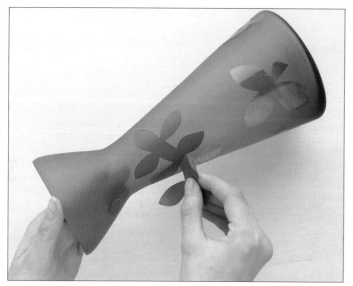

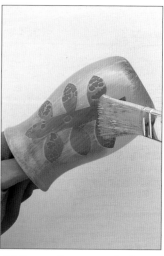

5 For a smaller vase, try using just one motif. Paint on the etching cream in the same way as for the large vase and leave it for 30 minutes.

4 Still wearing the rubber gloves, wash the etching cream off the vase with warm water. Leave to dry. If there are blotchy areas where the etching cream hasn't worked, simply paint the vase again and leave for another 30 minutes before washing it off. When you are happy with the results, peel off the sticky shapes. Wash the vase again to remove any sticky smears left by the plastic.

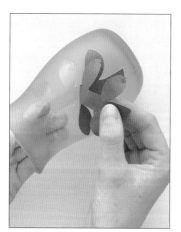

6 Wash off the etching cream and peel off the plastic motif to reveal the design, then wash the vase again. If there are any blotchy areas, paint the vase again with etching cream as in step 4.

7 For a striped frosted vase, cut out straight or wiggly strips of sticky-back plastic and stick them on to the vase. Paint on the etching cream as before and leave to dry for 30 minutes.

8 Wash off the etching cream, then peel off the plastic strips and wash the vase again to remove any sticky smears left by the plastic.

ART NOUVEAU HATBOX

An elegantly stencilled hatbox and matching shoe bag would be perfect for storing a bride's hat and shoes. Make a set for yourself or to give to someone special. And you needn't stop there: stencil a whole stack of matching hatboxes to use for stylish storage in a bedroom.

You will need

- round hatbox
- undercoat in white
- small decorator's paintbrush
- water-based woodwash in pale green
- masking tape
- tape measure
- pencil
- stencil card (stock)
- craft knife and self-healing cutting mat
- ruler
- spray adhesive
- stencil brushes
- stencil paint in dark green, royal blue and pale green

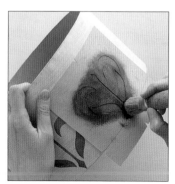

1 Paint the hatbox with two coats of white undercoat. Dilute 1 part pale green woodwash with 1 part water and apply two or three light washes to the hatbox, allowing them to dry between coats. Attach the lid with strips of masking tape. Measure the circumference of the box and divide by six or eight. Lightly mark the measurements on the lid and side of the box with a pencil.

2 Trace the templates at the back of the book. Cut the stencils from stencil card (stock) as described in Stencilling Techniques. Rule a pencil line across the bottom of the stencil to help align it on the box. Spray lightly with adhesive and position on the box. Using a stencil brush and dark green stencil paint, stencil the leaves and stem. Remove the stencil when dry, respray with adhesive and reposition. Continue to work around the box.

3 Reposition the stencil on the leaves. Add a shadow to the points where the leaves join the stem, using royal blue paint. Use a clean stencil brush to keep the colours clean. Repeat all around the box.

4 Using the heart stencil, add a pale green heart between each pair of leaves around the bottom of the box.

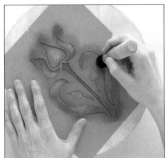

5 Stencil flowerheads around the rim of the lid in dark green following the pencil marks. Add a royal blue shadow as before. Stencil a whole flower motif in dark green in the centre of the lid.

6 Add decorative pale green heart motifs around the main motif, using a very small amount of paint for a delicate touch.

SNOWFLAKE GIFT WRAP

Create your own Christmas gift wrap and your friends and family will appreciate their presents even more than usual. This is one project where the finished effect is more important than accuracy and neatness, so it is quicker than you might think.

1 Trace the three templates at the back of the book and tape on to stencil card. Using a craft knife and cutting mat, cut each one out in a single piece. The cut-out shapes will be used to make a reverse stencil.

2 Load the stencil brush with white paint. Using the first stencil, block in a scattering of positive snowflakes across the sheet of wrapping paper. Leave enough space between them to fit in the other motifs, about six or seven shapes.

3 Fill in some of the spaces between them with positive stencils of the other two snowflake stencils, overlapping them if you wish.

4 To make reverse stencils of the three snowflakes, use a blocking action to work over the outlines and on to the surrounding background.

STAMPING
PROJECTS

Although stamping is often regarded as a type of stencilling, it is basically a very easy form of printing and produces a very different finished effect. You can make your own stamps from household sponges, or buy commercial stamps in a variety of shapes and sizes. It is a quick and effective technique – all you need is a stamp, a prepared surface and your imagination. As long as the surface is firm enough to take the pressure of the stamp, you can add details to almost anything, from walls to wrapping paper. The best results are achieved by holding the stamp steady and not letting it slide. This will take a little practice, so use a plain sheet of paper first.

ABOVE: Start with a simple, inexpensive project such as stamped wrapping paper and matching gift tags.

LEFT: Here a rose frieze is repeated with single rose motifs on the wall and a single motif on the chair.

SANTA FE LIVING ROOM

ztec motifs such as this bird are bold, stylized and one-dimensional, and translate perfectly into stamps. Strong colour contrasts suit this style, but here the pattern is confined to widely spaced stripes over a cool white wall, and further restrained with a final light wash of white paint.

1 Dilute the off-white emulsion (latex) paint with 50 per cent water and apply a wash over the walls using a sponge, alternating the angle at which you work. Allow to dry.

2 Using a large, dry brush, apply warm white emulsion to some areas to achieve a rough-looking surface. Allow to dry.

3 Starting 10cm/4in from one corner, and using a plumbline as a guide, draw a straight pencil line from the top to the bottom of the wall.

4 Measure 45cm/18in along the wall, hang the plumbline again and mark a second vertical line. Draw another line 10cm/4in away to create a band. Repeat all around the room.

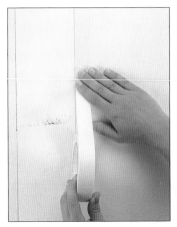

5 Apply masking tape to the walls on each outer edge of the marked bands.

6 Paint the bands in deep red emulsion using a medium decorator's paintbrush. Leave to dry.

8 Use a small roller to load the stamp with navy blue emulsion paint. Stamp the diamonds down the red bands, starting from the top and just touching at the tips.

7 Draw a 10 × 20cm/4 × 8in diamond shape on to medium-density sponge. Cut out the shape using a craft knife.

9 Copy the bird template at the
back of the book on to a piece
of high-density sponge. Cut away the
excess sponge using a craft knife.

10 Use the small roller to
load the bird stamp with off-
white emulsion. Print the birds upright,
roughly in the centre of the diamonds.
Make sure that they all face in the
same direction.

11 When the bird motifs are dry,
use minimal pressure and a large
dry paintbrush to brush gently over each
band with warm white emulsion (latex).
This will soften the bold colours.

SCANDINAVIAN LIVING ROOM

Create a cool atmosphere with this sophisticated Gustavian-influenced wall stamping. This project requires some preparatory work, but the elegance of the result justifies the little extra time. The stamps are cut from high-density foam or foam rubber which can be mounted on blocks of composition (mat) board with a small drawer knob added for easy handling, if required. Before you do any stamping, draw a grid down the wall using a plumb line and a cardboard square. If you find the effect of the two blues too cool, you can add warmth by applying a coat of tinted varnish to the wall, ageing the whole effect.

You will need

- wood glue
- 2 pieces of composition (mat) board, 9cm x 9cm/3¹/₂in x 3¹/₂in
- 2 pieces of high-density foam rubber, such as upholstery foam, 9cm x 9cm/3¹/₂in x 3¹/₂in
- tracing paper
- pencil
- spray adhesive
- craft knife
- ruler
- 2 small wooden drawer knobs
- plumb line
- cardboard 18cm x 18cm/7in x 7in
- plate
- emulsion (latex) paint in dark blue
- square-tipped paintbrush

1 Apply wood glue to the composition (mat) board squares and stick the foam rubber on to them. Leave to dry.

2 Trace and transfer the shapes from the back of the book. Spray with adhesive and place on the foam rubber.

3 Cut around the edges of the designs and remove the paper pattern. Scoop out the background to leave the stamp free of the composition (mat) board.

4 Draw two intersecting lines across the back of the composition (mat) board and glue a wooden drawer knob in the centre to finish the stamp.

5 Attach a plumb line at ceiling height to give a vertical guideline (this can be done with a piece of masking tape) on the wall. Mark a point 8cm/3¼in above the dado (chair) rail and place one corner of the cardboard square on it, lined up along the plumb line. Mark all the corners of the cardboard square on the wall in pencil, then move it up, continuing to mark the corners. Use this system to mark a grid of squares across the whole surface of the upper wall.

6 One of the stamps has a static motif and the other has a swirl. Use the static one first, dipping it into a plate coated with paint and making the first print on a sheet of scrap paper to make sure that the stamp is not overloaded. Then print up the wall, from the 8cm/3¼in mark.

7 Continue printing, working in a diagonal up the wall.

8 Change to the swirl motif, and stamp this pattern in the spaces between the static motifs.

9 Use a pencil and ruler to draw a line 3.5cm/1½in above the level of the dado (chair) rail, all the way along the stamped section of wall.

10 Fill the space between the pencil line and the dado (chair) rail with diluted dark blue emulsion paint, using a square-tipped paintbrush.

RIGHT: The flat blue wall with its stamp motif creates a dynamic background for the elegant mirrors and the delicate wooden furniture.

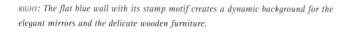

ART NOUVEAU ROSES

This stylized, flowing design is inspired by the rose motif found in the work of Charles Rennie Mackintosh, who used it repeatedly in his interior designs, on chairs, doors, leaded glass and textiles. Used here to link a chair with the wall behind it, it is equally effective as a single motif or as a repeating pattern.

1 Scale up the designs at the back of the book to the size you require and make templates. Cut a square of sponge to fit the rose and a rectangle for the stem. Cut two pieces of card (stock) to fit the sponge shapes and glue them on using PVA (white) glue.

2 Using a felt-tipped pen, transfer the designs to the sponge by drawing around the templates. Mark the top of each design on the card at the back.

3 Cut away the excess sponge from around the motifs using a craft knife. Make the stamp for the small dots by drawing around a small coin and cutting it out.

4 Using a pencil and ruler, and with the large stamp as a size guide, mark the positions of the bottom edges of the roses and stems on the wall, keeping the line parallel with the dado (chair) rail. Repeat for the upper line of roses, then mark the centres of the small dots directly above the lower ones, and on a line equidistant from the two rows of roses.

5 Using a medium artist's paintbrush, load the rose stamp evenly with a quantity of pink acrylic paint.

6 Match the bottom edge of the stamp to the marked wall and apply the stamp.

7 Load the small dot stamp with green acrylic paint. Stamp dots at the marked points on the wall.

8 Load the stem stamp with green paint and stamp at the marked points. Repeat to complete the rows.

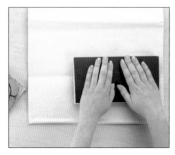

9 Remove the calico cover from the back of the chair and lay it out flat. Using tailor's chalk, mark the positions for the motifs along a line 5cm/2in in from each side. Load the stem stamp with green fabric paint and position the bottom edge on the marked line.

10 Load the rose stamp with pink fabric paint to complete the stamped design. Leave to dry, then rub off the chalk marks and fix the fabric paints according to the manufacturer's instructions.

PLASTER WALL TREATMENT

Add an extra dimension to stamping by creating a relief effect on your walls. For this technique, a mixture of paint and interior filler (spackle) is applied to the stamp and then pressed on to the wall, leaving a raised motif. A monochromatic scheme suits this look best.

1 Mix the off-white emulsion (latex) with 50 per cent wallpaper paste. Apply to the walls with a large paintbrush, working at random angles and keeping the effect quite rough.

2 Apply random patches of lime white emulsion, allowing the off-white base coat to show in areas.

3 Using the card (stock) square as a template and beginning in a corner of the room, make a small mark at each corner of the card. Reposition the card using the previous marks as a guide and repeat to form a grid of evenly spaced marks around the room.

4 Copy the template at the back of the book and transfer it to a piece of high-density sponge. Cut away the excess sponge using a craft knife.

5 Using a medium paintbrush, mix stone white emulsion with interior filler (spackle), using about 1 part filler to 3 parts paint.

6 Apply the mixture thickly to the stamp using a dabbing motion.

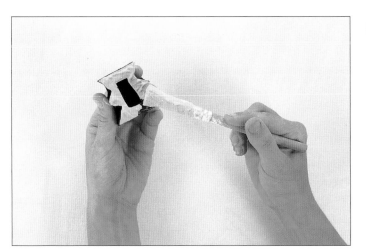

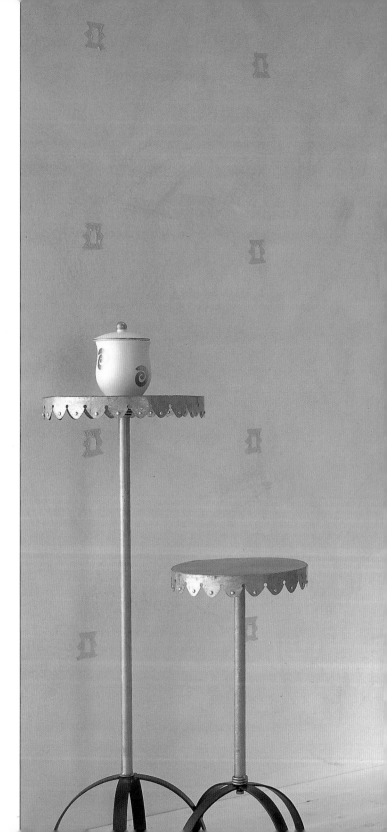

7 Print over each pencil mark, pressing the stamp quite hard and pulling it cleanly away – be careful not to smear the impression. Leave for about 4 hours to dry.

8 Dry brush a little lime white emulsion over each stamp, so that only the areas in highest relief pick up the paint. Do not attempt to make all the motifs the same – the charm of this technique lies in the slight irregularities.

GOTHIC DINING ROOM

Create a dramatic setting for candlelit dinner parties with purple and gold panels that will shimmer from deep velvety green walls. The effect is achieved by stamping the wall or walls with gold size and then rubbing on Dutch gold leaf which will adhere to the stamped motifs.

You will need

- 30cm/12in square of thin card (stock)
- ruler
- pencil
- scissors
- high-density sponge, such as upholstery foam
- felt-tipped pen
- craft knife
- matt emulsion (flat latex) paint in dark green and purple
- natural sponge
- plumbline
- small paint roller
- old plate
- gold size
- Dutch gold leaf
- soft brush

1 To make a template for the wall panels, draw a freehand arc from the centre top of the card (stock) square to the lower corner.

2 Fold the card in half down the centre and cut out both sides to make a symmetrical Gothic arch shape.

3 Copy the design from the back of the book and make a paper pattern with a diameter of 10cm/4in. Transfer the design on to a piece of high-density sponge. Cut away the excess sponge using a craft knife.

4 Apply dark green emulsion (latex) paint liberally to the wall or walls, using a sponge and working in a circular motion. Allow to dry.

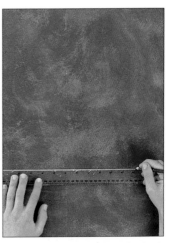

5 Using a plumbline as a guide and beginning 23cm/9in from a corner, mark a vertical line up the wall to a height of 1.8m/6ft.

6 Measure across the wall and use the plumbline to draw vertical lines every 60cm/2ft.

7 Measure out 15cm/6in each side of each vertical and draw two more lines to mark the edges of the panels.

8 Place the point of the card template at the centre top point of each panel and draw in the curves.

9 Use a small paint roller to load the stamp with gold size. Print each panel, beginning with the centre top and working down the central line, then down each side.

10 When the size is tacky, apply Dutch gold leaf by rubbing over the backing paper with a soft brush.

11 Once the panel is complete, use the soft brush to remove any excess gold leaf.

12 Using only the centre of the stamp, fill in the spaces between the gold motifs using purple emulsion paint.

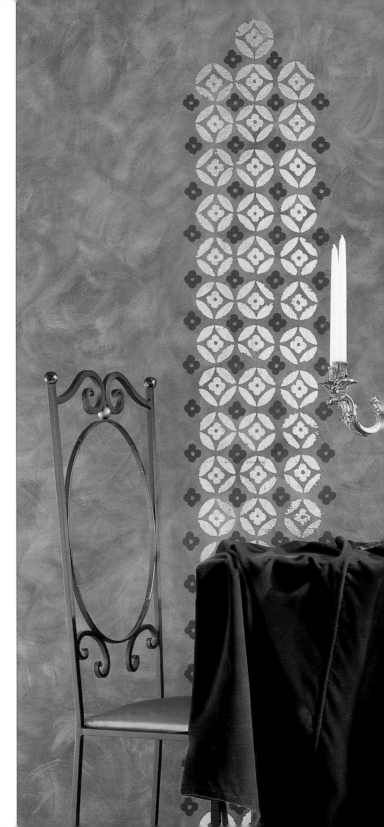

ROSE BREAKFAST ROOM

New homes are wonderfully fresh, but the perfectly even walls can look plain if you are used to details such as dado (chair) rails and deep skirting (base) boards. This project shows you how to retain the freshness of new pastel paintwork and add interest with a frieze at dado-rail height and a coat of colourwash below it. Don't worry about painting in a straight line for the frieze – just use two strips of low-tack masking tape and paint between them. You could even try doing it by hand, as it does add character to the decoration, even if you do wobble a bit! Wooden furniture is given a distressed paint finish in toning colours, and stamped with the rose designs to co-ordinate with the walls.

1 To prepare the furniture, rub each piece down with abrasive paper (sandpaper) and apply a coat of cream paint. Make a blue-green glaze by diluting one part paint with three parts water, then brush it on following the direction of the grain. Before the paint has dried, use a cloth to wipe off some of the paint.

2 Spread the dusky-blue paint on to a plate and run the roller through it. Ink the rosebud stamp and print the design on to scrap paper.

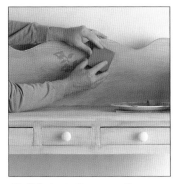

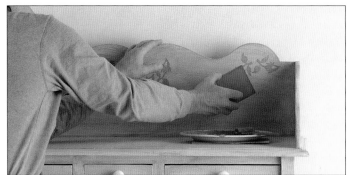

3 Referring to the paper pattern, stamp the design in the centre of your chosen piece of furniture.

4 Stamp more rosebuds on either side of the central design. Work with the shape of the individual piece of furniture to decide upon the best position and the number of prints to use.

5 If you are decorating a desk or dresser, unscrew and remove any handles, then stamp the pattern on the drawer fronts. Screw them back after the paint has dried.

6 For a small piece of furniture like this chair, a simple design is best. Paint the chair with cream emulsion (latex) paint, then print a single small rose in peach.

7 To make the colourwash for the walls, mix one part peach emulsion (latex) paint with one part wallpaper paste and four parts water. Make it up in multiples of six. It is best to make more than you need, so that you can do the whole room from the same batch to ensure a colour match. Unless the room has been painted recently, apply a coat of cream emulsion to the walls.

8 Measure about 90cm/36in from the floor and make a pencil mark on the wall. Tape the spirit level to the plank and draw a straight line all round the room 90cm/36in above floor level. Draw another line 3cm/1¼in above it.

9 Apply the colourwash below the line using sweeping random brushstrokes. If runs occur, just pick them up with the brush and work them into the surrounding wall. Aim for a patchy, mottled effect.

10 If you have a steady hand, paint a dusky-blue stripe on the wall with the square-tipped brush, otherwise use masking tape to guide you and remove it when the paint is dry.

11 Spread the dusky-blue and peach paints on to the plates and use the foam roller or paintbrush to ink the large rose stamp, using the colours as shown. Print with the stamp base resting on the top of the dusky-blue stripe. Continue all round the room, re-inking the stamp each time for a regular print.

RIGHT: Three rose stamps look very pretty used as a wall frieze and on matching painted furniture. This is an ideal way to decorate second-hand furniture.

GRAPEVINE FRIEZE AND GLASSES

This elegant repeating design is a combination of sponging and freehand painting – practise the strokes on paper before embarking on the wall, and keep your hand relaxed to make confident, sweeping lines. It's perfect for a kitchen or conservatory and is repeated on a set of glasses to carry the theme on to the table.

1 Copy the template at the back of the book and use to draw the leaf shape on a piece of medium-density sponge. To make the stamp for the grapes, draw around a small coin, or copy the grape template.

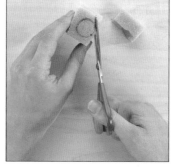

2 Cut out the sponge shapes using a pair of scissors or a craft knife and self-healing cutting mat.

3 Trace the template of the frieze design on to the wall where you want it to appear, carefully marking the positions of the grapes and leaves.

4 Mix together two shades of purple acrylic paint. Using a medium artist's paintbrush, load one side of the grape stamp with dark purple paint and the other with a lighter shade to give a shadowed effect.

5 Build up the bunch of grapes, starting with the top row and working downwards to avoid smudges. Position the grapes in succeeding rows diagonally between the ones above, as shown. Keep the dark side of each grape facing the same way.

6 Mix two shades of blue paint and load the leaf stamp, painting the outside edge in the darker shade. Stamp the leaf shape where marked on either side of each bunch of grapes. Paint the stems freehand in the lighter shade of blue, using a fine brush.

7 Before decorating the glasses with the grape motif, clean each thoroughly to remove any trace of grease. Leave to dry.

8 Mix two shades of purple ceramic paint and load the grape stamp as before, with dark purple on one side and a lighter shade on the other. Align the first row of grapes below the edge of the glass, keeping clear of the rim.

9 Continue to build up the bunch of grapes until it fills one side of the glass. Keep the dark side of each grape facing the same way.

10 Mix two shades of blue ceramic paint and load the leaf stamp as before. Stamp a leaf motif on either side of the bunch of grapes.

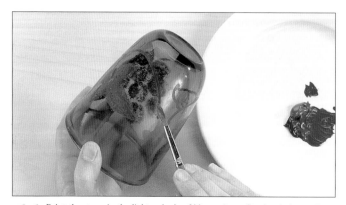

11 Paint the stems in the lighter shade of blue, using a fine brush. Leave the glass for 24 hours to dry completely. The glasses will withstand gentle washing but should not be put in a dishwasher or cleaned with an abrasive scourer.

PROVENÇAL KITCHEN

This kitchen is a dazzling example of contrasting colours – the effect is almost electric. Colours opposite each other in the colour wheel give the most vibrant contrast and you could equally well experiment with a combination of blue and orange or red and green. If, however, these colours are just too vivid for you, then choose a gentler colour scheme with the same stamped pattern. The kitchen walls are colourwashed to give a mottled, patchy background. Put some wallpaper paste in the colourwash to make the job a lot easier – it also prevents too many streaks from running down the walls.

You will need

- emulsion (latex) paint in deep purple and pale yellow
- wallpaper paste (made up according to the manufacturer's instructions)
- paintbrush
- plumb line
- cardboard measuring approximately 30cm x 30cm/12in x 12in
- pencil
- plates for palettes
- foam rollers
- rosebud and small rose stamps
- acrylic paint in red and green
- clear matt varnish and brush

1 To make the colourwash, mix one part deep purple emulsion (latex) with one part wallpaper paste and four parts water. Make it up in multiples of six. It is best to make more than you need. Then colourwash the walls. If runs occur, just pick them up with the brush and work them into the surrounding wall, aiming for a patchy, mottled effect.

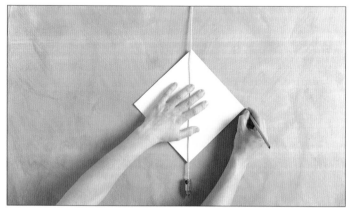

2 Attach the plumb line at ceiling height, just in from the corner. Hold the cardboard square against the wall so that the string cuts through the top and bottom corners. Mark all four points with a pencil. Continue moving the square and marking points to make a grid pattern.

3 Spread some deep purple paint on to the plate and run the roller through it until it is evenly coated. Ink the rosebud stamp and print a rosebud on each pencil mark until you have covered the wall.

4 If you wish to create a dropped-shadow effect, clean the stamp and spread some pale yellow paint on to the plate. Ink the stamp and over-print each rosebud, moving the stamp so that it is slightly off register.

5 Continue over-printing the rosebuds, judging by eye the position of the yellow prints.

BELOW: *Attach a wooden peg rail to the patterned walls to match the Provençal theme.*

6 For the cupboard doors apply a base coat in pale yellow. Spread some green and burnt orange paint on to the plates and run the rollers through them until they are evenly coated. Coat the rose with burnt orange and the leaves with green. (If one colour mixes with the other, just wipe it off and re-coat.) Print a rose in the top left-hand corner. Re-coat the stamp for each print.

7 Print the stamp horizontally and vertically to make a border along the edges of the door panel.

8 When you have printed round the whole border, leave the paint to dry. Apply two coats of varnish to protect the surface of the doors.

RIGHT: The stamping on the walls and the cupboards instantly transforms a plain kitchen into a busy working one, conjuring up images of delicious French dishes.

TUSCAN FRIEZE

Three stamps are used in this project to transform a dull space into a wall frieze that you will want to preserve forever. The finished wall will bring a touch of Tuscany into your home, even when the sky is a gloomy grey outside. The wall is divided at dado height with a strong burgundy red below and a warm cream above to visually lower the ceiling. The vine leaf pattern has been stamped on to a grid of pencil marks that is simple to measure out using a square of card (stock) and a plumbline. The lines are hand-painted using a wooden batten (furring strip) as a hand rest but you could also stick parallel strips of masking tape around the walls and fill in the stripes between.

You will need

- tape measure
- pencil
- ruler
- emulsion (latex) paint in cream, burgundy, terracotta, white and black
- large household paintbrush
- wallpaper paste, mixed according to the manufacturer's instructions
- plate
- foam roller
- grape, tendril and leaf stamps
- thin strip of card (stock)
- long-bristled lining brush
- straight-edged wooden batten (furring strip), 1m/1yd long
- plumbline
- card, 15 x 15cm/6 x 6in
- square-tipped artist's paintbrush
- clear gloss, matt (flat) or satin varnish and brush

1 Measure the height of a dado (chair) rail and draw a line around the wall with a ruler and pencil. Paint the wall above the line cream and the area below burgundy. Mix roughly equal amounts of wallpaper paste, burgundy and terracotta paint on a plate.

2 Run the roller through the mixture until it is evenly coated and ink the grape stamp. Align the strip of card (stock) with the top of the burgundy section. Rest the base of the stamp block on the card to stamp a row of grapes.

3 Ink the tendril stamp and stamp a tendril at the top of each bunch of grapes. Allow some of the prints to be paler than others as the paint wears off the stamp block, to give a deliberately faded and patchy effect.

4 Mix a little cream paint into some white. With the lining brush, apply highlights to the grapes and the tendrils. Let the brushstrokes vary in direction and weight to add to the hand-painted look. Support your painting hand with your free hand.

5 Hold the batten (furring strip) just below the top edge of the burgundy section and rest your painting hand on it. Slide your hand along the batten to paint a smooth, thin line in off-white. Practise this movement first and try to relax your hand to avoid jerky lines. A slight waviness to the line will not spoil the effect. Try to avoid having to paint over the line, as a single, fresh brushstroke looks better.

6 Attach a plumbline above dado height, just in from one corner and so that it hangs down to the skirting (base) board. Place the card square against the wall so that the string cuts through the top and bottom corners. Mark all the corner points in pencil.

7 Move the card down so that the top corner rests on the lowest pencil mark. Complete one column of the grid in this way, then move the plumbline across and continue until the lower wall is completely covered with a grid of pencil marks.

8 Mix a small amount of black paint into the burgundy to deepen the colour. Spread some dark burgundy paint on to a plate and run the roller through it until it is evenly coated. Ink the leaf stamp and make a print on one of the pencil marks.

9 Position the stamp just above or just below the pencil mark each time to create a regular pattern over the whole lower wall.

10 Move the batten about 2.5cm/1in from the cream dado line and use the square-tipped artist's paintbrush to paint a second, broader line. Keep the line as fresh as possible; visible brushstrokes are preferable to solid, flat colour. Apply a coat of varnish to the lower wall to seal and protect the paint.

RIGHT: *The grape motifs are printed with two stamps, one for the grapes and one for the tendrils. These are then highlighted by hand using a lining brush to create a hand-painted look. This technique can be applied to give extra depth and interest to other stamped designs.*

FLOWER POT FRIEZE

This witty frieze has a 1950s feel and creates an eye-catching feature above a half-boarded wall. Use scraps of left-over wallpaper or sheets of wrapping paper for the pots, then stamp an exuberant display of flowers to go inside them.

You will need

- matt emulsion (flat latex) paint in pale blue and white
- 2 large decorator's paintbrushes
- clean cotton cloth
- pencil
- wallpaper or wrapping paper
- scissors
- PVA (white) glue and brush
- acrylic paint in green
- fine artist's paintbrush
- stamp inkpads in a variety of colours
- large and small daisy rubber stamps
- cotton wool buds (swabs)
- scrap paper

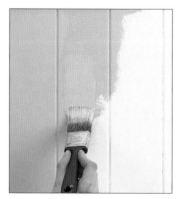

1 Paint the tongue-and-groove boarding or the lower half of the wall with pale blue emulsion (latex) paint. Leave to dry.

2 Using a dry paintbrush, lightly brush white emulsion over the flat colour. For a softer effect, rub the paint in with a cotton cloth.

3 To make the frieze, draw flower-pot shapes on to scraps of different wallpapers or wrapping paper and cut them out. Cut scalloped strips of paper and glue one along the top of each flower pot, using PVA (white) glue.

4 Glue the flower pots along the wall, at evenly spaced intervals. Alternate the different papers to create a pleasing random effect.

5 Using acrylic paint and a fine artist's paintbrush, paint green stems coming out of each pot. Leave the paint to dry before beginning to print the flowers.

7 Test the daisy stamps on a sheet of scrap paper before applying them to the wall.

6 Use coloured inkpads to ink the daisy stamps, using the lighter colours first. To ink the flower centre in a different colour, remove the first colour from the centre using a cottonwool bud (swab), then use a small inkpad to dab on the second colour.

8 Print the lighter-coloured flowers on the ends of some of the stems, using both the large and small daisy stamps. Allow the ink to dry.

9 Print darker flowers on the remaining stems. Allow the flowers to overlap to create full, blossoming pots.

MEDIEVAL HALLWAY

A welcoming hallway decorated with medieval patterns and colours will make a stunning entrance to your home. If your hallway seems dark and narrow, using two colours will help make it appear more spacious. A dark colour above dado (chair) rail height creates the illusion of a lower ceiling, while a light colour below, combined with a light floor covering, seems to push the walls outwards to give the impression of width. The crown pattern on the lower half of the wall is stamped in a diagonal grid, which is easy to draw using a plumb line and a square of card (card stock).

1 Draw a horizontal pencil line on the wall, at dado (chair) rail height. Paint the top half in blue-green and the bottom in buttermilk yellow emulsion (latex) paint. When dry, lightly sand the blue-green paint. Stick a strip of masking tape along the lower edge of the blue-green, and another 10cm/4in below. Apply light cream paint with a dry roller over the buttermilk yellow.

2 Stick another length of masking tape 2cm/5in below the one marking the edge of the blue-green section. Using a paintbrush and blue-green paint, fill in the stripe between the two lower strips of tape. Leave to dry and peel off the tape. Lightly sand the blue-green stripe to give it the appearance of the upper section of wall.

3 On a plate, mix one part blue-green emulsion (latex) paint with two parts pre-mixed wallpaper paste and stir well. Ink the diamond stamp with the foam roller and stamp a row of diamonds on the narrow cream stripe.

BELOW: Basic geometric patterns used at dado (chair) rail height are a useful decorative device to separate the different background colours, above and below.

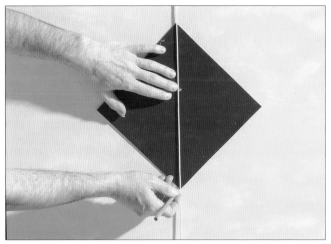

4 Use a plumb line and a card (card stock) square to mark an all-over grid on the cream half of the wall. This will be used as a guide for the crown stamps.

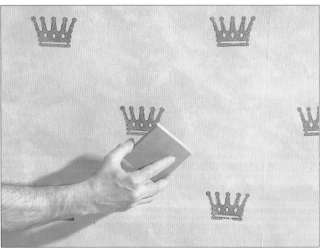

5 Ink the crown stamp with the blue-green emulsion (latex) paint and wallpaper paste mixture and stamp a motif on each pencil mark. Make several prints before re-inking to create variation in the density of the prints.

RIGHT: This themed hallway is perfectly complemented by a medieval-style cupboard with its heraldic stencilled panels.

MEXICAN HALLWAY

anish gloomy weather with vibrant sunshine yellow and intense sky blue in your hallway. With the heat turned up, add an ethnic touch by stamping an Aztec border along the walls. Use the patterns from the template section to cut basic geometric shapes from a foam rubber sponge, such as the ones used for washing dishes. Mix shades of green with purples, add an earthy red and then stamp on diamonds of fuchsia pink for its sheer brilliance. This makes a bold decorative statement.

Emulsion (latex) paint is available in a wide range of exciting colours. Try not to be tempted by muted colours for this border – it will lose much of its impact. Bright colours go well with natural materials, like straw hats, sisal matting, wicker baskets and clay pots.

You will need

- tape measure
- spirit level (level)
- pencil
- emulsion (latex) paint in sunshine yellow and deep sky blue
- paint roller and tray
- small amounts of emulsion (latex) paint in light blue-grey, purple, brick-red, fuchsia pink and dark green
- 5 plates
- foam rubber sponge

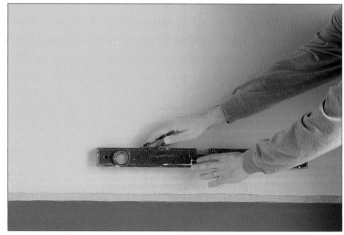

1 Divide the wall at dado (chair) rail height using a tape measure, spirit level (level) and pencil. Paint the upper part in sunshine yellow and the lower part in deep sky blue, using a paint roller. Then use the spirit level (level) and pencil to draw a parallel line about 15cm/6in above the blue section.

2 Use the templates from the back of the book to make the foam rubber stamps for this project. Then stamp a light blue-grey line directly above the blue section. Use this strip again to stamp the top line of the border along the pencil line.

3 Spread an even coating of each of the frieze colours on to separate plates. Use the rectangular and triangular shapes alternately to print a purple row above the bottom line and below the top line. Stamp on to a piece of scrap paper first to make sure that the stamp is not overloaded.

4 Stamp the largest shape in brick red, lining it up to fit between the points of the top and bottom triangles. There should be approximately 1.25cm/½in of background colour showing between this brick-red shape and the triangles.

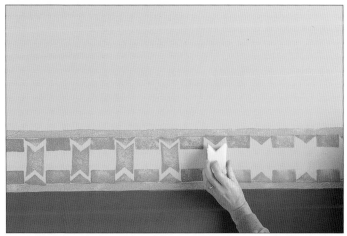

5 Stamp the diamond shapes in fuchsia pink, placing the stamps centrally between the brick-red motifs already stamped.

6 Finally, add a zigzagged edge along the top and bottom by overprinting dark green triangles along the light blue-grey lines.

RIGHT: *The rustic wooden furniture adds an authentic touch to this Mexican setting.*

MOORISH TILE EFFECT

Moorish wall patterns are based on abstract, geometric motifs which you can reproduce most effectively with stamps. In this wall treatment, a lozenge shape is incorporated in a subtle tile design on a cool colourwashed background.

You will need

- matt emulsion (flat latex) paint in mid-blue, off-white and terracotta
- wallpaper paste
- paint-mixing container
- Large and small decorator's paintbrushes
- thin card (stock)
- ruler
- pencil
- scissors
- medium-density sponge, such as a kitchen sponge
- felt-tipped pen
- craft knife
- spirit level
- fine artist's paintbrush

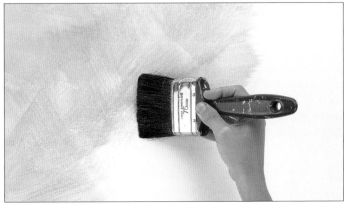

1 Mix the mid-blue emulsion (latex) with 50 per cent wallpaper paste. Apply to the walls with a large paintbrush, working at random angles and blending the brushstrokes to avoid any hard edges.

2 Mix the off-white emulsion with 75 per cent wallpaper paste and brush on to the walls as before, to soften the effect. Allow to dry.

3 To make a template for the tile shape, cut out a 30cm/12in square of thin card (stock).

4 Mark the sides of the card square 5cm/2in from each corner, draw a line across the diagonal and cut off the corners.

5 Copy the template from the back of the book and transfer it to a 5cm/2in square of medium-density sponge using a felt-tipped pen. Cut away the excess sponge using a craft knife.

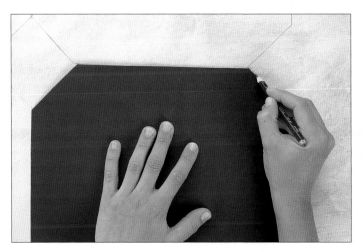

6 Using a spirit level, draw a horizontal line around the room where you want the top of the pattern. Place the top of the card template against the line and draw around it. Repeat all over the pattern area.

7 Use small decorator's paintbrushes to load the stamp with mid-blue and terracotta emulsion paint. Print the motif in the diamond shapes created by the template.

8 Dilute off-white emulsion with water to the consistency of thick cream. Using a fine artist's paintbrush, paint over the pencil lines.

SCANDINAVIAN BEDROOM

This delicate stamped decoration on walls and woodwork is designed to go with the pale colours and painted furniture that characterize period Scandinavian interiors. This is a scheme of great charm, restful on the eye and perfect for a bedroom.

You will need

- matt emulsion (flat latex) paint in grey-blue, off-white and red
- paint-mixing container
- wallpaper paste
- large and medium decorator's paintbrushes
- plumbline
- ruler
- pencil
- high-density sponge, such as upholstery foam
- felt-tipped pen or white crayon
- craft knife
- small paint roller
- fine artist's paintbrush
- matt (flat) acrylic varnish and brush

1 Mix grey-blue emulsion (latex) with 50 per cent wallpaper paste and apply to the walls with a broad paintbrush, working at random angles. Blend the brushstrokes to avoid hard edges.

2 Allow to dry, then repeat the process to soften the effect.

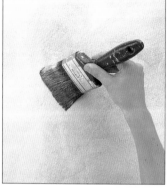

3 Mix off-white emulsion with 75 per cent wallpaper paste. Brush on as before. Allow to dry.

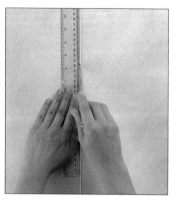

4 Hang a plumbline 2.5cm/1in from one corner and use as a guide to draw a vertical line down the wall.

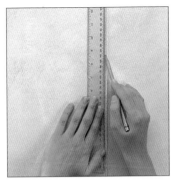

5 Measure about 40cm/16in across and draw a second vertical line, again using the plumbline as a guide. Repeat all around the room.

6 Trace the template at the back of the book and draw it on a rectangle of high-density sponge using a felt-tipped pen or white crayon. Cut away the excess sponge around the design using a craft knife.

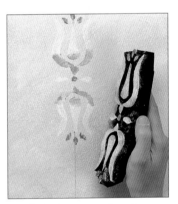

7 Use a small paint roller to load the stamp with off-white emulsion (latex) paint.

8 Add details in red and grey-blue, using a fine artist's paintbrush over the off-white paint.

9 Apply the stamp to the wall, positioning it centrally over the marked line.

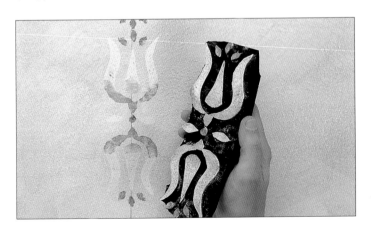

10 Repeat, positioning the stamp so that each motif is just touching the preceding one. Work down from the top of the wall.

11 Use the grey-blue wash mixed for the wall base coat to drag the door. Applying pressure to the bristles, pull down in a straight line, following the direction of the wood grain.

12 Apply the paint to the stamp as before, but this time loading only one flower motif. Stamp a single motif diagonally into the corners of each door panel as shown.

13 Add more paint to the grey-blue wash to deepen the colour. Edge the door panels using the artist's paintbrush. Leave to dry, then apply two coats of varnish to the door to protect the design.

COUNTRY GRANDEUR BEDROOM

Redecorating a bedroom can be as refreshing as taking a holiday, and stamping is such fun that it won't seem like work at all. First sponge over a cream background with terracotta emulsion (latex) paint and add a final highlight of pink to create a warm, mottled colour. Any plain light-coloured wall can be covered in this way. The two stamps are then combined to make a border which co-ordinates with an all-over pattern on the wall and a bedside table. You can also decorate matching curtains and cushions, or stamp the border on sheets and pillowcases.

You will need

- emulsion (latex) paint in dark salmon-pink, off-white and dusky pink
- plates
- foam rollers
- fleur-de-lys and diamond stamps
- card (stock)
- plumbline
- pencil
- long ruler
- small table, painted off-white
- pair of compasses
- black stamp pad
- scrap paper
- scissors
- paintbrush
- clear matt (flat) varnish and brush

1 Spread some dark salmon-pink paint on to a plate and use a roller to ink the fleur-de-lys stamp. Stamp a row of fleurs-de-lys above the dado (chair) rail, using a piece of card (stock) 7.5cm/3in wide to space the motifs.

2 Ink the diamond stamp with the dark salmon-pink paint, and print diamonds between the fleur-de-lys motifs. Use a card spacing device if you are nervous about judging the positioning by eye.

3 Cut a card square about 25 x 25cm/ 10 x 10in. Attach a plumbline at ceiling height, just in from one corner so that the weighted end hangs down to the border. Use a pencil to mark a grid for the diamond stamps.

4 Ink the diamond stamp with the dark salmon-pink paint. Print a diamond on every pencil mark to make an all-over pattern.

5 Spread some off-white paint on to a plate and run a roller through it until it is evenly coated. Ink both stamps and overprint the border pattern. To create a dropped-shadow effect, stamp each print slightly below and to the left of the motif that has already been printed.

6 Overprint the diamond wall pattern in the same way.

7 Lay the ruler across the table top from corner to corner in both directions to find the central point. Mark the centre lightly in pencil.

8 Set the pair of compasses to a radius of 10cm/4in and lightly draw a circle in the centre of the table top.

9 Increase the radius to 12.5cm/5in. Position the point of the compasses on the edge of the circle, in line with the middle of the back edge of the table. Mark the point on the circle at the other end of the compasses, then move the point of the compasses to this mark. Continue around the circle to make five divisions. Connect the marks with light pencil lines to make a pentagonal shape.

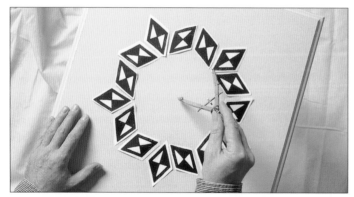

10 Use the black stamp pad to print 15 diamonds on paper then cut them out. Arrange them around the pentagon, as shown. Use the compasses to mark the inner points of the five inward-pointing diamonds.

11 Spread some dusky pink paint on to a plate and run a roller through it until it is evenly coated. Ink the diamond stamp and print the five inward-pointing diamonds at the marked positions.

12 Re-ink the stamp as necessary and print the rest of the pattern. Print an arrangement of three diamonds in each corner of the table top. Paint any moulding and handles on the table in the same shade of pink. Seal the table with a coat of clear matt (flat) varnish.

RIGHT: *Fleurs-de-lys and diamonds make an elegant combination. The circle of diamonds on the bedside table shows how a single simple motif can be positioned at different angles to create a complex design.*

COUNTRY QUILT FRIEZE

S tamp this friendly, folk-style frieze in a child's bedroom in soft pinks and a warm green. The pattern is reminiscent of an old-fashioned appliqué quilt, and the overlapping edges and jauntily angled birds accentuate its naïve charm. The colour scheme avoids the harshness of primaries, which are so often chosen for children. Green is a calming colour, but it can be cold. For this project use a sap green, which contains a lot of yellow, for warmth. The finished effect is bright enough to be eye-catching without overpowering.

You will need

- emulsion (latex) or artist's acrylic paint in green, sap green, pink and crimson
- paintbrushes
- pencil
- ruler
- spirit level (level)
- tracing paper
- spray adhesive
- medium-density sponge, such as a kitchen sponge
- craft knife
- 4 plates for paint palettes

1 Divide the wall by painting the lower section green, up to dado (chair) rail height. Measure 24cm/9½in up from the green section and draw a straight line using a pencil, ruler and spirit level (level) to act as a guide for the top border.

2 Trace the pattern shapes using the templates from the back of the book, then spray the backs with a light coating of adhesive. Stick them on to the foam and cut out with a craft knife. Press the straight strip into green paint and make a test print. Print a line along the pencil guideline, and another just above the green wall section.

3 Press the curved strip into the green paint, make a test print, then stamp curved lines to form a branch shape.

4 Press the leaf shape into the green paint, make a test print, then stamp the leaves in groups, as shown, two above and one below the branch.

BELOW: This charming frieze would work equally well in a playroom. Since the design is not too babyish it will last throughout early childhood.

5 Stamp pale pink birds along the branch – you need two prints, one facing each direction. Do not make the prints too uniform; aim for a patchy effect.

6 Clean the sponges, then press them into the crimson paint. Stamp the rest of the birds along the branch, alternating the direction of the motif as before.

7 Stamp a row of pink and crimson hearts above the top line to complete the border pattern.

RIGHT: The colours used on the walls are echoed on the door panel, which is painted freehand with a floral design, in keeping with the country theme.

ANIMAL FRIEZE

Alow frieze is perfect for a nursery as it concentrates interest at the child's own level. Children can't fail to be enchanted by this harmonious troop of animals all sharing the same flowery field, with clouds billowing overhead.

You will need

- emulsion (latex) paint in sky blue, grass green, yellow and white
- paint roller
- large decorator's paintbrush
- fine artist's paintbrush
- paint-mixing container
- stamp inkpads in black, brown and pink
- rubber stamps in cow, chicken, pig and sheep designs
- natural sponge

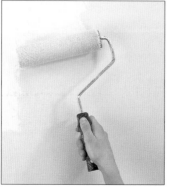

1 Paint the wall in sky blue emulsion (latex) using a paint roller. Leave to dry.

2 Paint the skirting (base) board in grass green emulsion.

3 Using the same green paint, apply wispy strokes up the wall to create the effect of grass growing up the wall. Allow the paint to dry.

4 Using a fine artist's paintbrush, highlight the grass with a lighter, yellowy green.

5 Paint small daisies in white emulsion at random in the grass. Add yellow centres.

6 Using a black inkpad and rubber stamp, stamp the cow motif randomly along the top of the frieze.

7 Print groups of chickens, using a brown inkpad.

8 Print the pig stamp several times facing the opposite direction, using a pink inkpad.

9 Print the sheep, using black ink. Using the fine paintbrush, fill in the body of the sheep in white emulsion. Do the same with the cows if you wish.

10 Lightly press a natural sponge into white emulsion and sponge cloud shapes on the sky blue wall above the frieze.

DECORATED TILES

These days you can buy wonderful decorated tiles in all shapes and sizes, but they cost a fortune! So, why not use stamps and paint to make your own set of exclusive decorated tiles? Acrylic enamel paint resembles ordinary enamel, but it is in fact water-based and does not include harmful solvents. If you are decorating loose tiles, bake them in a domestic oven following the manufacturer's instructions to "fire" the colour and give added strength and permanence. The fired tiles will be waterproof and resilient to non-abrasive cleaning. If you are stamping on to a tiled wall, it is best to position the design where it will not need too much cleaning – the paint will certainly withstand an occasional soaking and can be wiped with a damp cloth.

You will need

- plain off-white tiles
- detergent and clean cloth
- acrylic enamel paint in blue and green
- plates
- foam rollers
- small, large and trellis heart stamps

1 Wash the tiles with detergent and hot water, then dry them thoroughly with a clean cloth before you apply any paint. The tiles must be clean and grease-free.

2 Spread some blue paint on to the plate and run a roller through it until it is evenly coated. Ink the small heart stamp and print two hearts side by side at the top of the tile, with equal spacing on either side.

3 Align the next two stamps directly below the first. Take care not to smudge the first two when stamping the second row. Acrylic enamel paint dries fast, so you only need to wait a few minutes to avoid smudges.

4 To make another design, ink the large heart stamp and make a single print on another off-white tile. Press the stamp down, then lift it off immediately to get an interesting surface texture.

5 Ink the large heart stamp and print overlapping the edges, so that the point is at the top edge of the tile and the curved part is at the bottom.

6 Ink the large heart stamp and make a first print with the heart angled to the left. Leave it to dry, then print another heart angled to the right as shown.

7 Spread some green paint on to a plate and run a roller through it until it is evenly coated. Ink the trellis heart stamp and print a single heart in the centre of a tile.

8 Continue printing a single trellis heart in the centre of each tile. The texture will be different on every print, making the tiles look far more interesting and giving an expensive hand-painted effect.

RIGHT: If you prefer, stamp less tiles with the heart motifs and use them as individual highlights on a chequerboard pattern of plain tiles. See the Country Kitchen project for an example of how to position the stamped tiles.

SAILING BOAT FRIEZE

Use this charming yacht bobbing on the waves to decorate a bathroom with a nautical theme. It is better, if possible, to stamp tiles before fixing them to the wall, so that the ceramic paints can be made more resilient by baking in the oven. You can stamp and appliqué the same design, with embroidered details, on to your towels.

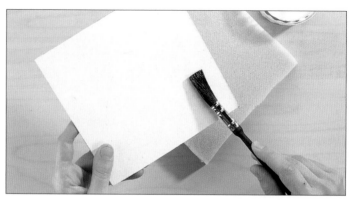

1 Cut a 15cm/6in square and a 15 × 5cm/6 × 2in rectangle of sponge to make the stamps. Cut a piece of card (stock) for each square and glue one on to each piece of sponge using PVA (white) glue.

2 Scale up the designs at the back of the book to fit a 15cm/6in tile and make paper templates. Draw around the boat, wave and seagull designs on to the square sponge stamp using a felt-tipped pen.

3 Cut away the excess sponge around the design using a craft knife. Repeat on the rectangular sponge to make the second stamp, positioning the waves so that they will fall between the first set of waves.

4 Load the boat stamp with ceramic paints, applying the colours to the different areas using a paintbrush. Clean any grease from the surface of the tiles by rubbing with a cloth dipped in methylated spirits (methyl alcohol). Allow to dry.

5 Press the square stamp over the tile. Allow to dry. Load the rectangular waves stamp and stamp another set of waves between the first set. Repeat the boat design on some of the tiles.

6 For the plain wave tiles, re-load the wave stamp with paint and position it 1cm/½in from the bottom edge. Apply the stamp, aligning it with the bottom edge. Print the seagulls at a 45 degree angle above the waves using one, two or three birds to give a varied natural effect.

7 For the appliqué towel panel, cut out a 17cm/7in square of plain cloth fabric and tape it on to the work surface. Mix fabric paints to match the ceramic paint colours and load the boat stamps as before. Stamp the design on to the fabric and leave to dry.

8 Fix the paints according to the manufacturer's instructions. Insert the panel in an embroidery hoop and work running stitch to pick out the clouds and details on the sail and boat in stranded embroidery thread.

9 Press under a 1cm/½in hem all round the panel and pin it in place at one end of the towel. Work blanket stitch all round the panel to attach it.

10 Stitch a pearl button to each corner of the panel, and one in the middle of each side.

COUNTRY KITCHEN

Specialist suppliers sell beautifully decorated tiles but they can be very expensive. So why not use stamps and paint to make your own set of exclusive tiles? The grape stamp is inked with two shades of green that blend in the middle in a slightly different way each time. Small touches such as the rustic hanging rail and the wooden plate add rustic authenticity to a country kitchen. The wood for the rail needs to be old and weathered. The nails banged into the rail as hangers are called "cut" nails, which are used for floorboarding. Attach the rail to the wall and hang fresh herbs from it, conveniently close to the cooker (stove). The wooden plate is stamped with different parts of the tendril motif to make a decorative border and central design.

You will need

- plain tiles
- detergent and clean cloths
- acrylic enamel paint in blue-green and yellow-green
- plates
- foam rollers
- grape, leaf and tendril stamps
- emulsion (latex) or acrylic paint in olive-green
- scrap paper
- weathered piece of wood, maximum 30cm/12in long
- long "cut" nails or hooks
- hammer or drill
- black stamp pad
- scissors
- wooden plate, sanded to remove any stain or varnish
- vegetable oil

1 Wash the tiles in hot water and detergent, then wipe dry to ensure that there is no grease on the surface.

2 Spread some blue-green acrylic enamel paint on to one plate and some yellow-green paint on to another. Run the rollers through the paint until they are evenly coated.

3 Ink the leaf stamp and the top and right side of the grape stamp with the blue-green roller. Ink the rest of the grape stamp with the yellow-green roller.

4 Stamp a bunch of grapes in the centre of each tile. Remove the stamp directly, taking care not to smudge the print. If you do make a mistake, you can simply wipe off the paint with a clean cloth and start again. Follow the manufacturer's instructions to "fire" the tiles in the oven if required.

5 For the hanging rail, spread some olive-green emulsion (latex) or acrylic paint on to a plate and run a roller through it until it is evenly coated. Ink the leaf stamp and stamp twice on to scrap paper to remove some of the paint.

6 Stamp on to the length of weathered wood without re-inking the stamp. The resulting print will be light and faded-looking, like the wood itself. Make as many prints as you can fit along the length. Hammer in the nails or drill and screw in the hooks to complete the hanging rail.

7 For the wooden plate, stamp several tendrils on to scrap paper using the black stamp pad and cut them out. Arrange them on the plate to work out the spacing and positioning of the motifs.

8 Spread some olive-green emulsion or acrylic paint on to a plate and run a roller through it until it is evenly coated. Ink the corner of the tendril stamp comprising the two curls that will make up the border pattern. Carefully begin stamping these motifs around the edge of the plate.

9 Ink the whole stamp and stamp two tendrils in the centre of the plate. Leave the paint to dry.

10 Dip a clean cloth into some vegetable oil and rub this into the whole surface of the plate, including the stamped pattern. You can repeat this process once all the oil has been absorbed into the wood. Each time you rub oil into the plate, the colour of the wood will deepen.

RIGHT: Stamp co-ordinating motifs on tiles and wooden accessories, using different paints and techniques appropriate to each surface. Position the grape tiles as highlights or create an all-over effect, as illustrated in the Decorated Tiles project.

FOLK COFFEE CANISTER

Rescue an old kitchen canister and give it a new identity as a piece of folk art. Painted tinware was very popular with early American settlers, and for years peddlers roamed the countryside loaded down with brightly painted cans, pitchers and bowls they sold from door to door. All these years later tinware is still a popular way of brightening up kitchen shelves. Prepare this canister by rubbing down the old paint with abrasive paper (sandpaper) to provide a surface for a fresh coat of emulsion (latex) paint. After stamping, bring out the colour and protect the surface with several coats of clear varnish.

You will need

- empty coffee canister
- abrasive paper (sandpaper)
- small household paintbrush
- emulsion (latex) paint in brick-red, black and bright red
- fine artist's paintbrushes
- plates
- foam roller
- tulip stamp
- clear gloss varnish and brush

1 Sand the canister. Paint the canister and lid brick-red. Leave to dry, then paint the rim of the lid black using a fine artist's paintbrush.

2 Run the roller through the black paint until it is evenly coated. Ink the tulip stamp and print a tulip on the side of the canister, tilting the stamp block around the curve of the canister.

3 Fill in the tulip shape carefully, using bright red paint and a fine artist's paintbrush.

ABOVE: Stamping works well on tin surfaces. In this project, the tulip shape is filled in using a fine artist's paintbrush.

4 Apply several coats of gloss varnish to seal and protect the canister. Allow each coat to dry completely before applying the next.

EGYPTIAN TABLE TOP

The beauty of this table top design lies in its simplicity. Just one colour was used on a bold background, with three similar images stamped in regimented rows. The table used here has a lower shelf, but the design would work equally well on any occasional table. The salmon-pink prints show up well on the rich background, making it look even bluer. The stamps are pre-cut and are taken from Ancient Egyptian hieroglyphs. The finished table could be one element of a themed room, or the surprising and eye-catching centrepiece of a room decorated in subdued colours.

You will need

- 3 hieroglyphic rubber stamps
- ruler
- 2 card (stock) strips, for measuring stamp positions
- felt-tipped pen
- set square (triangle)
- emulsion (latex) or acrylic paint in salmon-pink
- small paint roller
- piece of card or plastic

1 Use the stamp blocks and a ruler to measure out the stamp positions. Place a card (stock) strip along the vertical edge of the table. Mark as many stamp lengths as will fit along it, leaving equal spaces between them. Work out the positioning carefully so that the rows of prints will fit comfortably. Use the second card strip to mark the widths of the stamps.

2 Place the horizontal measure across the table so that it marks the position of the first row. The top of the stamp will touch the measuring strip. Use a set square (triangle) to position the vertical strip at a 90-degree angle to the first row. Move the vertical strip along as you stamp. Coat the roller with paint by running it through a blob of paint on a spare piece of card or plastic.

3 Use the roller to coat the stamps, then print them in sequence all along the first row. Position the stamps following the marks you have made on the card strips.

4 Move the horizontal measure up one stamp space on the vertical measure and stamp a second row of figures. Once again, the tops of the stamps will touch the bottom of the horizontal strip. Check that the card measures remain at a 90-degree angle. Continue until the pattern covers the whole table top.

BELOW: Vibrant colours turn an ordinary table into a main feature. You could also use subtle colours such as beige and brown.

SPOTTED FLOWER POTS

Customized terracotta pots will give a new, fresh look to your conservatory, patio or kitchen windowsill. Light, bright colours suit this project really well, but you can make them as subtle or as bold as you please. The end of a small sponge roller gives a neat, sharp image for the spot motifs.

You will need

- terracotta flower pots
- white acrylic primer
- medium decorator's paintbrushes
- matt emulsion (flat latex) paint in a variety of colours including yellow, white, red and blue
- paint-mixing container
- old plate
- small sponge paint rollers
- satin acrylic varnish and brush

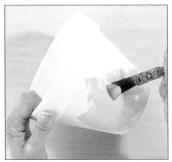

1 Make sure the flower pots are clean and dry. Prime them with a coat of white acrylic primer and leave to dry.

2 Dilute some yellow emulsion (latex) paint with water to the consistency of single (light) cream. Colourwash the first pot using a dry brush and random brushstrokes. Allow to dry.

3 Spread some white paint on to an old plate. Press the end of a small sponge paint roller into the paint, then press it firmly on to the first flower pot. Remove carefully and repeat all over the pot. Leave to dry.

4 Repeat using red paint over half the white spots, but position the sponge slightly to one side of each white spot to give a highlighted three-dimensional effect. Colour the rest of the spots blue. Leave to dry.

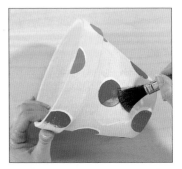

5 Repeat on the other flower pots, using different colour combinations. Seal the pots with two to three thin, even coats of satin acrylic varnish, allowing the varnish to dry between coats.

STRAWBERRY FRUIT BASKET

Strawberry motifs always look fresh and pretty, with their bright red fruits and shapely leaves, and the sponging technique used here suits the texture of strawberries particularly well. This decorative planter would look lovely on a kitchen windowsill filled with herbs or, of course, with strawberry plants.

1 Lightly sand the planter with medium-grade abrasive paper to prepare the surface for painting.

2 Apply two coats of white emulsion (latex) paint, allowing the paint to dry and sanding lightly between coats.

3 Copy the strawberry, leaf and calyx templates from the back of the book. Draw around them on the sponge with a felt-tipped pen. Cut away the sponge around the shapes using scissors or a craft knife and cutting mat.

4 Mark the positions of the strawberries on the planter in pencil. Load the strawberry stamp with red acrylic paint, then stamp the strawberries on the planter. Allow to dry.

5 Load the calyx stamp with green acrylic paint and stamp a calyx just above each strawberry shape.

6 Mark the positions of the large and small leaves on the planter. Load the leaf stamp with green paint and stamp the leaves, making the large leaves by stamping three times.

7 Allow the leaves to dry, then use a pencil to mark the positions of the stems. Paint the stems freehand using a fine artist's paintbrush and green paint.

8 Use the fine artist's paintbrush to paint yellow seeds on the strawberries. When the paint is dry, apply two coats of clear acrylic varnish, all over the planter to protect the design.

HERB BOX

Aminiature chest of drawers with decorations on a botanical theme makes a charming store for dried herbs in the pantry, or would look equally good in the potting shed, filled with seeds. Small, unpainted wooden chests are inexpensive and widely available.

You will need

- unpainted wooden chest of drawers
- 6 unpainted wooden knobs with screws
- acrylic primer in white
- medium decorator's paintbrushes
- matt emulsion (flat latex) paint in pale green and very pale green
- clear wax and brush
- medium-grade abrasive paper
- ruler
- pencil
- drill and drill bit
- rubber stamps in plant designs
- stamp inkpad in green
- screwdriver

1 Prime the chest, drawers and knobs with an even coat of white acrylic primer. Allow to dry. If the drawers have thumb-holes in their fronts, as here, reverse them when you replace the drawers later.

2 Paint the chest, drawers and knobs with pale green emulsion (latex). Leave to dry thoroughly.

3 Apply clear wax to the edges and corners, wherever the chest and knobs would receive most natural wear and tear. Allow to set for 10 minutes.

4 Using the decorator's paintbrush, paint on a coat of very pale green emulsion and allow to dry.

5 Using medium-grade abrasive paper, rub down the areas where the wax was applied to reveal the base colour.

6 Mark each drawer 2.5cm/1in down from the centre top in pencil and drill a hole for the knob.

7 Ink a rubber stamp using the green inkpad and press on to the drawer below the drilled hole. Choose a different herb or flower design for each drawer.

8 When the stamped designs are dry, screw the knobs to the drawers. Place the drawers back in the chest.

FOLK-ART CHAIR

Simple repeating designs on a white painted chair have a wonderfully naïve charm. Stick to a few bright colours in keeping with the folk-art style of this design, which any slight irregularities in the stamping will only serve to enhance.

You will need

- medium-grade abrasive paper
- wooden chair
- matt emulsion (flat latex) paint in white
- medium decorator's paintbrushes
- medium-density sponge, such as a kitchen sponge
- felt-tipped pen
- coin
- cork from a wine bottle
- craft knife
- pencil
- ruler
- acrylic paint in black, red, terracotta and blue
- paint-mixing container
- scrap paper
- clear acrylic varnish and brush

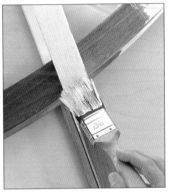

1 Sand the chair with medium-grade abrasive paper to remove any rough patches or old paint or varnish.

2 Paint the chair with two coats of white emulsion (latex) paint, allowing the paint to dry between coats.

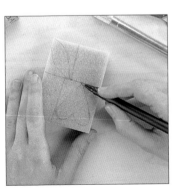

3 Copy the heart and leaf from the back of the book. Draw around the templates on to the sponge using a felt-tipped pen. Draw around a coin on to the end of a cork to make the spot stamp.

4 Cut out the excess sponge around the motifs using a craft knife. Cut out the cork spot motif.

5 Using a pencil and ruler, mark the positions of the leaves, 6cm/2½in apart, on the struts of the chair back and on the seat.

6 Load the leaf stamp with black acrylic paint, then stamp once on a piece of scrap paper to remove excess paint. Stamp along the struts at a 45 degree angle. Alternate the direction of the leaves on each strut.

7 Load the heart stamp with red acrylic paint, remove the excess paint as before and stamp a heart at the top of each vertical strut, across the back and front of the chair.

8 Load the cork with terracotta acrylic paint, remove the excess paint as before and stamp a dot between each leaf shape.

9 Wash the terracotta paint off the cork, load it with blue and stamp dots 2cm/¾in apart along the legs and all round the edge of the chair.

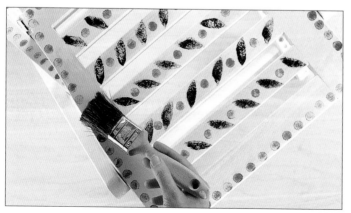

10 Leave the paint to dry, then apply two coats of clear acrylic varnish to protect the design. Allow the varnish to dry between coats.

STAMPED WRAPPING PAPER

Y ou can turn plain sheets of paper into fabulous hand-printed gift wrap using simple, bold linoleum-cut motifs and coloured inks. The designs are finished off using small rubber stamps. For the chequerboard design, position the linoleum block carefully to get an even pattern. Cut up a large sheet to make gift tags, threaded with narrow ribbon.

You will need

- linoleum board
- felt-tipped pen
- wood offcut
- linoleum-cutting tools
- water-soluble printing ink in a variety of colours
- small pane of glass or old saucer
- rubber ink roller
- plain wrapping paper
- metal spoon
- small star and spot rubber stamps
- stamp inkpads in a variety of colours
- hole punch
- narrow ribbon

1 Draw the star and star outline freehand on to paper. Cut out and copy on to two squares of linoleum, using a felt-tipped pen.

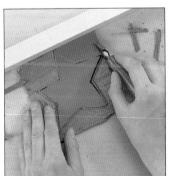

2 Butt the first linoleum square against an offcut of wood and place the wood against a wall on a flat surface, to prevent the linoleum from slipping. Cut away the area around the design using linoleum-cutting tools.

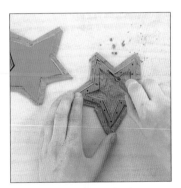

3 To cut out the spots for the star outline you will need a fine cutting tool. Place the point of the tool on a marked spot and scoop out the linoleum. Dust away the shavings.

4 Select a coloured ink for the star shape and squeeze a small amount on to a piece of glass or old saucer. Roll out the ink until it feels tacky, then roll it on to the star stamp. Do not apply too much or the linoleum will slip when printing.

5 Position the star stamp on the paper and press down, holding firmly in place. Smooth the back of the linoleum with the back of a metal spoon. Reapply the ink before printing each star.

6 Use a darker shade of ink for the star outline and line it up carefully over the plain shape. Smooth over the back of the linoleum with a metal spoon.

7 To complete the star design, use a small star-shaped rubber stamp and coloured inkpads to match the colours of the large stars. Stamp the small stars at random between the large ones. Repeat the motifs on gift tags, punch a hole with a hole punch and thread with narrow ribbon.

8 Follow the design in the picture to make a chequerboard stamp in the same way. Finish with a small spot-shaped rubber stamp on each square.

INDIAN VELVET CUSHION

Indian textile printing blocks are available in numerous designs. This is an opulent way to decorate cushions or other fabric accessories. Add metallic powders to fabric-painting medium to give a glittery effect with a hardwearing finish.

You will need

- 150cm/1½yd velvet
- tape measure
- scissors
- dressmaker's pins
- sewing machine and matching sewing thread
- 4 gold tassels
- bronze powder
- fabric-painting medium
- paint-mixing container
- medium paintbrush
- scrap paper
- Indian textile printing block
- 3 gold buttons
- sewing needle
- 56cm/22in cushion pad

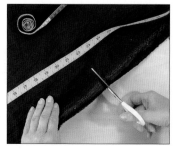

1 Cut out a 58cm/23in square and two rectangles 33 × 58cm/13 × 23in from the velvet. Turn in, pin and stitch a double hem along one long edge of each rectangle. Make three buttonholes, evenly spaced, in the hem of one piece.

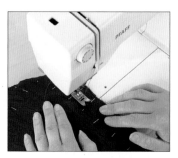

2 Right sides together, pin the button-holed piece to the square front on three sides. Pin the second back piece on top, stitched hems overlapping. Insert a tassel in the seam at each corner, facing in. Stitch and turn through. Flatten the seams and lay the cushion on a flat surface.

3 Add 1 part bronze powder to 2 parts fabric-painting medium and mix. Insert scrap paper inside the cushion to protect the other side. Prime the block with the mixture and position it along one edge of the cushion and press down. Repeat to complete the design.

4 Remove the scrap paper. Sew a gold button opposite each buttonhole on the back of the cushion cover. Insert the cushion pad and fasten the buttons.

ROSE CUSHIONS

Don't get your needle and thread out for this project – just buy plain cushion covers and stamp them with contrasting colours. New cushions revitalize existing decor and they can change the mood of a room in an instant. They are also a clever way to distribute a themed pattern round a room as they subtly reinforce the rosy look. Natural fabrics like this thick cotton weave are perfect for stamping because they absorb the fabric paint easily to leave a good, sharp print. Fabric paints can be fixed (set) with a hot iron after applying to ensure a long-lasting and hard-wearing finish.

You will need

- sheet of thin card (stock)
- natural-fabric cushion covers in 2 different colours
- fabric paint in white and blue
- plates
- foam rollers
- rosebud, large rose and small rose stamps
- scrap paper
- scissors
- iron

1 Place the sheet of card (stock) inside the darker cushion cover. Spread some of the white fabric paint on to a plate and run the roller through it until it is evenly coated. Ink the rosebud stamp and make the first print in the bottom right-hand corner of the cover.

2 Continue stamping in rows, using the stamp block as a spacing guide – use the top edge as the position for the bottom edge of the next print. You should be able to judge by eye after a couple of prints. Fill the cover with a grid pattern of rosebuds.

3 For the second, paler-coloured cushion cover, ink all three stamps with the blue fabric paint. Stamp each one on to scrap paper and cut them out. Use the paper patterns to work out the position of the rows of motifs.

4 Re-ink the large rose stamp and make the first print in the top left-hand corner. Use the paper pattern to help with the spacing between the motifs. Complete the row.

5 Ink the small rose stamp and complete the next row, again using the paper pattern for spacing.

ABOVE: Fabrics with woven stripes make it very easy to position the rose prints, and add to the overall effect.

6 Stamp another row of large roses, then print the rosebud stamp in the same way to complete the pattern. Finally, fix (set) the fabric paints on both covers with a hot iron, following the manufacturer's instructions.

SEASHORE THROW

Throws are indispensable accessories in every home – while adding glorious swatches of colours to any room, they also cleverly disguise any worn or stained patches. Throws can be thick and wintry or light and airy like this one, which could also double up as a sarong for a quick wrap-around. Crêped cotton has a fine, crinkled texture, which adds volume to the fabric and makes it drape well. Cotton or other natural fibres are the best choice as they absorb the fabric paint easily. So, have a go at this throw and make a luxurious gold design for your home.

You will need

- backing paper, such as thin card (stock) or newspaper
- length of crêped cotton or a ready-made plain throw
- drawing pins (thumbtacks)
- fabric paint in gold
- plate
- foam roller
- seahorse and shell stamps
- iron

1 Protect your work surface with backing paper. Lay the crêped cotton fabric over this and pin down with drawing pins around the edges.

2 Spread some gold fabric paint on to the plate and run the roller through it until it is evenly coated. Ink the seahorse stamp and make the first print in one corner of the fabric.

3 Print a border along the top and bottom edges of the fabric, alternating the shells and seahorse stamps.

4 Stamp widely spaced rows of seahorses between the borders, turning the stamp 180 degrees each print. The prints in each row should fall between those of the previous row. Fix (set) the fabric paint with a hot iron, following the manufacturer's instructions. Press directly down on to the fabric, ensuring the crêped cotton retains its texture.

ABOVE: Stamping is possible on many different fabrics, even the crinkled surface of crêped cotton.

STARFISH HAND TOWELS

hese seashore-style hand towels are made from a cotton/linen mix, similar to the fabric used for glass cloths. Fabric paints are ideal for the job because the colour is permanent once fixed with an iron and you can use the towels again and again. The stamps have been given a three-dimensional look by stamping firstly in green and then overprinting some areas in white.

You will need

- pair of cotton/linen hand towels
- iron
- backing paper, such as thin card (stock) or newspaper
- fabric paint in green and white
- plate
- foam roller
- starfish and seahorse stamps

1 Wash the towels to remove any glaze from the fabric as this may block the absorption of the colour. Press each towel flat with an iron.

2 Place a towel on the backing paper. Spread some green paint on to the plate and run the roller through it until it is evenly coated. Ink the stamps and print a border, alternating starfish with seahorses.

3 Stamp two rows of green starfish down the length of the towel. Ink half the stamp edges with white paint. Overprint each stamped starfish and seahorse by lining up one point of the stamp with the green stamped image, then positioning the rest of the stamp.

LEFT: *Making and decorating your own hand towels is surprisingly simple, and the towels will be very pleasant to use.*

VINEYARD TABLE NAPKINS

These stamped table napkins look great with rush mats on a wooden table top. They bring together even the most casual collection of plates, glasses and cutlery to look like a deliberate choice. You can buy a set of plain table napkins or make your own by sewing straight seams along the edges of squares of cotton fabric. The fabric paints can be heat-treated with a hot iron to make the pattern permanent. Always follow the manufacturer's instructions, which may vary from brand to brand.

1 Wash and iron the napkins to remove any glaze which may block the paint's absorption. Lay the first napkin on top of several sheets of newspaper. Spread some cream fabric paint on to a plate and run the roller through it until it is evenly coated. Ink the grape stamp and print a bunch of grapes in each corner of the napkin.

2 Stamp a bunch of grapes halfway along each edge, then ink the tendril stamp and print tendrils between the grapes. Stamp all the napkins in this way and leave to dry. Seal the designs with an iron, following the paint manufacturer's instructions.

LEFT: You could stamp a tablecloth border to match the napkins.

TEMPLATES

The templates on the following pages may be re-sized to any scale required. The simplest way of doing this is to enlarge or reduce them on a photocopier. Alternatively, trace the design and draw a grid of evenly spaced squares over your tracing. Draw a larger grid on another piece of paper and copy the outline square by square. Draw over the lines to make sure they are continuous.

HARLEQUIN SCREEN (how to mark the panels and apply the masking tape)
pages 262–265

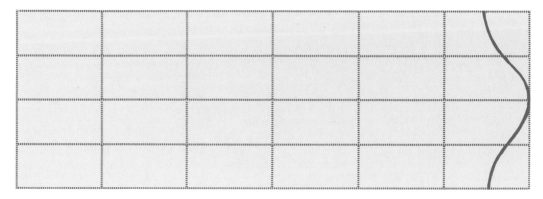

The pencil marks

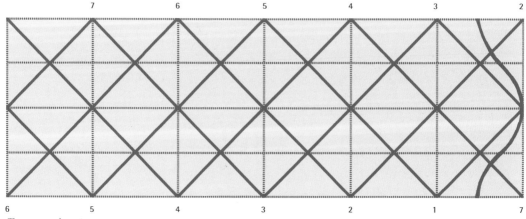

The tape marks

PENNSYLVANIA-
DUTCH TULIPS
pages 284–287

SCANDINAVIAN DOOR PANELS
pages 256–257

THROUGH
THE GRAPEVINE
pages 288–291

RENAISSANCE ART
pages 292–295

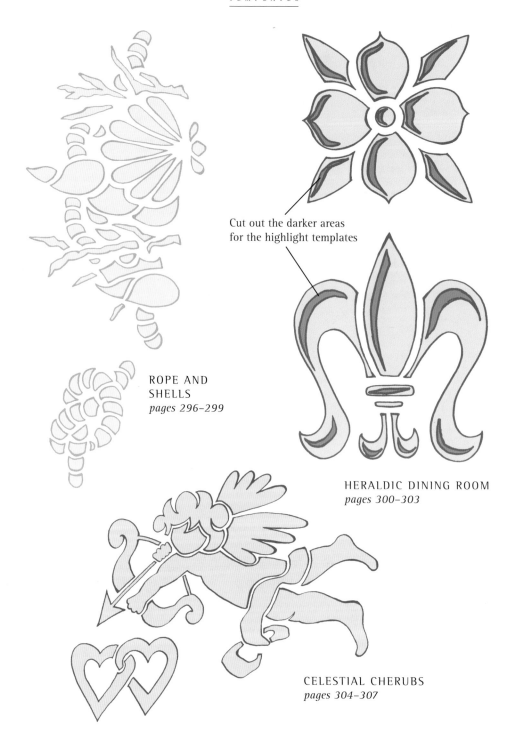

Cut out the darker areas
for the highlight templates

ROPE AND
SHELLS
pages 296–299

HERALDIC DINING ROOM
pages 300–303

CELESTIAL CHERUBS
pages 304–307

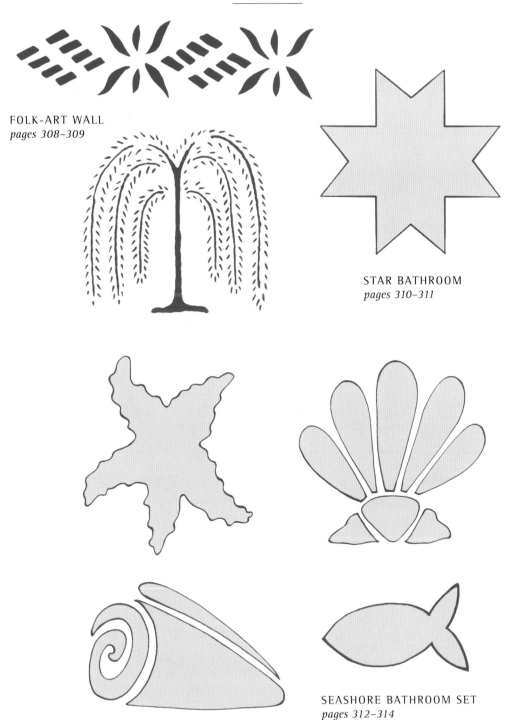

FOLK-ART WALL
pages 308–309

STAR BATHROOM
pages 310–311

SEASHORE BATHROOM SET
pages 312–314

GREEK URNS
pages 315–317

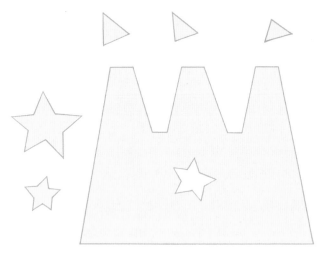

MAKING SANDCASTLES
pages 318–321

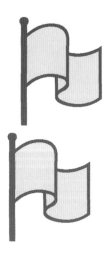

FLAG STENCILS
pages 322–323

CHILD'S SEASIDE ROOM
pages 324–327

PAINTED DRAWERS
pages 328–330

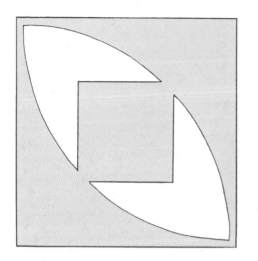

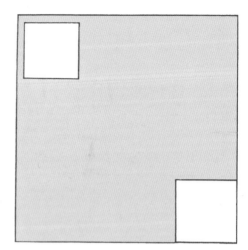

GEOMETRIC FLOOR TILES
pages 334–337

TROMPE L'OEIL PLATES
pages 338–341

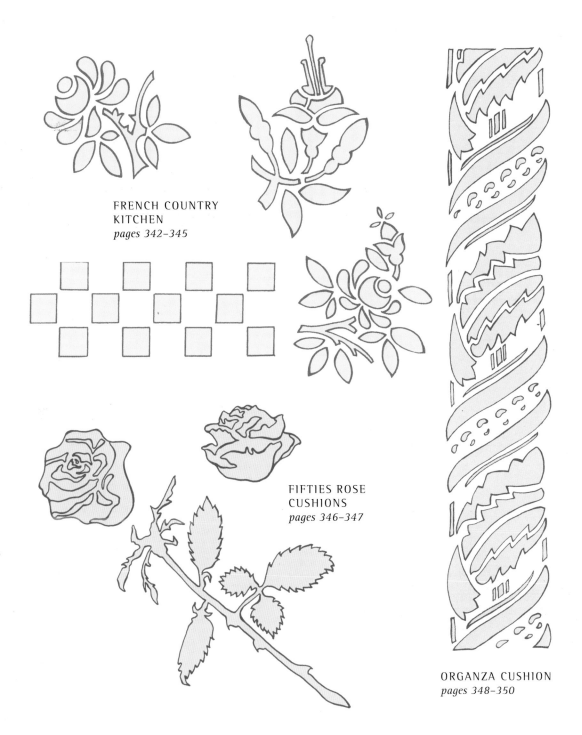

FRENCH COUNTRY
KITCHEN
pages 342–345

FIFTIES ROSE
CUSHIONS
pages 346–347

ORGANZA CUSHION
pages 348–350

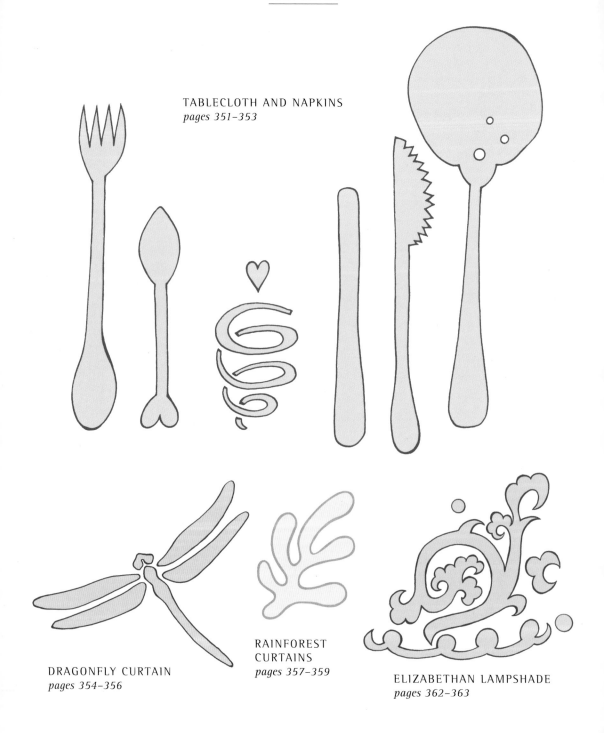

TABLECLOTH AND NAPKINS
pages 351–353

DRAGONFLY CURTAIN
pages 354–356

RAINFOREST
CURTAINS
pages 357–359

ELIZABETHAN LAMPSHADE
pages 362–363

LEAFY
PICTURE FRAMES
pages 364–365

CITRUS
FRUIT TRAY
pages 366–367

GILDED
CANDLES
pages 371–373

TRAY OF AUTUMN LEAVES
pages 368–370

FROSTED VASES
pages 374–376

**SNOWFLAKE
GIFT WRAP**
pages 380–381

ART NOUVEAU HATBOX
pages 377–379

SCANDINAVIAN
LIVING ROOM
pages 388–391

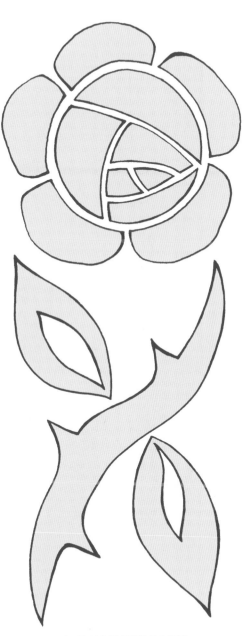

SANTA FE LIVING ROOM
pages 384–387

ART NOUVEAU ROSES
pages 392–395

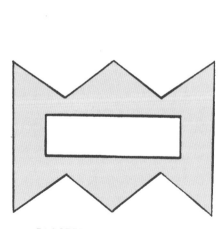

PLASTER WALL TREATMENT
pages 396–399

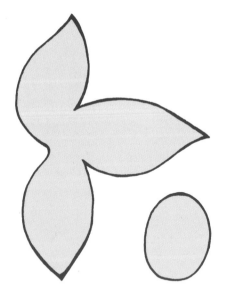

GRAPEVINE FRIEZE AND GLASSES
pages 408–411

GOTHIC DINING ROOM
pages 400–403

MEXICAN HALLWAY
pages 428–431

MOORISH TILE EFFECT
pages 432–435

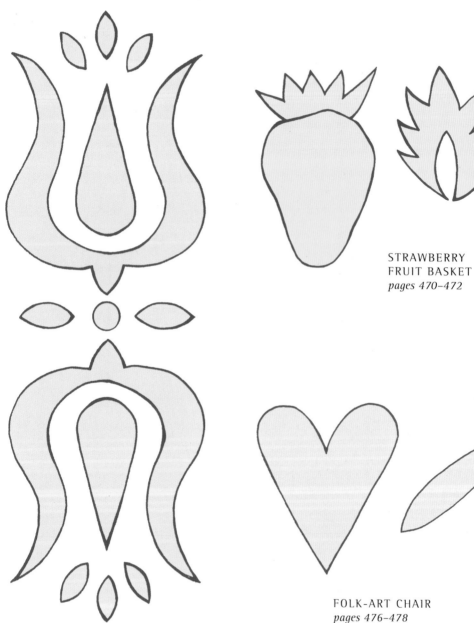

STRAWBERRY
FRUIT BASKET
pages 470–472

FOLK-ART CHAIR
pages 476–478

SCANDINAVIAN BEDROOM
pages 436–439

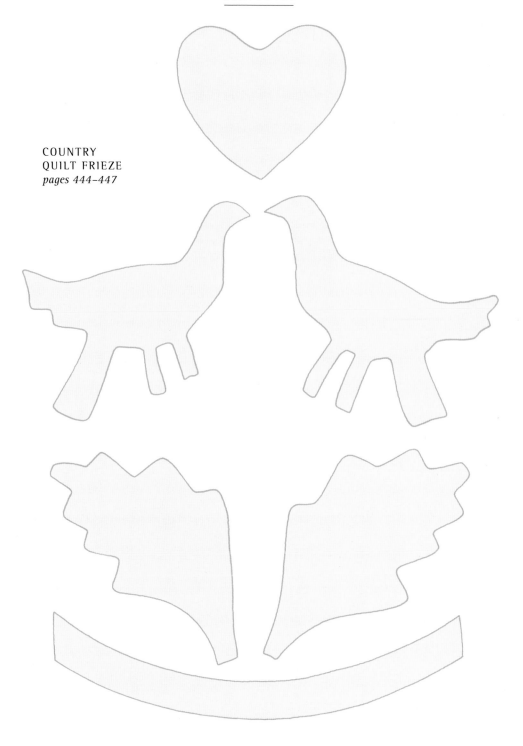

COUNTRY
QUILT FRIEZE
pages 444–447

SAILING BOAT
FRIEZE
pages 456–459

INDEX

SUPPLIERS

The publishers would like to thank Foxell & James Ltd, 57 Farringdon Road, London, for lending their equipment for photography.

The speciality materials and equipment that you will require for the projects featured in this book are available at any good art-supply shop.

USA

Adventures in Crafts
Yorkville Station
P.O. Box 6058
New York
NY 10128
(212) 410-9793

Art Essentials of New York Ltd
3 Cross Street
Suffern
NY 10901

Createx Colors
14 Ariport Park Road
East Granby
CT 06026
(860) 653-5505

Dick Blick
P.O. Box 1267
Galesburg
IL 61402
(309) 343-6181

Heartland Craft Discounters
Route 6 E
P.O. Box 65
Genesco
IL 61245
(309) 944-6411

Hofcraft
P.O. Box 72
Grand Haven
MI 49417
(800) 828-0359

Sandeen's
1315 White Bear Ave
St. Paul
MN 55106
(612) 776-7012

Stencil House of New Hampshire
P.O. Box 16109
Hooksett
NH 03106
(603) 625-1716

UNITED KINGDOM

Crown Paints
Crown Decorative Products Ltd
PO Box 37
Crown House
Hollins Road
Darwen
Lancashire

Blade Rubber Stamp Company
2 Neal's Yard
London WC2H 9DP

The Stamp Connection
14 Edith Road
Faversham
Kent ME13 8SD

Brodie and Middleton
68 Drury Lane
London WC2B 5SP
Brushes, lacquer, metallic powders, oil and acrylic paints and powder pigments.
Mail order.

Green and Stone
259 Kings Road
London SW3 5EL
Brushes, crackle varnish, linseed oil, scumble glazes, shellac, stencil card.
Mail order.

Stuart Stevenson
68 Clerkenwell Road
London EC1M 5QA
Gold and silver leaf and other gilding and art materials.
Mail order.

Farrow and Ball
Uddens Estate
Wimbourne
Dorset BH21 7NL
Specialist paint suppliers.

Fired Earth
Twyford Mill
Oxford Road
Adderbury
Oxon OX17 3HP
Specialist paint suppliers.

Grand Illusions
2-4 Crown Road
St Margarets
Twickenham
Middlesex TW1 3EE
Specialist suppliers of paint effects materials.

ICI Dulux
(01753) 550 555 for stockists of paint.

Homebase
(0645) 801 800 for stockists of paint and decorating materials.

Wickes
(0500) 300 328 for stockists of paint and decorating materials.

Do-it-all
(0800) 436 436 for stockists of paint and decorating materials.